My Life & 1,000 Houses

Failing Forward to Financial Freedom

Lone Horse Publishing – BMI
P.O. Box 171174, San Antonio, Texas 78217
210-669-7183

Dedicated to Tommi Stephen…

Who has changed more for me than anyone I know.

THANK YOU FOR LETTING ME CHASE MY DREAMS.

Read What Others Say About *My Life & 1,000 Houses* By Mitch Stephen

Mitch Stephen presents something unique—a decisive strategy that incorporates integrity and compassion into a determination to succeed. Here is an insider's look at the highs and lows of becoming one of the most respected real estate investors in Texas. Every investment association should recommend My Life & 1,000 Houses *to its members.*
— Tom Hennigan, Founder, National Real Estate Investor's Association

There's no shortage of books on building wealth from real estate. Hundreds of textbook-type offerings present all the business basics you could ever need, and plenty of how-to advice to go with them. This is not that book.

Mitch Stephen delivers a unique and practical guide to real estate success, one that examines the bigger picture. My Life & 1,000 Houses *describes Mitch's personal journey as a real estate entrepreneur, from his early struggles to his phenomenal success—success he achieved just one house at a time.*

More than 1000 houses later, Mitch delivers what few real estate books do: the personal insights of an entrepreneur who not only knows what to do but does it. Plus, he goes beyond the boundaries of business, revealing how his experiences affected his personal life.

You'll gain a rare insight into the challenges, setbacks, triumphs, and unexpected lessons that come from one man's venture into the entrepreneurial life. More importantly, you'll be inspired.

— Eddie Speed, Founder of NoteSchool· and Author of Streetwise Seller Financing

The San Antonio Real Estate Investors Association has dedicated its offices in Mitch Stephen's name. Although he never served as president, on the board, nor on a committee, Mitch has made a tremendous difference in the success of others by simply showing up and giving freely of his expertise. **My Life & 1,000 Houses** ***captures the essence of this man's business acumen and the personal history on which it's based. His book is as fascinating as it is entertaining. It speaks to you on levels far deeper than the issues of money, and demonstrates how success is much more than financial wealth. We'll always have a copy of this invaluable book at "The Mitch Stephen Investment Center."***

— Orlando Rodriguez, President of the San Antonio Investor's Association, San Antonio, TX

If only Mitch had written this book 5 years ago when I got started in real estate! I've read about a hundred books on real estate and attended dozens of seminars on the subject. But if I had to pick the one factor that helped me the most in moving from homelessness to financial freedom, it would be this book. Mitch's straight-forward, tell-it-how-it-is style blends the perfect amount of humor with serious and insightful content.

— Eli Call, Financially Independent Real Estate Investor, San Diego, CA

Mitch is a walking encyclopedia of information, and it shows in this long-overdue book. Rarely do you meet someone like this who has

the charisma, smarts, and initiative to take action in the direction of their passion. After reading this book, I find it much easier to accept life's challenges, take action, and push forward to success!
— Joseph Ponce, Retired Army Officer/Real Estate Investor, Ft. Bragg, NC

Bookstore shelves are packed with publications claiming to reveal the easy route to wealth. However, few address the struggles encountered and the life lessons learned during the pursuit of success. **My Life & 1,000 Houses** ***is that rare offering. With little more than passionate desire and initiative, Mitch moved from abject poverty to extraordinary riches. He takes you along on his amazing quest for financial freedom through real estate, without sparing the rich texture of setbacks and disappointments he experienced along the way. His tale of blood, sweat, tears and laughter is truly inspirational.***
— Michael Walloch, Co-Founder of www.IBuyHouses.com, Dallas, TX

My Life & 1,000 Houses ***is refreshingly different. I found myself enlightened and entertained at the same time. This book is a real achievement. It's a keeper!***
— Bill Bridges Jr., Regional Director, The Ritz-Carlton Club & Residences

When it comes to real estate, Mitch Stephen is the real deal. With single-minded purpose, hard work, and a devotion to his investors, Mitch has succeeded in numerous facets of real estate. His inspiring book delivers several revelations about life in this business. You'll laugh and cry and turn the last page with a smile.
— Bill Crawford, Author of 18 books including, Stevie Ray Vaughan: Caught in the Cross-fire and All American: The Rise and Fall of Jim Thorpe.

Austin, TX

My Life & 1,000 Houses *is not another get-rich-quick book. Rather, it's an inspirational story about thinking outside of the box, looking towards the future, establishing the right relationships, standing by your word, and continuing to challenge yourself. I saw myself in this book, and contemplated its content much more than I had expected. This book is a smooth, gentle read that keeps you turning page after page. I read it in just two days because I couldn't put it down.*

— Tommi L. Leonard, Vice President, Stillwater National Bank, San Antonio, TX

My Life & 1,000 *Houses is a must read for the serious or aspiring real estate investor. If Jack Canfield and Mark Victor Hansen of the Chicken Soup for the Soul® series ever decide to offer a book about real estate investment, this is the story they should use. I found myself laughing out loud on an airplane while reading it!*

— Mike Ochsner, Founder of the www.IBuyHouses.com Marketing System, Salt Lake City, UT

I've just finished reading My Life & 1,000 Houses *by Mitch Stephen. What a trip! I laughed, I cried, and I felt like I had been there myself. Mitch is a great storyteller. His descriptions of the hard times he encountered and how he got through them were a great education for me. I also reveled in the good times he experienced. With this book, you're in for a real treat.*

— Margaret Childress, Customer Support Assistant, One Advocate Group, San Antonio,

TX

TABLE OF CONTENTS

More Stories from

My Life & 1,000 Houses

"The master in the art of living makes little distinction between his work and his play, his labor and his leisure, his mind and his body, his information and his recreation, his love and his religion. He hardly knows which is which. He simply pursues his vision of excellence at whatever he does, leaving others to decide whether he is working or playing. To him he is always doing both."

James Michener

INTRODUCTION

• • •

The learning is in the living

My name is Mitchell Stephen. I am honored that you are reading this introduction. As you might imagine, I did not invent real estate, nor did I pioneer any of the techniques used to create wealth via real estate. While I may have a larger understanding of real estate than the average person, I've never considered myself to be a sophisticated person. I don't consider myself to be a genius or even above average in the mental department. I am sure that some of the movers and shakers out there would assess me as a slow learner, and that's ok. I'll say it first. My story is proof that I have to get hit in the head with a concept before I actually learn it. I don't believe I'm that much different from most people in that we don't learn when people tell us things. For us, the learning is in the living.

My light bulb didn't go off until I was in my mid 30's. Much of this book is about what it took for me to get my entrepreneurial skin thick enough to just survive. Long before I could find a deal in real estate, I had to find myself. It took a lot of persistence to find my place in the world. This is the point of the pages that follow: You don't have to have a Harvard education to accomplish or even exceed your dreams.

You are, however, going to have to work your butt off, just like the Harvard graduate. There is no easy money for anyone. Period! The late night, get-rich-quick infomercials are not driving that point home nearly as much as they are waving copies of big checks in your face. This would be a good time to ask for a refund if I've ruined your concept of real estate already. If that's the case, may I suggest you take the money and buy some lottery tickets, good luck! The rest of you will get my heart and soul. I can't tell you how anyone else did it, but I can tell you how I did it, for better or for worse. I am sure that at some juncture you'll begin to figure out that my particular journey was NOT the shortest path between two points. Perhaps you can shorten your journey by reading my story.

The intricacies of a deal can go on forever, and there's always more than one way to do things. There are plenty of gurus out there who will be happy to teach you every single one of those ways. Don't trip over the pennies on your way to the dollars. This is my story.

CHAPTER 1
THE ALL AMERICAN FAMILY

• • •

Sometimes you don't know how good you have it.

It's true: If you're born in Eden, you don't know you're blessed. My childhood was picture perfect and I thought the world simply ran like that. I thought that everyone's mother was beautiful and caring and everyone's father was handsome and hardworking. My younger brother, Kleat, and I were truly blessed. We had a father who never shunned one iota of his responsibility to provide for and lead his family, and we had a mother who stayed at home and nurtured us with the conscious and deliberate agenda to raise two strong, caring, and loving sons. Looking back I can't think of one thing we ever wanted for or that I'd change. Together, my parents provided a home and family right out of a 60's sit com, *Father Knows Best* or *Leave It to Beaver*. We were a family right out of Mayberry, but even better, we had air conditioning!

My father, Rod Stephen, was born in Eastland, Texas, and grew up 'round about the depression. He volunteered for the Marines and completed his commitment. By the time my brother and I were born, Dad was a coach for the Longview Lobos High School. My mother, Margaret Rita Turk (Rita), was raised in El Paso when she wasn't on the Indian reservation in New Mexico. Her grandmother (my great grandmother) was full blooded Mescalero Apache. We could all be stalking deer on the great hunting lands, but Great Grandma told the white man to stick their papers where the sun don't shine…and who could blame her? Mom would achieve education on her own but there is no doubt that her very special heart and soul was an extra special gift from God. In Okinawa, Rod accidentally on purpose fell in the pool next to Rita, and a few years later my brother and I were walking the planet.

My brother Kleat and I were born in Longview, Texas, and we had a very close relationship. We climbed trees, built forts, hunted and fished, played all kinds of games, and excelled in athletics together. Later, I'd wonder, did I ever have a girlfriend he didn't kiss? Generally speaking, we were two peas in a pod.

One time when we were in elementary school, I remember Kleat coming home all beat up. I asked him who did it and he told me that one of the twins down the street did it, but he didn't know which one it was. The twins were my age and bigger than most. I headed out the door and found the identicals laughing about the event on the street corner. When I asked which one of them beat up my brother, they refused to tell me. I couldn't tell them apart either. Heck, no one could tell them apart. So I beat them both up! After that I figured I needed to teach Kleat how to fight. I'm not so sure that was a good move. As brothers do, I'd have to fight him more than most. But we always got past it, as brothers do.

My family likes to hunt. My brother and I have hunted since we were very young. Of course, one of the primary concerns in the early years was that we not get hurt or hurt anyone else with our firearms. My father taught us verbally everything he knew how to about gun safety. He was constantly watching how we handled our guns, where the barrel was inadvertently pointed, how we loaded and unloaded our guns, whether the safety was on or off—always, always, always counseling us.

I'm the oldest and of course the first to start shooting. Carrying a full-fledged firearm was new for me. The responsibility of educating a young son about firearms and safety was new for Dad. He wasn't sure if I was getting it. Yes, I was hearing him, but did I really understand the importance and the huge responsibility of handling a rifle? He wasn't sure, and he couldn't rest until he knew without a doubt that I understood the full weight of the situation.

One day he asked me if I wanted to go to the shooting range. He said he wanted me to help him sight in his old 30-30 rifle. I was proud that he fancied me as a good shot, so of course, I said, "Yes." We hopped into the truck and off we went.

When we got to the range we set everything out on one of the shooting tables. Dad told me to take the rifle out of the case. I knew what he was waiting for. He was waiting for me to check immediately to see if the rifle was loaded or empty. It was the first rule of guns. "Never touch a gun without checking to see if it is loaded." You touch it, you check it. The last thing I ever wanted to ask my father was, "Is this gun loaded?" That question would get you lit up. You don't ask—YOU CHECK THE WEAPON YOURSELF! Dad watched me check the rifle's chamber for shells. I cocked the magazine open and gazed at the insides. He leaned in to look at the same time. He saw it was unloaded, same as I did, but still he asked me, "Is it safe?"

I answered, "Yes Sir." He made his point with his words and with an intent look directly into my eyes.

After we grabbed some sandbags, he instructed me to take a seat at the table. We made a few adjustments with bags while I was in the shooting position. Dad asked, "How's it feel?"

"Pretty good," I said. I had the butt of the rifle pulled in tight to my shoulder with my cheek down on the stock. With one eye shut, I could see that the barrel set nicely in line with the target one hundred yards ahead of us. I'd never shot his gun before. It was one of those sacred moments. Dad was about to let me shoot *his* 30-30 rifle.

As a marksman, I'd already achieved excellence with my Crossman "pump" BB gun. Carrying a gun or shooting wasn't new to me, but the big rifle was a bit intimidating.

DAD: Think you can put one in the bull's eye from here son?

ME: I reckon I can.

DAD: This trigger has a long draw on it. It takes some getting use to. I'm not a real fan of dry firing a gun, but why don't you try it once or twice and get a feel for it.

ME: OK.

I closed the magazine and got down on the target. I took a deep breath and pulled the trigger slow at first but, then, I yanked it. "CLICK." The gun dry fired. I knew, without a doubt, I would've missed if this had been the real thing.

DAD: You jerked it didn't you?

ME: Yes Sir, I sure did. That trigger does take a long time to go off.

DAD: Try it again. This time you'll know more what to expect.

I cocked the empty gun again and started to bear down on the target.

DAD: Take your breath and pull so slow you don't even know when it's going to go off.

CLICK. The hammer flew forward striking to the firing pin.

DAD: That was perfect! Cool as a cumber! You'd have leveled that deer.

ME: Yes Sir, I would've that time but sure is a long pull.

DAD: Awe, you'll get used to it in a few more times. Hey, let's take a break and go get us a cold soda-pop. I saw a machine around front. Here's some change. Go get us both one will you?

I disappeared around the front of the little house/office. When I got back, we sipped our sodas and talked about the upcoming deer season. It was starting to get hot.

DAD: Hey, what do you say we try this one more time before we start using expensive ammo.

ME: OK, but I hate to shoot your gun dry like that. Sure it's alright?

DAD: Yea, it'll be alright. I got it ready for you too. One more time won't hurt it.

I got into position while Dad was coaching me to take my time. "Nice and easy…take a breath and then…nice and slow…squeeze the trigger."

BANG! The gun went off! It roared like all the thunder I have ever heard in my life, all happening at once! The adrenaline shot through my body, *fear - shock - panic*. I jumped up off the gun and looked at my father with eyes that must have been big as saucers…more fear and panic, and then embarrassment. My heart had all but leapt out of my chest. My ears were ringing. I was stone cold, petrified. And stunned! My father grabbed me with one hand and the rifle with the other. Holding the rifle way away from his body with one arm, he clinched the front of my shirt at the collar and pulled me to him with his other arm. His face was within inches of mine. He had big tears in his eyes and he gritted his teeth. A single drop was forced from the corner when he closed his eyes and said, "Son, the gun is *always loaded*. No matter what you think, no matter what anyone tells you, no matter what you might suspect, the gun is *always loaded*, son. The last three words were barley audible but whispered directly into my ear I heard them, "It's *always - loaded*!"

My father had slipped a shell into the rifle when I went for the sodas. He did it to make an impression on me he feared his words were not making. I just thought I understood that my rifle could go off and kill somebody. I got a new understanding that day. All the coaching, all the fireside chats at camp, all thc talking in the world would not, could not, accomplish what my Dad did with one very carefully placed 30-30 shell that day.

A few days later, I asked him why he'd gotten choked up that day on the rifle range when the gun went off. He welled up somewhat again, "Because I love you. I love you so much and I don't want the potential of that gun to ruin your life. If your gun ever kills you or anyone else I will never forgive myself. I want you to enjoy the outdoors, to experience the wilderness and the thrill and cunning of the hunt. But it comes with a risk. That gun is dangerous. It'll kill you dead as a door nail in a heartbeat. It can steal all of those good times away in the flash of a muzzle."

Dad continued, "You see, when I was a kid, my gun went off. Unfortunately it was not orchestrated like yours was. I could have killed someone—anyone—who would have been standing in the path of my bullet. I got lucky and no one got hurt, but I have never forgotten that moment when my gun went off unexpectedly. It made an impression that has lasted all my life. I think, no, I know, it takes an unexpected discharge before that gun will ever get all the respect you can give it. When it happens you're almost sick with the realization of what could have happened. I wanted you to get that experience without having to take the chance I had to take to get it. I was overcome because I could tell by the look on your face when that gun went off that you had gotten that experience. I was relieved."

As a student of life, I've learned almost everything meaningful in this fashion. It has to happen to me in real time for me to get the lesson once and for all. Yes, for many of us, learning is in the living.

My high school days were picture perfect; all district this, most popular that, played drums in the local rock-n-roll band, and had a dang pretty girl friend. I drove a 1979 midnight blue Trans AM complete with T-Tops and an oyster white, leather interior, straight off the show room floor (thanks Mom and Dad!). I thought I was the coolest thing in town, but it was really just a very cool time. I'll never be able to thank my parents enough for all they gave me and did for me. It simply cannot be done.

I had average grades in school and excelled in football. I've often wondered what I'd be like today if it hadn't been for athletics in school. It's been said that athletics can build a strong inner fortitude. I'm certain that it did in my case. At 125 pounds, I was probably one of the smallest 4A starters in Texas. I started my first varsity football game as a sophomore at the running back position in 1976. At the time, in 4A high school, that was a big deal. I really had no business starting on a 4A high school team but, lucky for me, our team didn't have anyone better. I was never the fastest man on the field, but with a lot of help I managed to gain my fair share of yards. The main thing I had going for me was that my mind was right. It was not a conscious decision to prevail over my lack of size. Simply put, I was never told that I couldn't, so I did. After the graduation ceremony, we all went to the last "Class of '79 Keg Party." When I woke up the next morning the bleachers were empty.

It was only natural for me to try to find a new stadium. I spent the next year working out and training. When I walked on my first college football field in San Angelo, Texas, five years after my high school debut, I weighed a meager 165 pounds soaking wet. The front line was averaging over 300 pounds per man.

During some testing for quickness and speed, I found myself paired up beside a lineman to run the forty-yard dash. He weighed in at about 325 pounds. I thought to myself, *"This guy isn't going to push me to my best time."* Well, that was wrong. I barely managed to outrun the big man by 1/100th of a second. I wasn't *that* slow. The big man was just *that* fast! I watched as the other running backs got tested. The Astroturf all but rolled up behind the speed demons as they crossed the finish line. With every official time they recorded, my heart sank a little further. There was no way I could compete at such levels. In all my eighteen years, quitting football had never been an option, not even a remote thought, but the handwriting was on the wall. I was going to get cut from a football team.

My dreams of football were dashed. It was a very confusing time, and I lingered for awhile through 1980 and 1981. Eventually, I did what any red-blooded American boy would do. I packed up my Trans AM, took the t-tops off, cranked up *Boston* on the cassette stereo, and headed for California. Why, you might ask? Well, red-blooded American boys don't need a reason to go to California. They just go.

Stephen Family: Kleat, Rita, Rod, Mitch
(left to right)

CHAPTER 2
CALIFORNIA, HERE I COME... ALMOST

• • •

There's a lot to be said for a change of scenery.

Somewhere between Las Vegas, Nevada, and Bishop, California, I got side tracked it the tiny town of Tonopah, Nevada (probably because I ran out of money in Vegas). I ended up getting a construction job building a state-of-the-art molybdenum mining plant. To get to the job site, I had to go about three or four miles west down the main street of Tonopah, take a right on a newly paved two-lane road, and drive thirty miles down that road with nothing but tumbleweeds and sand for as far as the eye could see. When I finally reached that little black spec on the horizon, I had arrived.

On the right side of the road there was a mining facility and, on the left, there was a KOA Camp with a convenience store. Well, it was almost like a convenience store except that it had fifty concrete shower stalls in the back. The showers were there to accommodate over 2,000 workers living in every conceivable size and shape and make of RV, fifth wheel, camper trailer, and tent you could imagine. There were also more long-haired, leather-clad, earring-wearing, beard-growing, whisky-drinkin', dope-smokin', knife-wielding, tattooed men there than I'd ever seen or hope to see again. Being the red-blooded American boy I was, I decided to stay.

When I showed up to apply for a job on the first day, I got in a line to sign up for work. There were several lines with about fifteen to twenty people in each line. At the front of each line sat rough, husky men wearing hard hats, bossing everyone around and handing out paperwork and orders. I started talking to other guys in line to see what I was in for. I started with the guy in front of me in line.

ME: What's this line for?

STRANGER IN FRONT: This line's for laborers.

ME: How much do laborers make per hour?

STRANGER IN FRONT: Laborers get paid $12.00 an hour.

I looked over at a biker-lookin' guy in the line to my right.

ME: Hey man, what's your line for?

GUY TO MY RIGHT: This line's for welders, dude.

I didn't figure I could fake being a welder so I looked over towards the line on my left hand side.

ME: Hey man…what line are you standing in?

GUY TO MY LEFT: This line's for iron workers.

ME: What do iron workers do?

GUY TO MY LEFT: We screw together the metal as the building goes up

Now I was absolutely sure I could *screw up metal*, so I was encouraged.

ME: What do iron workers make per hour?

GUY TO MY LEFT: Iron workers make $15.00 an hour.

I nonchalantly drifted out of the laborers' line and into the iron workers' line. When it was my turn to talk to one of the leathernecks, he started asking a bunch of iron worker questions I didn't know the answers to. Still, I did my best to muddle my way through. With every question, I got deeper and deeper into a hole. Mr. Leatherneck had had just about enough of my non-iron-working B.S. when this scrappy looking, one-eyed guy tapped him on the shoulder and said, *"I'll take him."* Old "Uno" had his head cocked down so that his good eye was looking over the top of his reading glasses and right at me. He eyeballed me up and down, from head to toe, like I was a cow at auction or something. He never cracked a smile. Finally, he pointed towards his truck and told me to wait for him over there. So I hauled my newly appointed, iron-working butt over to my new boss's truck. Along the way, I waved at the guy I'd met in the Laborer line as they were handing him a broom. He shook his head and pointed his finger at me as if to say, "You son-of –a-gun! I *should have done that too."*

My boss said he picked me because he'd seen me switch lines, and he liked my decision-making process. Amazing! I'd escaped detection from everyone else in the building but the guy with one eye caught it! I was more of a gopher for Cyclops than I was an iron worker, but for $15.00 an hour plus overtime, you could call me anything you wanted to—anything but laborer. We worked twelve, fifteen, sometimes eighteen hours a day. We worked hard and played hard too. Every Friday evening, the 2,000-plus construction workers stampeded the 2,000 residents of Tonopah and proceeded to burn that poor town down to the ground. It was like a scene from Kevin Costner's movie *Water World*, but instead of being in the middle of the water it was in the middle of the desert—lawlessness run amuck!

I was twenty years old. The legal age in Nevada was twenty-one. That probably kept me out of some trouble, that and the fact that two old timers had taken me under their wings. I have always been blessed in that way. The good Lord usually places me in good company. Moose was a huge, burly man (as you might suspect by his nickname), and my boss, One-Eyed George, was lean and mean. They never looked for trouble but when it came-a-knocking, it promptly left when Moose stood up and turned his baseball cap around backwards. It was a very rough place, and I made it a point to stick close to Moose and One-Eyed George.

During the workweek there was not much to do in camp after work but read. In that little convenience store, I purchased my first *Entrepreneur Magazine*. The magazine had all kinds of ideas on how to start your own business, but the one that caught my eye was an article about striping parking lots. I must have read that article a dozen times. I started to formulate a plan: Sell my drum set for $750 and purchase a striping machine. I'd exercise that plan sooner than I thought.

I still don't know how I did it, but three months after I'd arrived in Tonopah, I was packed up and headed back to Texas, tattoo-less! I got home and heard that Moose had fallen from high in the structure and hit his head on one of the steel I-beams on his way down. It messed him up really bad. I thought about going to see him, but his wife said that he didn't even know who *she* was and not to waste my time. Still, I regret not going. Today, I do not know where he is or how he is, but I would like to take this opportunity to thank Moose for watching over me back then. Thank you too, One-Eyed George.

This is me after a hard day's work in Tonopah, NV

CHAPTER 3
MITCHELL STRIPING

• • •

Doing the work is just half the battle…
You have to collect your money.

Shortly before I plunged into entrepreneurship, I was fortunate enough to be able to ask a very successful builder a few questions about starting a new business. He informed me that most businesses fail in the first two years due to lack of work ethic and/or lack of money (under capitalization). He also told me that my life wouldn't be my own for the first two years if I were going to make it work. I was about to learn exactly what he meant. To this day, I always seem to underestimate the start-up costs and the time it takes to establish a new business. (Hey, at least I'm honest about it!)

No one in San Antonio would talk to me about the striping business. I needed to know what type of machine to buy, what type of paint to use, how to bid jobs, etc. And the thought of actually painting a straight line on the pavement terrified me. What if I painted this ugly, crooked line on someone's parking lot? Finally I called some guys in Austin, Texas, and offered to work a week for free if they would teach me a little bit about the business. I promised not to do any work in Austin in return for their consulting. They had me painting straight lines in no time. When that week was over, I returned to San Antonio and purchased my first machine from the Perry Shankle Store with the money I'd received from selling my drum set. Every now and then, I'd be asked to go to Austin and do a job. True to my word, I never did any work in Austin, even after I'd lost track of the guys I'd made my promise to.

Business was good, but the dang construction companies took their sweet time paying me. *Entrepreneur Magazine* forgot to mention collection problems in their articles. I had to pick up some kind of part-time job so I could afford to buy the paint and gasoline I needed while I waited to get paid. Doing the job was one thing. Getting paid was another. The lessons were coming at me quick but I liked it like that. I was learning more per month about real life business than I could have learned in a year of college. For the first time in my life, I could actually feel myself growing intellectually.

I ended up taking a bartending course so I could get a part-time job as a bartender. I needed a job that paid me immediately so I could mitigate the time between striping pay days. Bartending seemed to fit the bill.

I got fired from my first two bartending jobs (both times on the first night). The bartending institute did a great job of teaching me the ingredients of all the drinks, but they forgot to teach us how to run a cash register. What kind of deal is that? I'm just thankful it was bartending and not flying lessons.

ME: Mitch to Tower. Do you read me? Over.

TOWER: We read you loud and clear, Mitch. Over.

ME: Request permission to land on runway 3. Over.

TOWER: Runway 3 is clear for landing. Over.

ME: Tower, I have one small problem. Over.

TOWER: State your problem. Over.

ME: The jerks at the "Institute of Flying" forgot to teach me how to land.

TOWER: Copy that. They only teach people how to *fly*. We'll notify the fire department and the ambulance crew. You're clear for landing. Over.

Nothing's ever as easy as it looks. There's always more than meets the eye.

After a short stint at the cash register institute, bartending was great! I was 21 years young, loving the nightlife, and making $100 to $150 per night, four nights a week. I was in the hottest bar in town, The SK Stampede. An eight-hour shift passed like a ten-minute roller coaster ride: fast and furious, with no time to look at your watch. I'd leave the bar at 12:00 or 2:00 a.m. and go stripe parking lots while they were still empty. Before I knew it, the sun would be coming up—and that's how I liked it. To this day, I have trouble looking at my watch when I'm working.

I bought my first property about that time. It was a one-bedroom efficiency condo that the seller financed for me. It cost $28,000 with $2,000 down. Shortly after I put my John Henry on the papers, I was a man about town. I had my own business, my own car and my own place. Not bad for a twenty-one year old I thought. Life was good!

I quickly took on a partner in the striping business. On that fateful day, I'd spent half the morning broom sweeping by hand just a fraction of a lot I intended to stripe. Then this stranger walked up from out of nowhere with a blower on his back and finished cleaning the rest of the entire parking lot in ten minutes. He showed me how to use the blower, and I showed him how to put a stripe on the ground. That was the beginning of my partnership with Jimmy Allison. Jimmy was even a few years younger than I was. He had wild, curly, red hair and freckles and, together, I suppose we looked like two outcast members of *Spanky and Our Gang*. Many of the construction foremen didn't take us seriously when we'd ask to bid on their jobs but, eventually, we'd striped every parking lot in San Antonio, no joke. Jimmy and I became the best of friends and we worked like you've never seen two guys work in your life.

We did the regular business stuff during the day like banking, sales, collections, bidding, etc. At night we would stripe our butts off. Mitchell Striping was pounding out the work but, just like before, the money was fast going out and slow coming in.

Once we got called into Frost Bank by then Vice President, Ken Herring. We thought we were going to get a loan or something good like that, but it turned out much different. When we got to Frost Bank we were met by none other than the FBI.

FBI: Are you fellows kiting checks?

ME & JIMMY: No.

FBI: Do you know what kiting checks means?

ME & JIMMY: No.

FBI: Kiting checks is when a person deposits money at one bank and then withdraws that money the same day and goes to another bank and deposits it in such a fashion to show the money in both banks on the same day.

ME & JIMMY: Well, sir, we're doin' the *Hell* outta that!

As I've mentioned, the huge companies we worked for took their sweet time paying us. First it would be thirty days, then sixty days, then ninety days. The slow pay was killing us cash flow-wise, so we started getting creative. Texas State Bank's daily clock ticked over at 3:00 p.m. but Frost Bank's clock didn't click over until 4:00 p.m. So, we started making deposits at Texas State Bank before 3:00 p.m., and then we'd take the money back out at 3:30 p.m. and run the funds over to Frost Bank and deposit it before 4:00 p.m., just to float payroll.

Those badge waving men in suits scared us to death until I caught my account rep trying to contain his laughter outside the fish bowl office. When I caught the agent himself trying not to laugh I assessed that they were just giving us a little scare. I didn't let on, but I knew we weren't in any real trouble at that point, so I played along, letting them have their fun with us. They knew we didn't mean any harm. In our young, naïve, business minds we thought we were being smart, creative businessmen until we could get paid. You know, if it feels wrong…it probably is.

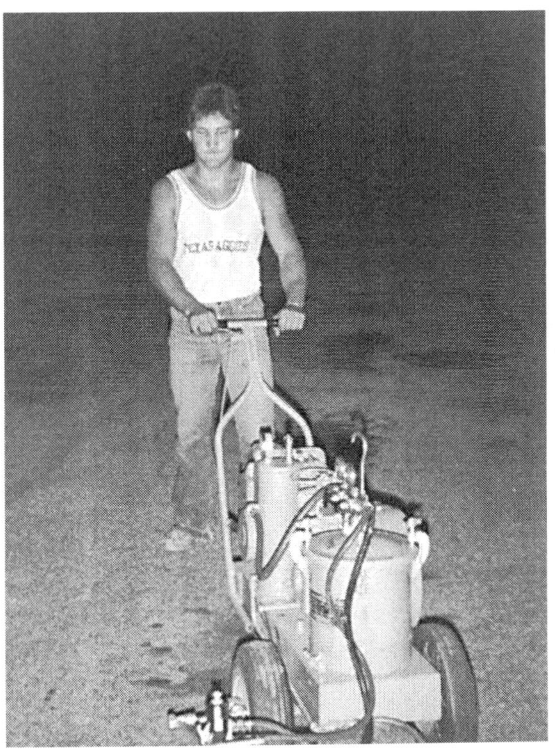

Learning to paint a straight line on asphalt (Mitch)

CHAPTER 4
ANGELS AMONG US

• • •

Sometimes only a stranger can tell you.

Around 1982, the pace of that twenty-four hour a day business started to take its toll on me. I'd go to sleep at night and wake up two days later, with everyone pissed off at me. I started finding it increasingly difficult to make it through a day without busting into tears (when no one was looking of course). Hey, I played football. My father's a former Marine. We don't cry about a dang thing! I didn't know what was happening to me. I'd quit football, and now I was crying like some baby all the time. What's next? I stop liking girls? When it came time to cry, which could be anytime, anywhere, and always right out of the blue, there was no holding it back. There was little warning, and within seconds, I'd break like a cheap water balloon on the windshield of an oncoming car, floodgates wide open!

As luck would have it, the bar I worked at wasn't much different than that of the sitcom *Cheers*. We had regulars you could set your watch by: The kind of customers who frequented happy hour every day of the week and always arrived at the exact same time, sat in the exact same spot, and ordered the exact same drink without fail! I served this one particular customer everyday for months but never bothered to ask what he did for a living. I was always too busy promoting my own business to worry about what anyone else did for a living. (It's a character flaw I still have, but I'm working on it.) I remember bragging to him about sleeping on the sofa for over two days straight without ever getting up to take off my clothes or to use the bathroom. No drugs. No alcohol. I just fell asleep on the sofa watching TV and didn't wake up for forty-eight hours! Looking back, my customer started asking me questions shortly after that. I thought nothing of it at the time. I guess it was the way he asked. His questioning came off as idle conversation.

"Hey workin' man, how long did you end up working yesterday?"

"Are you going to get some rest tonight or are you going to work straight through 'til daylight again?"

"Hey, Mitch, I haven't seen you for a few days. Did you fall asleep for forty-eight hours again?"

"You're looking a little stressed my friend. May I buy *you* a drink? Is everything okay with you?"

"Mitch, how long have you been in the striping business?"

"What do you do for fun? Do you have some fun?"

"When was the last time you took a day off? Do you ever take a vacation?"

One day I was stuck behind the bar talking to this customer when suddenly the dam started breaking. I couldn't run anywhere to hide so he caught a glimpse of me starting to crack just before I ducked down below the bar. I stayed down on my knees as if to count liquor bottles or something. Really, I was just crying. I'm sure he could hear me sobbing but at least he couldn't see me. More importantly, I did not have to see him seeing me. I thought the attentive customer had just been keeping up with me over the months through conversations across the bar, but really he had been diagnosing my condition. I guess my unraveling was the last straw for him.

On my next shift, he arrived as usual before the rush. He placed a rather thick book on the bar in front of him. The manager of the bar approached me shortly thereafter and instructed me to go sit with my customer at an out-of-the-way table while he took over my bartending duties for a while. It was early. Business was slow. I thought it was odd but what the heck.

I sat down at the table with my customer, and he explained that he was a psychologist. For the past ten years, he had been working for the state prison system helping men with life sentences cope with their reality. He went on to explain that he admired both my entrepreneurial spirit and my work ethic, but he was beginning to worry about my health. He asked me how often I cried like the other night. I told him, "Well, at first it was once a month, then later it was twice a month, then once a week and now (I was embarrassed to say and had looked down at the table) almost every day." A lump grew in my throat as I spoke and I worked hard to choke it down.

He asked me to read a few pages from the book he'd brought in. Highlighted on a page was a list of symptoms I recognized all too well. I don't know why the revelation struck me so hard. Maybe it was the relief of finding an explanation. Whatever the reason, I could not contain myself for another second. There I sat during happy hour, tears rolling down my face, crying for all I was worth.

Now, finally, I knew what was happening to me. At twenty-two-years of age, I was having a nervous breakdown. I was trying so hard to be successful that I was wearing my poor body plumb out. My will was stronger than my flesh and bones, and even some parts of my mind (like the part that needs sleep). I was pushing so hard, apparently too hard, and for way too long. The only symptoms I had not experienced were black outs or loss of memory. Then again, for the life of me, I cannot remember that good doctor's name. I hope I bought him a drink afterwards because I now understand that a nervous breakdown can be a lot worse than just tears. So, whoever you are, wherever you are, "Thanks, Doc."

I still struggle with this problem today. You can only work so much. Sooner or later, if you are going to grow big or bigger, you have to leverage money or human capital or both. If you don't have balance between work and play, things can go to Hell in a hand basket and fast! I'm not telling you I'm good at it. I simply telling you, I've come to know it's true.

I took a month off. When I tried to come back, I fell into the same routine and, within a week, I was breaking down every day again. Completely drained and desperate for rest, I gave up my half of Mitchell Striping. Letting Jimmy down hurt me, and I was starting to feel like a real loser.

The next few years (1983–1985), with Jimmy at the helm and me back at the bar, Mitchell Striping grossed as much as $1.7 million a year. Shortly after that, my best friend Jimmy died. Dr. Denton Cooley, the famous heart transplant surgeon, had given Jimmy a replacement heart but for whatever reason, it just didn't take after awhile. At the time, he was the youngest active heart transplant patient ever. They said his initial heart problems had nothing to do with the stress or the workload, but I've always wondered. He was a real go-getter, a great friend, and I miss him to this day. I could tell plenty of stories about Jimmy and what a genius he was despite his young age. I *will* tell you this: If heaven has yellow lines on their parking lots, Jimmy Allison painted them.

"TRAINS"

Written by Mitch Stephen and Billy O'Rourke

Daddy worked the railroad 30 some-odd years
On the train that was the center of our town
Never had to wonder where on Earth he was
We'd just close our eyes and hear that whistle sound
The Railroad Commission sent the suits one day
And they tore up all the tracks
The whole town starrin' at their golden watch
Like that train, is sometime comin' back

CHORUS:
Baby that train, it don't stop here anymore
It's been moved on down the line, for one reason or another
And it's got plenty of, our memories aboard
But it won't be comin' back
'Cause baby that train, it don't stop here anymore

Jimmy was my best friend and the first to get his car
And we'd cruise the town each Friday night
I could always count on him to get me to the dance
Or around the Dairy King a thousand times
Then his mother got a letter, with a folded U.S. flag
She sent me the keys to his Fairlane
Sayin', Jimmy would've really wanted that"

(REPEAT CHORUS)
'Cause baby that train...

BRIDGE:
This year the angels took my Brother
And I've known no greater pain
Lord meet me early at the station
'Cause lately I've been missin' far too many trains

MODIFIED CHORUS:
'Cause baby those trains, they don't stop here anymore
They've been moved on down the line, for one reason or another
They've got plenty of, our memories aboard
But they won't be comin' back... No they won't be comin' back
'Cause baby those trains, they don't stop here ...anymore

Listen: http://www.mitchstephen.com/trains.asp?music=on
Sung by Kevin Hughes

www.MitchStephen.com

Jimmy Allison poses on a newly purchased water blaster rig

CHAPTER 5
ADVERSITY UNIVERSITY

• • •

I eventually graduated from La Calle (the Street) U.

From then on things started going down hill. I had more jobs and I tried to start more businesses than I care to count. Everything failed. Texas was in a recession, and I was getting further and further behind little by little. I sold cars. I sold knives. I sold advertising. I sold mobile homes. I played in a band. I tried the lawn mowing business, the health club business, telemarketing, a roofing business. I was an apartment manager, worked in shipping and receiving, copier sales, the window tinting business, and onsite real estate sales. You name it, I tried it. I either recognized that the job was going nowhere or I flat out failed, but either way I was perpetually moving on. Looking back, I'm sure it didn't help that in my early twenties I looked like I was sixteen. Who wants to buy a car or a home from a guy who looks like he's sixteen years old?

Fast Forward: Somewhere my Momma has a stack of business cards about three inches thick. She brought them out and showed them to me once when I was talking about how lucky I was to have so much in life. She said that being grateful was a wonderful trait but that she was not sure at all about how "lucky" I'd been. I was about to protest when she handed me that stack of business cards tightly wrapped with a rubber band. I released the rubber band and began to flip through all the different cards. I got quiet as I revisited every failure one at a time. There were so many failures, and many I'd forgotten about. Once I saw them I remembered every single job or venture, and the disappointment wrapped up in them. Mom broke the long silence, "I know you and I've saved these cards for this day. You've been busting your little tail end ever since I can remember. Be grateful for your health or your parents or your God-given abilities but don't give luck too much due…You've fought for every inch of your success."

As I travel through this life I find myself saying this more and more, "God Bless Mommas."

I just couldn't find myself. I couldn't find what I was supposed to do to make a living. Every time I'd start out excited in my new career, reality would set in, and it was over. The cycle was making me doubt myself. I'd been so successful in high school and now so many failures coming one after another.

During the lows, I always managed to make ends meet. I don't know how but I also always managed to keep my good credit. I never asked my parents for any money, but Dad would slip me a $100 every now and then, figuring I could use it. He wasn't wrong. More importantly, both my parents were supportive. Their emotional support ran deep and wide. I don't ever recall them laughing at any of my crazy business ideas. I don't ever remember them saying, "That won't work," or even, "Are you sure about this?" They always said something to the affect of, "Great, it sounds exciting! Let us know how it's going…let us know if we can help." My parents were always enthusiastic and always encouraged me. I can only imagine how they must have worried about me. I was falling down so often.

Somewhere in my failures, I began to see how easy it would be to be homeless. I completely realized how often I was just one paycheck away from being in the street. It seems like that should've tamed my capacity for risk but really it emboldened me. You see, I had a net and I knew it. I always knew I could go home if things really got bad. On the day I moved out, Momma was standing in the driveway waving goodbye in tears as I left, and I never moved back in. I knew I could have moved back if I'd needed to. I knew that. That one thing alone could well be the reason for the way things turned out in my life. It would be a bold face lie to say that having such a net didn't immensely change the way I looked at risk. I might have been young, dumb, and failing, but I was smart enough to know that now was the time to try and fail. I knew that I would never go hungry or have to sleep in the rain as long as I had my wonderful mother and father and I could make my way to them. To this day, I am grateful for that net. Change that little ingredient and my life might taste very different today. I am very grateful for the parents God gave me. And as sure as age comes to all of us, I can assure you that neither my mother, nor my father, will ever go hungry or sleep in the rain, not if I am alive and can function. I pray they will never need me, and they probably won't, but that is my promise to them. That is their net.

CHAPTER 6
STAY OUT OF THE RUTS

• • •

Take some chances...choose a path less traveled.

The bartending kept me afloat, but I didn't want to get caught in that routine like so many others. I've witnessed it first hand. I worked with several guys and gals that'd been in the bar biz for twenty years or more. Bartending was great at twenty-something but I just couldn't imagine being a bartender at forty or fifty years old working for $2.00 an hour plus tips. I always had two things going: The bar job and my new business of the month.

Along the way, someone told me that owning rental houses was the way to get rich. So, I rented out my first condo and purchased another larger one across town on Powhatan Street. My new two-story condo had two bedrooms and two baths and a kitchen and a den with a fireplace. I rented out the second room of my new condo to a roommate, and that money, together with the positive cash flow from my first condo, made the payments on both condos a non-issue. As long as I had a roommate and my first condo was rented out, I was living for *free*! Eventually the volatility of condo association fees would drive me away from condos, but for awhile there I really enjoyed this condo ownership thing I had going.

I also bought some property out in Boerne, Texas, around that time. A man sold me a lot high up on a hill and financed it for me. The day I closed on it, I drove my mother out to see my latest conquest and to celebrate the occasion. We picked up a bottle of champagne and two long-stemmed champagne glasses along the way. We got there and hiked up to the very highest point. It was beautiful there and we could look out over the countryside for as far as the eye could see. I popped the cork on the champagne and we made a toast to the beautiful Texas hill country and my new purchase. The day was sunny and clear and the view was fantastic—then Mom slipped!

In reflex, she grabbed hold of me, but I wasn't prepared. Off we went, like two square bowling balls, rolling down the hillside in a cloud of dust and tiny bubbles. I could've saved myself some serious bruising but I wouldn't let go of the bottle or my glass or Mom. Finally, we came to a stop at the bottom of the hill right next to each other. The dust was settling over us, and in a silent gesture I immediately offered up the bottle for another drink. Mom offered up her champagne glass, but the cup part had shattered on the way down, and the only thing left was a stem. We laughed until we cried. I laughed until champagne came out my nose. Mom thought that was really, really funny, and she laughed so hard she inadvertently belched like a sailor. Now, I don't think I'd ever heard my mother burp in my entire life so that launched me into a category of laughter way past hysteria—way, way out there somewhere where *you can't breathe* kind of laughing happens.

We started to gather our composure after awhile but lost it again when we began to dust each other off and pick the debris out of each other's hair. I didn't think we were ever going to get off that piece of property. The next morning we were both pretty sore. I don't know if it was from the fall or from laughing so hard for so long. I suspect it was a bit of both. In all honesty, we were lucky we didn't get hurt.

CHAPTER 7
REAL ESTATE MAKES MONEY?

• • •

I bought my first properties because I wanted to be an owner. Actually making money on real estate wasn't even on my radar screen.

Eventually, I sold the land for what I paid for it and recouped my $3,000 down payment. I made a mental note; *"It's hard to get raw land to pay for itself."* Simply put: I needed money. I was broke until I sold the land and got my $3,000 down payment back, plus I sold the Powhattan Condo for another $12,000 worth of profit. $15,000 was more money than I'd even seen in one place in my life! To me it was the world, and I was dancing on top of it. The ink wasn't even dry on my deposit slip when I learned two new real estate words to add to my vocabulary. The words were *balloon payment*. Yep, repeat after me: *ballooooonnn paaaaaymeeeent*.

Mortgage companies were scrambling to get out of certain types of loans, and condo loans were at the top of their list. Apparently, the balance on my first condo note was due immediately. I barely had enough to cover the call. Luckily, I had been making extra principle payments during the good times so I had decreased the balance radically. Despite my good pay history, no one would refinance me. It took everything I had to pay them off. Rich one day then broke again the next. But at least I had one condo free and clear.

Although the experience of feeling *loaded* with cash was brief, I liked the feeling of having a large bank account. My thoughts were racing when I came to the conclusion that if I sold my first condo for what I'd paid for it I would have $28,000 back into my account. No problem I thought. Wrong.

I didn't know how lucky I was to sell the Powhattan condo. The recession of the 80's was in full swing. It seems that condos were worth about half of what they'd been, and I couldn't sell it for anything close to what I had in it. Now I knew why no one would refinance me. (I was a little slow back then.) It didn't help that my condo association fee went up. Then, when the tenant skipped out, I moved back in. Since I'd paid it off, all I had to pay was the monthly condo association fee, which was only $135 per month at the time. I was sick that my investment had decreased in value so drastically, but living cheap wasn't so bad. After checking out the apartment rates, the decision to move back into my old condo was real easy.

I made another mental note: When a recession hits and/or interest rates go up, fewer people can qualify to buy properties. As a result, rents go sky high. In the simplest of terms, if the market ain't buyin', they're rentin' (or they're owner financing). This is perhaps one of the most important lessons I've ever learned concerning the economics of cash flow properties. In the years to come this simple truth will save my buttocks more than once. It bears repeating; if the population is not buying, they are renting…or they are buying via "Owner Financing."

During the recession of the mid 80's, I kept bartending at night, and during the day, I took a job working for a pair of judges who had an on-going real estate law practice. Did I mention that I worked very hard when I was young? I always had a day job and a night job. (I'm not saying that's right but that's what I did). These two judges owned about forty low-income rental units. Did I say low-income? What I meant to say was low, low, low-income rental properties. It was there, at that job, I learned some of the most valuable lessons in real estate.

CHAPTER 8
THERE'S A NEW LANDLORD IN TOWN

• • •

Higher yields on the lesser side of town.

To the best of my knowledge the term, low income, refers to the income of the tenants, or maybe it refers to the rents as being low. Whatever the case, it doesn't take long for me to discern that it *does not* refer to the amount of profit being made by the landlord. Owning low-income properties creates a unique opportunity to make big, if not huge, rates of return on your investment on paper.

To actually collect that profit, you have to mitigate the turnover rate, the delinquencies, the eviction costs, and the maintenance and repair costs. That is not as easy as it may seem, but it can be done if you stay on top of the business. And you can't be afraid to walk on the poor side of town.

These two judges would buy a giant, run-down house that use to be a magnificent mansion, but instead of renting it to one person for $800 per month, they'd section it off into eight, one-bedroom apartments and rent each room for $50 per week. Thus the property would produce $1600 plus per month. (Remember: there are more than four weeks in a month.) Also, let's not forget, a $10 late fee was added to each week if the rent is not handed over promptly every Friday. These late fees make a considerable difference in the yield. In this particular situation, let me tell you, everybody—and I do mean *everybody*—was always late if not downright behind.

That's where I came into the picture. Drum Roll Please. TA-DA. SUPER MANAGER! Yep, that was me. The lawyers had been busy lawyering, and the rents (or the lack thereof) had gotten way out of hand. I was hired to straighten things out. My job was to kick out the bums, fill the vacancies, collect the rents, enforce the late fees, and keep up with regular maintenance. Did I mention I had no experience at this whatsoever? That didn't seem to bother the two judges and it dang sure didn't bother me. I collected more money—cash money—than I'd ever seen in my life. And I collected it on a weekly basis! Once I realized the potential of my job, I was a man possessed. Look out boys, there's a new landlord in town and he's taking no prisoners. I was good to the good ones and bad to the bad ones. It didn't take long to get a reputation. You paid or you were out!

Every now and then, a tenant would ask for an extra day or two with the rent. I'd give them one chance. I wanted to be fair and understanding, but it usually got us screwed. I learned to tell them up front, if they broke their promise *one time*, I'd never take their word again. Everybody got one chance. They could never call me unfair and know it to be true in their heart of hearts.

What amazed me was that, most of the time, all the apartments shared one common bathroom down the hall. I had to see it to believe it, but it worked as long as I worked it.

The average rate of return on your investment is much higher when you deal in cheaper income-producing properties. Do the math: What has a higher rate of return?

A. An $80,000 house with 8 rooms at $50 per week... $1,600 per month

B. An $80,000 house that rents for $800 per month…$800 per month

I use a quick formula to size up the potential of an investment. Suddenly the math problems I'd struggled with in high school were making sense.

Formula: Annual Income divided by CASH Investment = Return On Investment
Example A: $1,600 X 12 divided by $80,000 = 24% ROI
Example B: $ 800 X 12 divided by $80,000 = 12% ROI

This is a cash-on-cash calculation that lets me know how long it will take to get the original investment back. This simple formula has been close enough for me to decide to buy or not to buy for most of my career. I just recently purchased my first real estate calculator after ten years of investing, but I think I'm going to return it. I like to keep things real simple. Today, when the cash-on-cash rate of return is around 25%, I start looking at the investment really hard. When the rate of return gets up into the 30% bracket, I start grabbing for my wallet. When the rate of return is into the 40% bracket, or over, I am literally running to the bank. All of that being said, never forget, a super high rate of return could mean that there are hidden problems concerning the property or that there are a lot of moving parts to keeping the cash flowing.

I learned so much about real estate and people while working for those two judges, it was life altering. Just like the days spent starting Mitchell Striping, I was growing a million miles per minute again. Although I wasn't exactly getting rich in either business, the feeling of personal growth made the work invigorating. Earlier in life, my parents had offered to pay for my college education, and I didn't get one (my decision). Now I was getting paid to get an education and it was meaningful. I could actually *feel* my personal growth happening. As far as I was concerned, I could learn more pertinent stuff in a month of hanging around entrepreneurs than I could in four years of math classes, or history classes, or even economics classes. The best education happens in real time and in real life. I made it a point to hang around the thinkers and the doers, the movers and the shakers, and the people who were successful.

CHAPTER 9
THE CARWASH AT SPRIGGSDALE & COMMERCE

• • •

Sometimes you're just outnumbered.

By 1987, my efforts in the rental management department really started to show up in the form of profits for the two judges. Because I'd been responsible and trustworthy with their business and their cash, the judges offered me a percentage of a carwash if I could get it up and running. The old carwash was in a very rough part of town and had long since been abandoned. The judges already owned the little strip center and the land it sat on, so it was an easy decision when they offered me a 33% share of the profit if I could turn it around for a reasonable amount of money. They'd put up the money and I'd put up the work.

I did a lot of research and running around for a few weeks. I researched equipment and installers and tried to salvage everything I could in the old place. I pulled together a simple business plan and budget and the project was approved by all of us in short order. We were off to the races! I was about to own 33% of a carwash! My dreams were aloft.

I worked hard to get the carwash opened by the deadline we'd set. I was in completely uncharted waters but that was starting to be normal for me. When "Grand Opening Day" arrived we ordered up some helium balloons and put them out around our grand opening sign. We sat out, off in the distance, and watched as the first customers rolled in and started putting quarters into the machines. First there was one customer and then two customers and then two more and, well, I was amazed! I was finally going to get some mail box money of my own.

We were all excited so we came up with a plan to celebrate at one of the fanciest restaurants in town. There we could get some well deserved relaxation and service and toast to our new venture. It was a great evening. We laughed and joked and speculated as to how many golden eggs our new goose was going to lay. We went on and on into the evening and stayed out way too late and had way too much fun. I could hardly sleep because it was my job to empty the machines in the morning and report how much money we'd made on our first day. The morning came way sooner than I wanted it too. Seemed like I went to bed for five minutes and then it was time to get up again. I was a hurtin' unit!

Once I got an ice cold Big Red and a couple of *chorizo con huevo* tacos in my belly I started to feel a bit better. The anticipation of collecting cash at the carwash had me pushing the speed limit down Interstate Highway 37 South. I weaved through a few side streets and approached the carwash. The closer I got the worse I started to feel. No, it wasn't from the fun we'd had the night before. It was from looking at the gaping hole in the side of our freshly painted carwash. The new $3,000 change machine had been ripped completely out of the brick wall.

Upon further inspection, I could see where the steal vault machine had been dragged down the street by a vehicle of some sort. There were scratch marks in the asphalt the whole way. The tracks kept going and going, but I figured I'd let the police find out where the trail ended. It was headed into a part of town I really did not want to go into by myself, unarmed as I was.

The police arrived, a report was filed, no one was ever arrested, and we closed the carwash. There was simply no way to stop people from stealing while you were away. I can't tell you how disappointed I was. We were all disappointed but I was still struggling financially and this deal was going to be the answer to my prayers. Obviously, there were other plans in store for me. As everyone left the carwash it started to rain. I remember thinking, "A little rain would have been good for business."

CHAPTER 10
POWER OF THE WRITTEN WORD

• • •

To this day I am amazed at the amount of power the written word can possess over the actions and emotions of the human spirit.

About this time, around the end of 1988, my personal life started to unravel. I was watching and helping others build their fortunes but I was still struggling in the financial department. Financial stress and my basic immaturity led to my demise. I'd been in a relationship spanning better than five years, but it was simply taking too long for me to find myself. When my significant other left, so did a large source of continuity. The endless string of business failures, the stress of living paycheck-to-paycheck, losing the woman I loved, it was all too much, and I went crashing to the bottom emotionally. Not like the breakdown I had experienced from over working. That was a different breakdown. This breakdown had to do with confidence. I was beginning to doubt myself—with conviction.

In an effort to fight my depressed state, my mother begged me to read some used books she'd found at garage sales or flea markets. She pleaded with me constantly, "Just read ten pages a day." This went on for days. Finally I decided to humor her. I picked up a stupid little book written by some nerd named Napoleon Hill. The book was titled *Think and Grow Rich*. I began to read the first ten dumb pages. The ten pages rolled into twenty and then into thirty pages before I knew it. Each day it would take a concerted effort for me to get started on just ten pages, but I never stopped at ten pages. I always felt better during and after reading. I learned that just a few minutes of reading about the possibility of being successful could actually make me rise above it all for a moment. I recognized the healing power of this diversion called reading. I didn't read much before that in my life. I never liked reading. But now its effect on me was undeniable. I've said it before and I'll say it again, *"God Bless Mommas."*

Think and Grow Rich was absolutely life altering for me. It gave me hope and a direction at a time when I was meeting with more rejection than I could handle. It helped to hear that many of the successful people documented in that book had failed many, many times before their ships came in. It showed me that many of the most successful people in the world didn't have a college education. Author, Napoleon Hill, was hired by Andrew Carnegie to find and prove up the common denominators for success. Instead the book seemed to prove that success could come from anywhere and everywhere and that there was no right or wrong way. It suggested that success was something that you learned over a long period of time and that if you set certain priorities in your life that your chances for success would be immensely increased if not predestined. The real trick was to make those priorities part of the fabric of your life and not just a garment to wear for a while. I studied those priorities, I agreed with them, and then I wove those new fibers into the fabric of my own life. Over time they formed the cloth that is ME today. I'd heard about such things before but apparently I wasn't ready to learn it then. I learned it when I picked up the right book at the right time in my life. I learned because I was ready to learn it. Someone once said, *"The teacher will appear when the student is ready."* I know this to be true in my life.

We'd all be better off if we paid more attention to what our minds hear, see, and think. More importantly, we need to listen to how we talk to ourselves. The greatest life lesson I've ever learned has been to listen to my inner voice. I listen to what it is saying to ME, and if it's not positive, I start immediately to change that. In a perfect world my inner voice would never say anything bad to me or about me. The worst thing my inner voice should ever say to me is, "You'll do much better next time, Mitch, and you will get there because you have or will be presented with everything you'll need to do it."

There is no doubt about it. We become what we feed our minds. May I suggest, the most important thing you'll ever do in your life, will be to recognize your inner voice when it speaks, monitor that voice, and control the message you're sending yourself millions of times a year. The thing we hear more than anything in our entire life is our inner voice. What are you saying to yourself? Are you telling yourself that you can, or are you telling yourself you can't? Let me tell you a little secret: If we are limited in any way it's because the message we are sending ourselves is wrong. Change your self talk and you will change your life! Its incredible how many people never take control of their inner voice.

One day, when things weren't going my way, my father showed his intuitive nature. He left me a note that read, "Life is 10% of what happens to us…and 90% of how we handle what happens to us."

I don't know where he got his statistics but that statement was good enough for me. It rings true even when we're not listening for a bell.

One of the teachers that appeared in my life was Maxwell Maltz, M.D., F.I.C.S. If you haven't read *Psycho-Cybernetics* by Maltz, DO IT! I'll assure you I'm not making any money off that book. I will also assure you I would have been well served if I had found his works earlier in my life.

A large part of the books I read, I read on the road. Shortly after the collapse of my love life, I ended up working for Spencer Engineering (out of Spencer, Massachusetts). Just prior to that job, I was trying to sell cars. Have you ever tried to sell something when you had a broken heart? If you have then you know, you ain't sellin' crap, Jack! I was sitting on the showroom floor going broke when I decided it was time to talk with the man upstairs. I remember that moment as clearly as if it were yesterday.

CHAPTER 11
THE POWER OF PRAYER

• • •

Say what you want, I know what I know...
and be careful what you pray for.

Anyone who knows me well knows I have a strong faith. Unfortunately, like many of us, I get a stronger dose of religion when things aren't going my way. About this particular time I was going broke trying to sell cars, so I asked God for help. I prayed that if He would show me a way to make $40,000 to $50,000 a year that I wouldn't waste the opportunity. I am a chronic doodler and, during the prayer, I scribbled the numbers "$40,000 – $50,000" on my desktop calendar. (Yes, I believe God hears me…even if my eyes are open and I doodle during my prayers.) After saying, "Amen," I left my desk for a cup of coffee in the break room. I was pouring cream into my cup when the receptionist announced over the intercom that I had a call on line one. I picked up the call on the break-room phone. It was a friend of mine, Steve Whitaker.

ME: Hello

STEVE: Hey Mitch, it's Steve. I heard things aren't going so good for you.

ME: That's an understatement, Steve.

STEVE: I thought maybe you'd like to get the heck out of town and make some money.

ME: I really need to do something. I'm going broke fast. In the condition I'm in right now, I couldn't sell water to a man on fire.

STEVE: Look, I took a job with this company up North and we're short handed. I heard about your situation and thought you might be primed to take off and try something new.

ME: What kinda work you doin'?

STEVE: You'd be installing telephone wires and networking computers in chain stores all over the country.

ME: Steve, I don't know anything about installing telephone wires or computers.

STEVE: Don't worry, you've always been a quick study and you like to work hard. I'll teach you everything you need to know. You don't have to do it forever, but I'll need you to commit to at least six months. The pay is good and all the gas, food, and rooms are paid for. All you need is $130 to buy your tools.

ME: What if I don't have $130?

STEVE: I'll loan it to you.

ME: How much is the pay?

STEVE: A good man could make about $45,000 a year counting the overtime. Think about it. Call me back. Don't wait too long!

I wrote Steve's phone number on the back of one of my business cards and under it I wrote, "$45,000." When I hung up the phone I was thinking of only one thing. If I took the job, I'd be headed out of town for an extended period of time. I would positively lose any chance of winning back the person I was pining over. I still wanted to fight for her. If I left San Antonio, I would be out of the picture. Any chance I had with her would be put on ice.

I strolled back over to my desk and plopped down in my chair. I held the business card in front of me and stared at it for quite sometime before I closed my eyes and shook my head no. Then, in the darkness, like some Las Vegas blackjack dealer, I inadvertently flicked the card onto my desk. With my hands now free I could therapeutically massage the stress from my forehead. Eyes still closed, I rolled forward in my chair so I could rest my elbows on the desk and rub my face and eyes. I continued to massage my face and forehead as I pondered my life. When I opened my eyes, I was looking down at my desktop. The card had landed right next to the numbers I had scribbled in doodle fashion during my conversation with God. The numbers on the desk calendar read, "$40,000 – $50,000." The number on the card read, "$45,000." It was plain as day. It was right there in front of me.

Within a matter of minutes, I was being given exactly what I'd prayed for. I thought to revise my prayer and ask God for a good job in San Antonio, but I immediately rejected the idea. God had given me exactly what I'd asked for, nothing more, nothing less. I'd emphatically promised God that I wouldn't waste the opportunity if it were given to me. If I was going to keep my word to God and to myself, I had to take the job I'd asked for and was being presented with right now.

This was gonna hurt. The axe was about to fall on my heart. I dialed Steve's number:

ME: Hey Steve, when can I start?
STEVE: When can you leave?
ME: How 'bout right now?

STEVE: I figured you'd be quick to make up your mind. I just finished checking the flights. Delta Flight 2874 leaves in four hours. Is that fast enough?

ME: I'll be there!

STEVE: Hey Mitch, don't you want to know where you're going?

ME: I don't give a damn, Steve.

(CLICK…I hung up the phone.)

WACK! The axe landed hard and true. It was done. I knew it for sure. It hurt like any amputation without anesthesia would. Game over. She was gone. I'd lost her for sure now.

Shortly after that conversation, I landed at the airport in Worcester, Massachusetts, and I hopped into a red Ford Econo van with someone I'd never met before in my life.

I remember my first day with Spencer Engineering. I remember that night it was brutally cold and my turn to ride in the passenger seat. We were driving to the next job somewhere around Lake Erie, Pennsylvania. There was a hole in the floorboard on the passenger side, so I crawled to the back of the van to get away from the artic blast coming up from the floor. I curled up in a sleeping bag in the back to stay warm. It dawned on me that I was twenty-eight years old, and I was sleeping in a cold, rickety jalopy like some homeless person. It was true. I had no home by then. I had no car. The only possessions at hand were packed in one duffle bag which I was using as a pillow. It was embarrassing.

The only thing that made it tolerable was that nobody around me really knew me. I was ashamed, but I took comfort that no one I loved could see me this way. I wanted to say I was better than all this but in fact I wasn't. I would not have been there if I was *better*. I had lost my love to a "Gentleman rancher" and I was sure they were out living "the good life" while *life* in general was kicking the living dog crap out of me. In some accidental stroke of genius or common sense, I never blamed *him* or *her*; I blamed me. That made my reality even tougher. I had only thought I was at the bottom when I left the car lot. This was substantially lower and colder. This was the bottom of the bottom and no one to blame…but me.

It was there, that night in the cold, in that rickety, red van, that I made a decision. I was going to have to start all over, from the ground up, in every aspect of my life. No one could help me, and I wasn't about to ask for help anyway. I was going to have to rebuild myself by myself. Being in this situation pissed me off! I was never ever, ever, ever going to go backwards again. If you think you are getting to the core of what makes Mitch Stephen tick, you're real close, baby.

Looking back I can see how the books I'd been reading were affecting my life decisions. I'd shown great integrity (if only to myself) by taking the job with Spencer Engineering. I opened my mouth and asked for it, prayed for it, even promised to do well by it. If I hadn't have taken the job, I'd have been a *schmuck* to myself! Being a *schmuck* to yourself will absolutely kill your self esteem. You just can't have it! Something else was beginning to happen as well. One of the most basic of all success principles had already started to thread its way into the fabric of my life. I was taking full responsibility for my life and everything in it, and everything that happened in it. By holding myself accountable, I was taking all that power away from everyone else, and that was giving me power. It is a very real power and I could feel it. I don't know if I was getting it from the books, or what, but I was beginning to hold myself accountable. Then again, it had to be the books. I didn't know nor think about those kinds of things before the books.

I also began to recognize that there is a considerable amount of freedom at the bottom. It is a terrific place to reinvent *you*. You have nothing to lose and there is usually no one around to talk you out of it. (All the opinions givers tend to leave when you run out of money.)

Over the next weeks and months, my convictions grew stronger: If I had to crawl to Hell and back on my hands and knees, I was not going back to San Antonio until I could go with my head held high, not if I had anything to do with it. If I returned before then, it'd be in a pine box. I made up my mind not to quit Spencer Engineering until I was successful, whatever that meant. I really didn't know what success was or even what I wanted to be successful at. All right, so what? With my financial needs met, I was going to stay out on the road until I had it figured out. I needed knowledge, and that fit right in with my therapeutic reading. I could get knowledge and therapy at the same time. I'll work and read, read and work. I'll work and read myself right out of this mess—Damn it!

"ACCEPT SHE'S GONE"

Written By Mitch Stephen & Billy O'Rourke

I've played it over in my mind
Around and 'round a thousand times
"Could have", "Would have", "Should have done"
The words, "I'm Sorry Love", are right here on my tongue

CHORUS:
Except she's gone
I could be lovin' her tonight
Except she's gone
I could have stars in my eyes
I don't wanna tell myself the truth
It's been the hardest thing to do
And I just don't know how to...
Accept she's gone

A broken vase, a stranded rose
The reason's why, God only knows
I hate to see things end this way
And I'd give anything, just to make her stay

(REPEAT CHORUS)

TAG:

I don't wanna tell myself the truth
It's been the hardest thing to do
And I just don't know how to...
Accept she's, gone
Accept she's gone
I just can't accept she's gone
Oh, accept she's gone

Listen: http://www.mitchstephen.comacceptshesgoneasp?music=on
Sung by Kevin Hughes

www.MitchStephen.com

CHAPTER 12
FEATHER IN THE WIND

• • •

I was born on the corner of Freedom Drive and Opportunity Lane but I was learning to think like an immigrant.

Over the next five years, I worked in almost every mall in the United States and most of them at least twice. Traveling to the malls introduced me to all the big cities of America. We'd do a prototype for a chain store like The Foot Locker, and then they'd award Spencer Engineering a contract to do 6,500 Foot Locker locations across the nation and abroad. Most of the time a single job would only take two to four hours and then we'd be off to the next mall.

I visited every nook and cranny of the United States of America, Puerto Rico, St. Thomas, and St. Croix. We pulled thousands of miles of cable in chain stores like Foot Locker, Lady Foot Locker, The Gap, The Kids Gap, Kenny Shoes, The Limited, Structure, Marians, Marians Plus, Spencer's Gifts, Victoria's Secret, Talbot's, Lazarus, and the list goes on and on. Along the way I saw Mt. Rushmore, the Golden Gate Bridge, the Grand Canyon, Niagara Falls (both sides), Gettysburg, the Big Apple, Times Square, Harlem, the Bronx, Central Park, New Orleans/Mardi Gras, the Little Big Horn, the White House, the Washington Monument, the Lincoln Memorial, The Wall

(Vietnam Veteran's Memorial), and hundreds of other places I'd read about in books or seen on TV or in magazines. The change of scenery across this great nation kept my eyes and my ears and my mind occupied as old man time worked to fix the inherent throws of a broken heart.

"THE JOKE'S ON ME"

Written By Mitch Stephen and Billy O'Rourke

I was looking through the attic, for a fishin' pole
When I reached to move a box, and the bottom broke
And every photograph of you, I ever owned
Was starrin' straight up at me from the floor

Well I tried not to look down, as I knelt to pick them up
But my fav'rite one was burning holes in me
And it led me to the reason's why, I had to pack them up
And no, I didn't get much fishin' done that day

CHORUS:
And just about the time I think it's over
Oh just when love, is dead and gone...
There you'll be, Standin' in my memories
'N' there I'll go, Feelin' like it use to be
Just about the time, I think it's safe to laugh at love
The joke's on me

I'd loaded up the ice chest, for a weekend at the coast
I was gonna drink some beer, and soak some sun
When just outside the driveway, A DJ raised your ghost
And played a tune that hurt to sing along

Well I should've turn it down, Hell, I should've turned it off
But it sounded just to much like you and me
By the time I'd learned the words and chords, All the beer was gone
And no, I didn't spend the weekend at the beach

(REPEAT CHORUS)

BRIDGE
:
I almost made it out to Vegas
But I found your Negligee, In our honeymoon suitcase

(REPEAT CHORUS)

Just about the time, I think it's safe to laugh at love
The joke's on me
I was lookin' through the attic, for a fishin' pool

Listen: http://www.mitchstephen.com/jokes.asp?music=on
Sung by Kevin Hughes

www.MitchStephen.com

About the time I got used to the malls, Spencer Engineering picked up a contract with Rite Aid Pharmacy. Rite Aid was buying up all of the mom and pop pharmacies in the eastern part of the U.S. We went to work converting about 2,700 pharmacies from the old NCR register systems to the newest, latest and greatest IBM register systems. Rite Aid introduced me to hundreds and hundreds of little townships up and down the east coast and then inland towards the middle of the nation. The Rite Aid jobs didn't take much longer than two to four hours either. We traveled like the wind, never sleeping in the same bed.

The way it worked out, we never stayed in the same hotel for more than one night. Ninety days on the road, ninety hotel rooms, ten days off. Luckily, we'd get about thirty-five days off at the end of the year. We'd go home for Thanksgiving and stay home through the Christmas shopping season. Nobody wanted us working in their stores during the holiday rush. Work started back up again around January 3rd. We got paid overtime for actual hours spent working over forty hours per week but straight (flat rate) time for driving hours. My time card registered between 100 to 120 hours per week. Ten or fifteen or twenty of those hours would be overtime wages. The only thing that made this many hours possible was that one person could sleep while the other was driving.

We logged thousands and thousands of miles a month. I would drive for one tank of gas and then I would sleep or sit in the passenger seat and read while my co-worker drove one tank of gas. When I wasn't sleeping, I read. I read to fight my depression, I read to fight the boredom, I read to fight the fear of uncertainty, and I read to fight my broken heart—thousands of miles every month. All the while the books were working on me. I continued to read books because they gave me hope, they encouraged me, they occupied my mind, and they were beginning to change my thought process at the very core. I'm definitely a "Roads Scholar."

I read about success: Autobiographies of successful men, successful selling, successful negotiating, how to be successful, etc. I picked up books about real estate and read them all. I read books on how to build a rent-house business, how to make a million dollars in real estate, how to create notes, how to buy property, how to sell property. At the time, I thought I might want to be a professional songwriter so I even read every autobiography of every country music icon I could find. Although I couldn't read while I was driving, my heart was still broken while I was driving, so I purchased cassette tapes. I listened to gurus of real estate like Ron Le Grand, John Schaub, Lonnie Scruggs and Jimmy Napier. They kept telling me, "I could do it! I could do it just like they did!" Sometimes I just wanted to explode. I wanted to try their ideas and techniques so badly, but I was in a van going to some town with a name I wasn't sure how to pronounce. Have you ever been to Schuylkill, PA? You had to think about it didn't you?

The books I was reading about the music business taught me a lot as well. Most of the famous people I grew up listening to on the radio seemed to have the life to envy. After reading their stories, I learned that most of them grew up poor as dirt. Many of them lived in the most meager environments early on: Homes with dirt floors, no electricity or running water. Yes, they were famous now, but the road had been long and hard for all of them. Their roads were hard just like my road was hard, so I took solace in their stories. From Ronnie Milsap, Randy Travis, and Willie Nelson to Johnny Cash, Hank Williams, and Hank Jr., to Dolly Parton, Tammy Wynette, Conway Twitty, and Merle Haggard, they all had it tough. All we ever see is the glory and glamour once they've garnered acclaim, but after reading their stories I had a much greater respect for a music person's success, whether I like their music or not. I related to their struggles and it made me more comfortable with my own.

Eventually, I would choose real estate over music, but I often wonder what might have happened if I'd dedicated myself to being a great songwriter. I guess to wonder "what if" is normal. Writing music is the only thing I have saved from my childhood. Writing has been a great release for me. I turn to my music in my deepest, darkest hours, and it has given me great comfort. It is a *venting* of sorts and a very real *release* for me. I find myself much lighter when I have completed a song on a certain topic or specific emotional event. It is as if I can *let go* when that personal emotion has been documented in song…my song. Songs have a way of taking a person back to a very specific point in time and putting them in exactly the same emotional state as when they were then. By creating my own songs, I am able to let go of some things much easier because I know if I ever want to go back, I simply pull that song out of my head and sing it to myself

One book that might well be responsible for my choice of real estate over music came as a personal revelation to me. The book was *Nothing Down* by Robert G. Allen. Allen had the audacity to suggest that I didn't need money to buy real estate (or to buy anything for that matter). Talk about timing? I had more *nothing* than anybody I knew! If *nothing* could buy real estate then I had enough *nothing* to by the whole darn town over the weekend! I had *nothing* but *nothing*, so that book and I connected the minute I read the title. Although I didn't agree with the author's propensity to over leverage, I was struck by the potential of creative thinking. It also taught me to ask many more questions during negotiations than I used to.

The truth of the matter was this: I wouldn't actually take the power of *Nothing Down* as my own for another six years. Controlling real estate with little or no money is an easy concept to read about. It is very easy for *their* lips to say and for *your* ears to hear, but, it is a life altering revelation when you actually come to *own* the concept.

Once you actually *own* the concept, there is no limit to what you can buy.

At Spencer Engineering, I was the brunt of a lot of jokes. I had my books and my tapes and everyone was a comedian. Last I heard, some of those guys are still there.

During my travels I read a book called *Self Made in America* by John McCormack. That author pointed out something that impacted me so strongly that I could almost swear I felt the revelation physically hit me with a thud. The book centered on the many immigrants who'd come to the USA with nothing, and I mean *nothing*, not even the language, and became financially independent in a relatively short period of time. Most of us born into this great country can't seem to get past buying designer clothes and all the luxuries available to us. As the author pointed out, the reason was obvious. The immigrants were used to having nothing. Sleeping on the floor of the donut shop while they saved enough money to buy the donut shop didn't faze them. They were emotionally able to sacrifice at a tremendously higher level than all of us wimps born here smack dab on the corner of *Freedom Drive* and *Opportunity Lane*. Not only that, immigrants recognized the opportunity offered in America as golden: a genuine gift sent from the heavens…the opportunity of a lifetime. Just like when I made that promise to the man upstairs, when I walked off of that showroom floor and on to that airplane to anywhere, those immigrants bound for success in McCormack's book were not going to squander the chance they'd been given. They came from places ruled in socialism or communism, even genocide…and now, here in the U.S. of A., they had a chance to control their own destiny.

Through *Self-Made in America*, John McCormack made me feel much better about the sacrifices I was making. Suddenly, I wasn't ashamed of sleeping in the back of that van in the freezing cold. I had finally culled myself from the herd. I had finally refused to travel with my nose in the butt of the cow in front of me. That was a good thing, not a bad thing. I was on the right track. The majority of the world had it all wrong this time, not me! I was choosing a road less traveled and man-o-man, *Life* was starting to smell a whole lot better!

I hope some day to meet Mr. McCormack. When I do, I'll tell him that his book made a difference in at least one person's life, mine! *Self Made in America* struck a chord way down inside of me and changed my shame into pride and conviction. It played an important roll in altering my life for the better. His lesson was there for me when I was ready to learn it. He explained exactly what I needed to know at that time, and I am grateful for Mr. McCormack's insight. If you know Mr. McCormack, tell him I'm looking forward to meeting him.

CHAPTER 13
ESCAPING THE DEBT TRAP

• • •

In some parts of the world people believe that debt is part of the Devil's plan. I completely understand how they could feel that way.

It took me the better part of a year working on the road to pay off all the credit card debt I'd amassed. For months I simply sent my pay checks to Texas. Mom had volunteered to handle my mail and my bills. I'd asked her to pay out every penny I made towards my debts. I got to where I didn't ask how much further I had to go, and Mom got to where she didn't say. All I knew was; I was making enough money to make a difference. Once I saw that I could do the job for Spencer Engineering and that I'd be gone so much of the time, I scuttled everything I didn't need or that cost me money every month. The company paid for all my rooms, food, and transportation. I sent every last dime I made home to pay my obligations. Every dime! It was hard. I worked, read, drove, ate, and slept. I put my head down and didn't look up. The less I thought about it the easier it was.

On the surface, my new job didn't pay all that much. What I found was that my new lifestyle, created by my job, allowed me to save money like I was making $100,000 per year. Think about it. I only made $45,000 per year, but I didn't need a place to live, I didn't need a car, I didn't pay for gasoline, I didn't pay for food or utilities. Many times I would be able to save money out of the per diem allotted for living expenses on the road. Not to mention, we worked all the time! I found when I worked long and hard, I usually had a bunch of money stacked up at the end of the pay period. Working this job had a dynamic I'd learned to recognize: The more I worked the less I spent. When I was working I wasn't spending. Many of the other guys seemed to find ways to blow their money, but I tried hard to save mine. Others would buy new cars or boats or take vacations that cost a fortune. I wanted my *freedom*. I was not going to settle for anything less than freedom. I wanted financial freedom. I'd been paying the price, and slowly I was beginning to see it working.

After about a year or so, in a routine call home, Mom announced she had very good news. She was excited and I could hear it in her voice. I'd about given up hope of ever being caught up on my bills, so I didn't suspect what she was about to tell me. She had been struggling right along with me all the while and she was so happy to finally say, "Honey, you don't owe anybody a penny. You are a free man." I had escaped the debt trap and those words made me happier than I'd been in a long, long time. I had made up my mind to change things and slowly they were changing. I gave my Mom the next $1,000 I made for helping me get through all those bills and for being there for me during the hardest part of my life to that date. She certainly never asked for any pay. She never does, nor does she ever expect any but I needed to give it to her for my own reasons, and I was happy she accepted it. Dad was proud, too, and he let me know it. You can't put a price on that. You sure can't put a price on that.

On the road I began to realize that my former life and relations would've never been able to survive the sacrifices necessary to become debt free. Nor could I have accomplished such a feat in any reasonable length of time with all the expenses associated with a normal life of living and working (at least not on what I was capable of making at a job). I could sleep on the floor in a sleeping bag. If it were just me, it'd be no problem. But somehow I could never ask a wife or child to do that with me. During this time of personal soul searching, sacrifice, work, reinvention, and healing I was alone. I could do it *by myself*. Somehow this time alone was making me stronger. There was some little voice whispering, "You've made huge concessions. You've sacrificed. What you are doing is right. You deserve good things to happen to you."

Despite the obvious hardships, I have to admit, the first two years of traveling were exciting. The last three years took their toll. By the end of that career, I could hardly feel anything. In the name of financial success, I'd given up the need for personal affection and a sense of belonging and community. I'd been emotionally alone for so long that I was completely flat. In self defense, I'd learned not to get high and not to get low. I ran a constant medium. I worked when I had to work. I slept when I could work it in. I enjoyed the excitement of my travels at every opportunity. I went home when it was time to go home. I made it a point never to count the days, and so I didn't.

CHAPTER 14 THE DIFFERENCE BETWEEN HAM AND EGGS

• • •

There's commitment...and then there's commitment.

In 1989, the tide started to turn. Inside I was beginning to smile back at those laughing at me with my satchel of tapes and CDs and books. I started to see how I could win at my own financial game if I set my own pace and did it my way. Who cared what anybody else thought? They could drive an expensive car or buy an airplane for all I cared. The masses could spend their money how ever they wanted and for whatever they wanted. I would not measure myself by those symbols of success. I wanted my freedom. I was alone, still relatively young and strong and getting my spirit back. I was thinking like an immigrant. I was full of hope and eager for what the future had in store for me.

I even began to pretend I was an immigrant. Thus, I started to become grateful for the opportunity instead of being ashamed of my position in society. Losing my former life and being alone on the road was truly a gift from God, and I was not going to waste it, not one minute of it. My check was coming in every Friday because I took and *did* the job I'd asked God for and was given. I had made a personal promise to myself and to the man upstairs and I was sticking to it, and that decision was transforming me from a boy to a man.

I was beginning to realize that extraordinary success calls for extraordinary sacrifices. The majority of the world does not understand the simple concept of sacrificing for the future. Therefore, it's even harder to sacrifice because you're going against the grain of everything the masses are doing. Regular people look at you like you're nuts. Now I had a different reason why I was glad no one I knew could see me during my years of personal struggle. I was sacrificing at a level they just wouldn't understand and, honestly, I would not have been able to explain it to them at the time. All I knew then was that I was where I needed to be. No matter how hard or uncomfortable it was.

I still didn't have a clue as to *how* I would become successful, but I was ready to take on some type of challenge. Yes, I'd been reading about music and songwriting, but it seemed like too much of a fantasy. I could not get my arms around how people in the music business got paid: Three cents for every song played on the radio? Who keeps track of that? And how the heck would I be able to hold them accountable? I remembered my experience at Mitchell Striping and how hard it was to get compensated for work I had legitimately completed. I'd been reading about real estate, and that business seemed to have an answer to the collection problem. If you didn't get paid, you simply kept the money your buyer had given you and took back the property so you could sell it again. Even I could understand that! I valued real estate's ability to make a person whole again.

Nevertheless, I was still intimidated by the problems of time and distance created by my job. I'd been reading about controlling real estate without money, but I'd not come to own that concept in my heart yet. These thoughts led me to my next decision (right or wrong): I figured that building my home would be something I could commit to and handle.

By the late 80's, all my debt had been paid and I started to save some money. Every time I turned around I was putting at least another $600-$800 in the bank. Since I didn't know what I was meant to do with my life, I figured if I built my home one stick at a time with cash, it would be the same as putting money in the bank, maybe even appreciating more than money in the bank. I couldn't lose anything if I built a house…my home. I poured the slab in the summer of 1989. It was a beautiful day, and I was proud of the 32' x 70' concrete slab curing on the hillside. It had hardened just enough to walk on when Dad came to visit me.

DAD: Gott'er poured did you?
ME: Yes Sir!
DAD: How much did this cost you?
ME: $8,356.72
DAD: Well, I'll be. How much do you have left?
ME: Exactly $53.27 to my name.
DAD: You're the pig now, ain't ya?

The comment triggered that father/son power struggle thing we sometimes fall into when we are growing up.

ME: *Pig?*
DAD: Yeah. PIG! Do you ever order ham and eggs for breakfast?
ME (agitated): Of course I've ordered ham and eggs before, Dad. What's that got to do with the price of tea in China?
DAD: Do you know the difference between the ham and the eggs?

ME: All right, Dad. What's the difference between the ham and the eggs?

DAD: The chicken is involved, the pig is committed. Son, you are the pig today. *You* are committed.

ME (my agitation now replaced with pride, unable to stop an emerging smile): I guess I am. I'm the pig today. I'm dang sure the pig today!

Dad put his arm around my neck, resting his wrist on my shoulder. Then, without looking at me, he calmly spoke.

DAD: You'll make it, Son.

ME: You sure?

DAD: I'm sure.

If you are a father, don't ever underestimate how powerful your show of confidence can be. I was scared, and he knew it. I was in way over my head, and he knew that too. One short sentence, "*You'll make it Son,*" was exactly what I needed at that moment. It produced immediate and long-lasting courage. At least there were two people in the world who thought I could do it: Mom and Dad.

If I credit my mother with my emotional survival during my adolescent trials and tribulations, then I must give my father credit for my backbone and my ability to take a blow and then stand back up. As I said earlier, he's a former Marine (if there is such a thing) and as tough as they come. He has been both tough and soft at the same time. As early as I can remember, my father placed little notes anywhere and everywhere for me to find when I was alone. Somewhere there is a stack of encouraging "I Love You" notes and letters at least ten miles high. Throughout my life, I would find those little notes under my pillow or in my suitcase or on the windshield of my car, in my chest of drawers, or in my closet amongst my clothes, in the pocket of my pants or my shirt, in my football helmet or in my shoe, I would find them. More often than not they were anecdotal or euphemisms, always ending with his undying belief in me. I recall one of my favorites;

"There are no great men, just great challenges that ordinary men are forced by circumstance to meet."

I see people in this world who've never had that kind of father in their lives and I can't imagine how they ever make it. I cannot imagine my life without this man who always let me know he loved me and that he was watching me and pulling for me, if even from a distance. Although those little notes don't come as often these days (and I am sure because I don't need them as much), he still leaves them for me from time to time. You can believe it or not but, as God is my witness, I got one from him today as I write this chapter. It is August 1st, 2008. I am forty-seven years old.

That's me in the white t-shirt and dad in the white shorts…just before I learned "the difference between ham and eggs"

CHAPTER 15
HOW DO YOU EAT AN ELEPHANT?

• • •

One bite at a time.

I began to focus my extra energy and dream power on building my new home. It was a good diversion for me while I was on the road. I'd read home magazines and started paying attention to the different types of building materials and how much they cost, etc. I'd hit the road for ninety days, save my money, get my contractors lined up from afar, head home for ten days or so and try to get another step closer to actually getting the home livable.

I was building the place out of my pocket, one dollar at a time, one stick at a time, and it was not a very fast process. It was a big mistake not to use the power of leverage, but I'd just gotten out of a life of debt and I wasn't mentally prepared to owe anybody anything at that particular time. The task of building that house got overwhelming and I remember a few times being overwhelmed to the point of being paralyzed: So far to go and everything moving so slowly. There were times I thought it would never even get close to being finished.

Once the structure was dried in, things got really frustrating. Everything cost so much, and when I started adding it all up I'd get completely overwhelmed. I was about to throw my arms up when Mom suggested something to me. She suggested that I do the house just like I'd done everything else since I'd decided to change my life: One step at a time…and don't even think about the parts you're not working on. From that day forward, I would pick one room or even one aspect of a room and stay with it until it was beautifully complete. I started with the master bedroom, so I would have at least one fully functional room in the house I could retreat to at night when the day's work was done. Mom's suggestion made a huge difference. I sought my reward not in the finished product but in every small job well done. Our elders hold a great deal of knowledge from their experiences. Some if it is so simple we just can't see it when we're young. How do you eat an elephant? One bite at a time! I had finished the walls of my master bedroom. Next I finished the master bathroom and then the closets and then the floors and ceilings. When it was finished I was in heaven, as long as I didn't open the door to the living room and the rest of the house. It took me, and later us (my future wife and daughter), years to finish that house. You should see it today. It's almost finished! (It keeps improving.)

A lot of people pitched in to make that house livable. I'll use the word "livable" loosely because my family and I lived in this house for months on concrete floors when we could see every 2x4 in the walls and every 2x6 in the ceilings. When I started the sink was set into a piece of 4' x 8' plywood held up by raw wooden 4x4 legs. Some of the friends I'd made at Spencer Engineering lived in nearby San Antonio and came to wire the complete house in one weekend. It was winter and very cold, but they bundled up and knocked it out. Thanks to Steve, Kevin, Brian, and Tino (my Spencer buddies), heat came just in the nick of time. It was a cold winter that year, and I remember thinking how grateful I was that they'd helped me.

That Christmas, I simply couldn't wait for Santa Claus to arrive. For the first time in a long time, I actually got things I wanted, or better stated, things that I *needed*, and boy did I need a lot of things! Ceiling Fans. Door Knobs. Windows. Doors. Sinks. Faucets.

You name it, I needed it! And let's not forget the tools! Tim the Tool Man had nothing on me come Christmas time. That was one of the things I was counting on when I poured that slab a few years back. I was counting on the idea that if people saw me with my head down working and sweating against impossible odds, somehow help would show up when I needed it.

Taking on the task of building a home was a complete leap of faith. As it turned out, I never had to ask for help. People just tended to show up. I think it had a lot to do with the passion I had for the project. I'm also sure that it didn't hurt that, in the past, I'd tried my best to show up when others needed help.

My heart was still in ill repair but, by now, I was not daydreaming about winning *anyone* back. I was mourning through my music more or less and therapeutically documenting my lament in song. I was piling up a number of songs I needed to get off my chest. Songs I wanted get out of my head and committed to tape. I am fortunate enough to be able to create my music from within so I can do it while I'm driving or while I'm working, and sometimes, while I'm sleeping. I really wanted to hear what my art might sound like with a real production, talented players, and talented singers. It was a freshman effort and it showed, but the energy I got from seeing the art in my head develop into a full fledged, ready for sale, cassette tape gave me tremendous energy. Although the project was yet more work heaped upon my other work, it was a respite from the grinding thoughts of debt, money, and financial freedom. It was a labor of love, and I chose to steal the time. I'd get home from the studio tired in the wee hours of the morning but somehow invigorated and rejuvenated at the same time. While deep down I knew the money spent completing the album, *Some Fires Never Die,* would never come back, the dream of hearing my music overruled my fiscal side. I spent countless hours and $10,000 on that project. It came at a time when I was saturated with the idea of making every penny count towards my independence, but I also instinctively knew I had to take care of myself emotionally. I was hurting in that department, and my music seemed to subdue the pains that ailed me. Some people have a stack of therapist bills at the end of a relationship. I ended up with a cassette tape. It was money well spent as far as I was concerned.

I don't mean to get sappy, but it is relevant to my story and everyone's story. In life, things we don't want to happen—happen. Fortunes get lost, loved ones pass, limbs get amputated, and hearts get broken. The point is this. I'm no different than anyone else. During this time of personal and financial struggle and of self discovery and growth, I had my own personal crosses to bear, just like everyone else. The sun is going to come up in the morning. It is going to come up in the same place it always comes up. The sun is going to set. When it does, it will set in the same place it always sets. In between, we have the choice to sit down or stand up. For whatever reason, I was choosing to stand up. I was not, however, choosing to ignore my pain or bury it in negative ways. I was confronting it through my music. If everyone could get over their losses by writing songs we'd have a lot more music to listen to, instead of headlines about killings, suicides, and addictions.

It doesn't take a genius to see I was writing myself out of a hole. One day I was driving the Spencer Engineering van through the Dakotas by myself. It was about ten degrees below zero, windy and snowing so bad I couldn't see past the hood of my van. Just when I didn't think it could get any colder my cellular phone rang. It was a friend from San Antonio letting me know my first true love had just gotten married. And I thought it couldn't get any colder. Shoot!

SAY "I DO"

Written by Mitch Stephen

Say, "I do"
And don't think about thee others anymore
Or me and you, just set us aside
And live the rest of your life
Happily ever after, I'll hear your laughter
Every night

Walk that road of love
And don't take the byways
Walk it straight
Don't ever you look sideways
And live the rest of your life
Happily ever after, I'll hear your laughter...

But tell me won't you tell, if that road's too long
Tell me won't you tell me, if things don't turn out right
I shouldn't be sayin' these things
The night before your wedding night
But waiting's been a lifetime
I couldn't just let you pass me by

Bridge:
And I'll be there behind the last row
Watching as the rice gets thrown
And I swear I'm gonna wake up at night
To the sound of that march
And thee echo of the words

So say "I do"
And don't think about the others anymore
Or me and you, Just set us aside
And live the rest of your life
Happily ever after, Happily ever after
I'll hear your laughter, Ev'ry night

Listen: http://www.mitchstephen.com/sayido.asp?music=on
Sung by Kevin Hughes

www.MitchStephen.com

CHAPTER 16
YOU CAN'T PLAN EVERYTHING

• • •

Just when you start getting comfortable…
Things will change. I think it's a law of some sort.

About two years into building my house, a lot of things were starting to change. I was seeing changes in the Texas real estate market, and my social life was starting to pick up. Life's opportunities were shifting on all fronts. In 1990, I drove a Spencer Engineering van to Dayton, Ohio, to meet with Steve Whitaker (the guy who'd hired me) to size up a job. Apparently we were about to rewire a six-story department store called Lazarus, and it was not at all what we were used to doing. A rewire for us usually consisted of two to six registers in stores like Foot Locker or The Gap. Those stores had modern mall construction. We'd use space above the standard hanging grid drop ceilings to run the wires from the registers (up front) to the controller in the manager's office (usually located in the back). Those were quick and simple jobs we did over and over hundreds of times.

After previewing the job in Dayton, the word "overwhelmed" would be an understatement. The physical store stood six stories tall and took up one entire city block. The structure was a mix and mess of many, many old buildings mutated together over the past hundred years. Our mission: To connect 200 cash registers with phone lines spread out over six floors covering one city block, to the controllers located in a third-floor computer room. We retreated to a nearby

T.G.I. Friday's to find out just how many beers it would take to figure out the logistics of that job.

It was about 5:00 p.m. when we arrived at the restaurant, and the local business crowd was filtering in. No sooner had we sat down at the bar when we heard the crash of glass hitting the floor and some hustle and bustle not far from our seats. Turns out, an inebriated man had just spilled a fancy cream drink all over a nice looking lady dressed in a blue silk business suit. The man was being obnoxious and, within seconds, we small band of Texans had maneuvered between the lady and her nemesis. Steve staved off the staggering patron while the manager and Tino (another Spencer man) hailed a cab and deported the menace in record time.

Meanwhile, I tackled the dubious job of helping the poor lady. My first effort was to help the deluged woman get some relief from the drink with which she'd been plastered. I couldn't help but notice how nicely she was dressed and just how beautiful she was. I guess she caught me staring at her wet torso because, when I looked up, she had that "you're so busted" look in her eyes. Since I was already, well, busted, I figured a little situational humor couldn't hurt.

"Hi, my name is Mitch Stephen, and I own a dry cleaners store just down the road. If you'll take off your clothes and give'em to me, I'll have'em dry-cleaned and back to you in less than one hour—no charge!"

Luckily, she thought that was pretty funny. Her laughter was very contagious and soon we were both laughing. She was about to catch her breath when she asked me, "Do you really own a dry cleaners?" She and everyone else awaited my answer. I looked her straight in the eyes and, without saying a word, shook my head ever so slightly, *No*, and the laughter started all over again. Shortly thereafter she left for the gym and a racquetball appointment, but before she did I managed to get her name and her business card. Her name was Phyllis Marsh.

The evening had just gotten started for the boys, though. We stayed on into the night eating and drinking and generally carrying on. The usual stuff you do when you're on the road with nothing else to do: telling jokes, talking to strangers, talking to the bartender, talking to the waitress, and every now and then talking about how in the heck we were going to tackle that huge Lazarus job downtown. I had been incessantly flipping that pretty lady's business card through my fingers all night long, but I guess it was about closing time when I stopped toying with the card and actually looked at it.

Apparently Phyllis Marsh was the sales rep for a temporary service that supplied day labor workers to businesses in need. An idea hit me like a ton of bricks right then and there.

The next morning I made contact with Ms. Phyllis Marsh at her work place. Phyllis set up a meeting with the manager and another top-level corporate person, where we promptly worked out an agreement to obtain day labor services through her and the company. We would work closely together in the months to come.

I also managed to talk Ms. Marsh into letting me join her in a friendly game of racquetball from time to time. She was an avid competitor and played religiously. I didn't tell the Spencer guys about these meetings for awhile. I kept these *dates* to myself and passed off my trips to the gym as just that, trips to the gym. It'd been a long time since my athletic days and my physical conditioning over the past ten plus years was, shall we say, less than stellar? I dreaded the actual game 'cause little Ms. Marsh would beat me like a drum for an hour and a half. It'd be everything I could do not to fall down from exhaustion. It was actually quite embarrassing for an ex-athlete like me. I didn't realize just how out of shape I really was. When the game finally ended, we'd get to what I considered to be the good part. We'd have a smoothie and talk.

One time the crew caught me returning from the gym with my racquetball racquet in my hand.

CREW: How was the game?

ME: It was good.

CREW: Did you win?

ME: No.

CREW: What was the score?

ME: 21 to 2.

CREW: Wow. You really got creamed!

ME: Yep, pretty much.

CREW: Who'd you play?

ME: Phhh…PhhhTom…TOM.

I couldn't say "Phyllis" had beaten me so badly. I'd never hear the end of it!

Then one weekend off, the gang and I were at Creaser's Creek barbecuing. I'd invited Phyllis to come join us, but I didn't really expect her to show up. When she did arrive, I introduced her to everyone. "Gentlemen, I'd like you to meet TOM." The cat was out of the bag. Everyone knew who she was. "TOM" was really the lady we'd met at Friday's, and the person we were getting our laborers from. She was also the one beating the tar out of me in racquetball. I didn't hear the end of it for a long, long time! And Phyllis would never be Phyllis again. She was officially dubbed "Tommi" by the Texans and the nick name would stick for the rest of her life. (You know Texans love girls with guy's names!)

Before it was all over, Spencer Engineering ordered over $100,000 worth of day laborer services; the Spencer crew and a pool of labor workers fitted over fifteen miles of cable into that Lazarus building, and I married that pretty lady, Phyllis "Tommi" Marsh on March 12th, 1991. Tommi and her daughter, Shannon, (now *my* daughter), moved to Texas. Tommi's son, Michael (a fine young man), was on his way to college and opted to stay near Ohio. There was a small wedding and I hit the road again. Tommi and Shannon would wait for me to come off the road for another three years.

CHAPTER 17
HONEY, I'M HOME!

• • •

...and I'm not leaving.

There are at least two different kinds of lonely. There's a loneliness that happens when you have no one to love, and there's another kind of loneliness that happens when you can't be with the one you love. My days on the road began to get long the minute I fell in love with my future wife and had to be gone for months. Just before I actually slammed that door and shouted, "Honey I'm home," I wrote of my commitment to get there and stay there. No, I wasn't a trucker. Yes, I was gone much longer than ten days at a time. Still, this song summed up how I was feeling.

"I WON'T BE LEAVIN' ANYMORE"

Written by Mitch Stephen & Billy O'Rourke

I've been runnin' hard so long, don't think this road will let me off
Chasin' tomorrow, all my yesterdays, back down the road somewhere got lost
That mileage gage keeps turning, over and over.
Those wining wheels keep saying, "Go to her. Go to her"
That roaring engine thunders, "You're not getting any younger ..."
"You better go while she's still there"

CHORUS:
And as I ramble down this road, like a thousand times before
Are those white lines getting longer
I am pressed to find a way, to knock upon her door ...Oh, Oh and say
"I won't be leavin' anymore"

When I was young I caught a fever, for 18 wheels and shifting gears
I landed my dream job that summer, now it's rolled into 18 years
I've got a wife that waits at home, 3 days off for 10 days on
She says she needs me now, I've got to find somehow
To ditch this rig when I get home

(REPEAT CHORUS)

BRIDGE:
I look hard at ev'ry sign. Omens or are they in my mind
But this rig keeps pulling left, as if to say, "Don't go west
...Go south where you belong

(REPEAT CHORUS)

(REPEAT CHORUS)

TAG:

I won't be leavin' anymore
I won't be leavin' anymore
I won't be leavin' anymore ...

Listen: http://www.mitchstephen.com/iwontbe.asp?music=on
Sung by Kevin Hughes

www.MitchStephen.com

CHAPTER 18
KNOCK - KNOCK

• • •

Opportunity rarely shows up when we're ready.

Meanwhile, back on the real estate front, I was watching a trend form. I'd read about how the real estate markets go through cycles, and you wanted to buy real estate in the down cycle or the down market. What was the most interesting part? The hottest down market in the country was now in my hometown, San Antonio, Texas. I didn't want to stop building my home because by now I had a wife and child living there, but on the other hand, I really needed a break from it. My common sense said I would be able to finish the house faster if I stopped working on the home and starting investing instead. Why? Because the new materials for my new home were costing me top dollar and used material already erected in the form of a pre-owned home was going for pennies on the dollar. Why should I pay top dollar to build a new home when the time had come to buy complete pre-owned homes at half price?

My rationale was this: If I bought enough of the used houses at fifty cents on the dollar, I would eventually be able to sell a few of them when the market turned around and pay to have my new home completed in short order. The problem was, I'd never done any of that before. I'd been reading and studying and preparing for a career in real estate and although the timing was bad because I hadn't finished my new home, the window of opportunity was opening wide for investing in pre-owned homes. I knew that window wouldn't stay open forever. I don't know about you, but for me, opportunity seldom knocks when I am ready. I wasn't ready when I walked off that show room floor to work for Spencer Engineering, and I wasn't ready when the real estate *down market* showed up in San Antonio, Texas. Ready or not, I was learning to jump!

Now, instead of saving to build, I was saving to buy. There were houses being auctioned off at the rate of 600 per week by the FHA and VA institutions! Decent tract homes with 1,200 square feet, three bedrooms and two baths that once sold for as much as $65,000 were now selling for as low as $17,000 each. And that was after they'd been completely remodeled by the government! You couldn't buy a lot and pour the slab and driveway for that price if you were building new. You *could* buy the *Real Estate Owned* (REOs) from the institutions for that amount. The minute I saw that with my own two eyes I was on it like flies to cow dookie…and there was no stopping me!

With Tommi at home it was now possible to begin building a business in Texas. She got a job working for a headhunting agency (job placement for professionals) making about $40,000 per year. With two incomes coming in, we were able to save money even faster as long as we could curtail our desires to improve living conditions at the house. During my short stints at home, I went to work buying up as much rental property as I could get my hands on. I met a real estate broker named Dick Gilby, and he helped me tremendously.

I'd call Dick just before leaving for home, and when I hit the ground in San Antonio, we'd be off to the lesser sides of town. Dick Gilby was, and is, a consummate professional. He was the only person in the world taking my investing aspirations seriously. I valued him because he was the kind of guy you could trust. Don't ask me how I knew that because I won't be able to tell you. But I knew I could trust him from the very first day I met him. I have not been wrong about that for more than twenty years.

I knew these little properties weren't making Dick rich, so I tried to be quick and decisive. Every time I'd come into town, I'd always buy one or two houses from him. He always made it easy for me. I only had ten days off most of the time so the pace was fast and furious. Gilby knew the buying criteria, and he'd have five or six properties lined up for me to look at. Within a day or so I'd decide on which one(s) to buy. We'd work so hard on my days off at home that I'd have to go back to work on the road to get some rest. After I'd return to work on the road, Tommi would get the properties rented in her spare time (which meant she had no spare time at all). I was a huge fan of her efforts. I finally knew how I was going to work my way off the road. Through reading and working and inspired by my wife's work ethic, I'd come up with a plan for success. I was going to stay on the road until I had enough money coming in from the rentals to replace my income from Spencer Engineering. I was determined to gain my financial freedom.

Tommi and I working on the house

CHAPTER 19

THE MOAT THEORY: KEEP SOMETHING SACRED

• • •

Financial freedom happens when your wants and your needs are exceeded by your passive income.

In the days I spent traveling, I was trying to put together my own personal plan for financial freedom. The first thing I had to do was get off the road. The endless travel was good money for me but it was no life for me. It was very hard to invest in real estate from a distant hotel room as far as I was concerned. Now that I had an ally at home, my wife, Tommi, I could finally see how things might be workable. I'm a simple man. I needed to break things down into the simplest steps to freedom. What do I do first? I had ideas coming at me from all directions due to the books I'd been reading. There were so many good ideas; it was difficult to decide which ones to follow. My satiated state was compounded by my own thoughts and twists on the subjects I'd been reading about. My own thoughts led to even more ideas. I was beginning to get confused. I was becoming paralyzed with a bad case of information overload.

I thought back to the other times in my life I'd become overwhelmed. What did I do then? I remembered how I'd paid those entire debts one bill at a time. I remembered how I conquered being overwhelmed with building an entire house by deciding to take it one room or project at a time. I came up with a plan to get me off the road and on a path to financial freedom. It was centered on something I'd read that was a revelation to me. Once I read it, I just could not stop thinking about it.

"Financial freedom happens when your wants and needs are exceeded by your passive income."

When I first read the above statement, it said several things to me. It said that there is a defining moment when financial freedom happens. Until I read that sentence, I was not sure how much money I wanted or needed or what I wanted money for. It also said; if I kept my wants and my needs reasonable, then the amount of passive income I'd need to achieve financial freedom would also be reasonable. I'm not suggesting we keep our dreams and aspirations low. I am suggesting that the sooner we get to even the most meager level of financial freedom, the sooner we will be working on our dreams and aspirations *full time*!

I formulated a simple little scenario in my simple little head, something I called the Moat Theory:

I imagined this little kingdom with everything we needed to survive in it: our home, utilities, cars, food, insurance, living expenses, entertainment and everything necessary for a reasonable life. I imagined it to be in medieval times: my castle, my horse, my chickens, my goats, my armor. Next, I imagined building a moat all the way around that little kingdom and those necessities. Then, I filled the moat up with water first and then with alligators and crocodiles and piranhas and such to guard what was inside the moat. Everything I needed to be comfortable in life was to be protected, safe inside the confines of that moat. Then, I calculated exactly how much it would cost per month to maintain everything inside the moat. I came up with a number. At that time, the number was $3,500 per month. Finally, I had something I could measure by. The day my passive income equaled $3,500 per month I would be financially free. I could leave my bosses and my J. O. B. (that's how entrepreneurs say the dirty word "job") the day I had $3,500 a month coming in, rain or shine, if I got out of bed or not. If I could accomplish $3,500 a month passive income, my kingdom, my lifestyle, would be paid for in full. The minute my lifestyle was paid for in full, was the minute I could start chasing all the dreams of my life *full time*!

My first goal became singular in focus. I had one solitary mission to complete. All the ideas I'd been reading about were to be used to create one single outcome. I had to create enough *passive income* to support what was inside my moat. I'd decided to create $3,500 a month positive cash flow from rental properties. If I could do that, I could come off the road and go home with my head held high. I would have all the time in the world to become wealthy after that. First step: Cover my overhead! Cover the expense of everything inside the moat. Become financially free at a very modest level.

CHAPTER 20
THE MOAT THEORY: FREEDOM TO FALL

• • •

Every bad business move that doesn't break us makes us smarter.

If you could try and fail without going broke, how long would it take you to try and succeed?

Imagine being able to sit inside the safety of your own moat, in your castle, with your expenses paid and the drawbridges up and locked. Imagine being able to live comfortably while you think and plan your next strategy, never having to worry about making a living or having a J.O.B. Do you think you would come up with a good idea? Do you think you would be rested? Do you think you might even get restless? Do you think you might be ready to engage in an endeavor, an adventure, with energy and vision and vigor, outside the castle walls and the moat?

Now, imagine that one day you have this great idea you are dying to try out. You've calculated everything and you're ready for your inquisition. You sound the trumpets, drop the drawbridge, and go forth, beyond the safety of the castle walls and over the moat. Without risking the assets that provide for your life inside the moat, you charge out into the world to prove the value of your new idea.

Now, let's say things don't go well. The enemy wasn't where you thought he'd be. There were too many of them. They had weapons you'd never seen before. You flee back towards your castle and along the way you gather many arrows in and about your backside. As you race back across the moat and into your castle, the draw bridge is abruptly lifted, closed, and locked. You are wounded and out of breath but safe again in your sacred place of refuge.

Because you did not risk the assets that pay for the expenses inside the moat, your kingdom is still there for you. You spend time inside your kingdom removing the arrows from your backside. You spend time healing. You spend time thinking, pondering: What went wrong? You think even more: What did I do and what should I have done? What will I do different next time? You rest. You replenish your energy and your stocks. You adjust your ideas and your plans. You create a new, improved plan.

The next time you charge outside the gates you are successful. Instead of returning in a sprint with arrows in your backside you arrive at the drawbridge on a horse that is gingerly walking. You are smiling proudly. You are traveling with the spoils of war slung over your shoulder. Your family cheers as you cross the moat. The village celebrates your victory with a fine feast.

Now ask yourself this question: If you had a castle and a kingdom like that one, how long would it be before you were wealthy beyond your dreams? If you had the income to cover your kingdom's expenses every month, while you planned and studied and honed your craft, how long would it take to become the person you've dreamed of becoming? If you could fail forward what might your future look like? Would you learn to fly? Start a Church? Learn to play the piano? Open a sky-diving school? How long would it take *you* to get where *you* were at peace? Suffice it to say, you could take all the time you needed! The real question at that point would be, "Could you even stop it?"

For me, it all started with a modest castle, a relatively small moat, and the passive income to pay for it all. From that position, I've been able to fail at things without my whole life going down the crapper. From that position, when I had ideas that cost more than I'd planned on or that took three times longer than I'd predicted, I was able to ride it out. I didn't need that *extra* money to live on. In fact, if my ideas completely failed and I lost everything I'd put in, I was still okay. Everything inside the moat was still okay, and life there was very sufficient.

The castle represents your safe place of refuge. In the beginning, it is simply the place you survive in reasonable comfort without having to worry about a job. This has been one of the keystones to *my* success. I'm well aware that my way is not the only way. Remember, this is a book about my life, so I can only tell of how I did it. But I observe so many people that obligated their first financial successes to huge house payments or such that essentially squashed their ability to chase their real dreams. So many people are so busy working to pay for their beautiful stuff that they don't have time to realize their real dreams: To become an expert in a field, to go to college and become that doctor, to become a pilot, or to chase their artistic or their entrepreneurial ambitions or to be philanthropic. I know what it is like to be too busy working to get rich. Believe me; I know how you can get trapped in that routine. That's why this concept was such a revelation for me.

The Moat is what defines your wants and needs. Where are we going to draw the line (or the circle as it may be)? The smaller the moat and the smaller the kingdom, the less passive income you will need to become *free*. Being free from your job and free to think is the key. The sooner we don't have to have a job, the sooner we will be chasing our dreams. The sooner we start chasing our dreams, the sooner we will accomplish or even exceed those dreams. It's indirectly about money, but more importantly, it's about self fulfillment. Can you temporarily suspend your material wants and needs to fulfill your life's endeavor?

The drawbridge represents passive income, and it is the gate that allows you to move from being content to experiencing growth (financially, spiritually or otherwise). It is the buffer between being comfortable and being challenged. Contentment is on the inside of the drawbridge, and your dreams and all the wealth in the world are yours for the taking just outside the moat over the bridge. The drawbridge also represents where you draw the line when you are assessing risk. Once you have it, you never risk what pays for your lifestyle inside the moat! NEVER! Those assets are what make it possible for you to explore and fail without fear of failure. Am I making sense?

The way I see it, there are two ways to become free: Learn to do without material things and basically shun traditional societal lifestyles or learn to create enough wealth to have the material things you desire and still have time to enjoy them. You can become a monk, or you can learn to win at the monetary game. I believe that either choice can be accomplished in a Christian fashion. But rolling the dice with everything you own every time you want to try something new is crazy! I'm certain a town in Nevada called Las Vegas thrives on those who don't know when to keep a certain amount of victories sacred. The only way you'll ever win in Vegas is if you leave the table when you're ahead: Those who don't get eaten up by the odds.

CHAPTER 21
ON THE OTHER SIDE OF THE CLOCK

• • •

Can you believe it's the 1st already?!

Most people in the world are on the wrong side of the clock. They get up every day, go to work, and then go home, just to do it all over again the next day. If they're lucky, they get Saturday and Sunday off. Still, many people these days work through the weekends to make ends meet. My father was a straight commissioned sales person most of his adult career. He did cold call sales, the hardest job in the world as far as I'm concerned. Talk about having to be mentally tough! That being said, the Stephen family never wanted for anything, ever! He was being interviewed for a company newsletter when the owner of the company he worked for asked, "Rodney, what is it that motivates you to sell so effectively?

My father answered, "The postman."

The owner queried again with a puzzled look on his face, "The postman?"

To which my Father replied, "Yea, the Postman…the son-of-a-gun keeps bringing bills to my mailbox."

I venture to say, all of us know exactly what my father was talking about.

When you are on the *wrong side* of the clock, you race to pay the bills every thirty days. You look up and say, "Oh no, it's the first of the month and time to pay my bills again, ALREADY!"

When you get on the other side of the clock, by creating passive, positive streams of income, you look up and say, "WOW, is it the first of the month? A bunch of people owe me a bunch of money again? Already?" Time is very different on the other side of the clock. On the other side of the clock, time is your friend. Time is working in your favor. Yes, finally, time is working for *you*!

May I suggest: If you're going to have to work, why not work on something, anything, that will get you on the other side of the clock? If what you're doing right now to make a living is *not* going to get you on the other side of the clock, re-assess what you are doing for a living! It's just a thought (but I can hear the light bulb going off in your head). When that concept finally reached my brain and my light bulb finally went off, the light was so bright I couldn't see for two days!

If you are not on the "Other Side of the Clock" ask yourself this question: If getting on the other side of the clock was your life's endeavor, how long do you think it would take *you* to achieve that goal?

If you stopped concentrating on the new car you want or that boat you just can't live without, how long would it take you to be financially independent? I know one thing for sure: The sooner you start, the sooner you'll get there. If you focus on the time or the effort it'll take, it might demoralize you. If you visualize over and over the result, the victory, you just might persevere. It is a matter of what you choose to concentrate on. It is a law of the mind. Focus on the work as drudgery and it will become drudgery. Science of the mind says that if you focus on the labor, you will most likely fail. Focus on the dream, and every step of work gets you closer to the brass ring. (I know I'm harping but if you haven't read Maltz yet, I suggest you read it.)

Some things in life just won't happen unless we make a plan to achieve that something. It amazes me how fast things start to come together when the peripheral stuff is set aside, and the main objective is brought to the forefront. When I learned to keep the main objective in the forefront, I was on my way. It is just a matter of time and money, no matter what the objective.

Tommi, enjoying some time on the other side of the clock

CHAPTER 22 MONEY CAN'T CHANGE EVERYTHING

• • •

Money magnifies who we really are.

Passive income is ultimately what we need to be free in a traditional society. Money isn't the object, it is the vehicle. *Freedom* is the objective. If we could buy freedom with jellybeans then this would be a book about collecting jellybeans. Unfortunately, it takes money to become free in most of today's societies.

A favorite partner and friend, Carlos Balido, once told me, "The only thing money will buy you is the freedom of movement."

If you have money you can generally get to anywhere in the world you want or need to be in a timely fashion. Money does not buy happiness. If you find out a dear friend has passed away you can buy an expensive flight that same day and make the funeral in the nick of time. I can almost guarantee, you won't be happy at the funeral. It may not be the best example, but I am confident we will all eventually come to the same conclusion; there are things money can't change. If you were a sad person without money, chances are you'll be a sadder person if you're rich. If you were a jerk without money, success will make you an even bigger jerk. Money tends to magnify who we really are. That is a major reason why it's so important to have strong foundations in many aspects of life before our fortunes are made.

I consider myself lucky to have had to fight for my success. Have you read the horror stories about lottery winners? Stories abound of divorce, bankruptcy, addiction, depression, family alienation, even suicide. Why? Because financial success demands maturity, discipline, responsibility, personal/emotional strength, and integrity on hundreds of different levels. A person who has achieved personal, financial freedom easily or overnight is especially challenged in many arenas. Truth is, we are all challenged by external forces, financially free or not. Imagine the troubles and temptations you could find if money was no object. A bunch of money can be dangerous in the hands of people who are not rounded by the struggles of achievement and grounded in their humility. Having money does not stop the challenges of life. Challenges never end and I contend we are all graded on a daily basis as to how we handle them, forever.

CHAPTER 23
BREAKFAST WITH A STRANGER

• • •

People know when you're committed

In the late 90's I had the good fortune to know the late Ken D'Angelo, founder of *Homevestors* and of the "We Buy Ugly Houses" fame. I unintentionally met him one morning at Echo's Mexican Food Restaurant in San Antonio. There I was eating my *juevos rancheros* when this man, walking with conviction, appeared in the middle of the restaurant. He boldly asked, for all the world to hear, "Who owns the blue Chevy pickup outside in the lot with the Cash4Houses. NET stickers on the doors?"

I had some egg and half a tortilla in my mouth when he looked over at me so I raised my hand. I had to raise my hand. I had a half a tortilla in my mouth and I couldn't say anything. Anyway, this man strolled over to the table and asked if he could join me? I still wasn't finished with that tortilla so I shook my head *yes* and began clearing off a spot for him on the other side of the booth. I was happy to finally swallow that tortilla and ask him what he wanted because he had a very serious look on his face and I thought I was in trouble or he'd hit my car or something. Turns out, that wasn't the case at all.

We introduced ourselves and he handed me a business card. He said he was passing the restaurant when he saw my car signs and he just had to turn around and see if those signs were what he thought they were.

KEN: "Do you know why your signs are so important to me Mitch?"

I shook my head no.

KEN: "*Your* signs are not magnetic signs. *Your* signs are permanently attached to your truck."

Now I'm thinking, "This guy has some kind of problem with my truck signs."

KEN: "Do you know what those signs say to *me* about *you*?"

ME: Now look here mister…I can put whatever signs I want too on my truck.

Ken started laughing.

KEN: No, no no…you've got me all wrong. Your signs say that *you* are serious about the house business. You're not trying this business on for size...YOU ARE *IN* THE BUSINESS!

Well, come to find out, Ken had started a little company called Homevestors and he was looking for franchisees to open the San Antonio area. Later that month I'd fly up to Dallas and he'd give me and some others the Homevestors grand tour. It was really an impressive company and Ken was telling us everything about everything. He was holding nothing back. About 10:30am I started feeling bad because I wasn't sure I was going to sign up to buy a franchise. I'd already bought and sold well over two hundred houses and I just wasn't ready to change my formula. Still, he was giving me all this great house buying/selling information. Finally I had to pull Ken over to the side and tell him.

ME: Ken, I'm going to have to stop you. I'm not sure I'm going to buy a franchise and you're giving me all your trade secrets. As much as I don't want to steal your ideas, I'm never going to be able to erase them from my mind.

Ken looked directly at me. He had a grin of supreme confidence. Then he said, "Mitch, I am building a franchise across the entire nation. I'm not worried about little ol' Mitch Stephen. But I appreciate your honesty…I knew I was right about you." Well, I just had to laugh. Even though I'd told Ken I was not a likely franchisee, he still insisted I finish the tour. I've never forgotten his unique spirit. It was very refreshing.

Several years later I'd speak with Ken D'Angelo again at a Christmas Eve party. It was late and we'd gotten into a rather deep discussion about our businesses and how entrepreneurs don't plan for the end results as much as they commit to being determined. He told me that he'd come to recognize something about entrepreneurs: "Entrepreneurs rarely end up making their money from the idea they start out with. It's the nature of an entrepreneur to adapt and adjust on their way to the money. Typically, eventually, they find a most rewarding path with the least amount of resistance." It was a revelation to me at the time. "Entrepreneurs rarely end up with the business they start with."

It was true for both of us. Ken talked about how he'd stumbled into the idea of franchising the house-flipping business because he liked flipping houses. I too had experienced a metamorphosis of sorts. I'd started out buying rental houses, but ended up owner financing houses and then selling the notes. It made sense; most entrepreneurs evolve into their success.

CHAPTER 24
PLANS CHANGE

• • •

When things take longer than you planned, it's usually because you're wanting more than you started out asking for.

At the beginning of my journey, I made a conscious choice *not* to permanently return home from the road until I'd purchased enough income-producing properties to cover the cost of my tiny, tiny kingdom. It was a tall drink of water for me, but I started sipping on it one day at a time. When I finally arrived home five years later, I was potentially a free man. I had twenty-five rental properties, and on paper I was supposed to make enough to sit down and enjoy life a little more.

That brings me to my next set of realities. I had replaced my income, but I had not replaced my new wife's income. Yes, we could have cut down and lived within a strict budget and, on paper, things would have worked out. Luckily, my wife wasn't ready to stop working, and I chose to keep the passive income rolling into a savings account in the name of growth. My new goal was to replace two incomes inside our moat within the next two years.

From 1994 to 1996, I took on a job at Emerald Recording Studios thinking I could compound our saving ability and progress towards taking my wife out of a job as well. It didn't make sense for me to be free and have a wife tied to a J.O.B. After being on the road ninety days at a time and managing business from afar, managing the rentals in my spare time from home wasn't any challenge at all. I took on a large portion of the daily responsibilities of running our rental properties and tried to maximize how much the rentals could generate in profit. That decision also gave my wife a well deserved respite. It was a good thing we made the choices we did because I was about to get a rude awakening. The income I had projected on paper wasn't happening.

On paper my twenty-five units were supposed to clear $300 in positive cash flow each.

25 units x $300 = $7,500 per month

It seemed like enough to be able to save a ton. I knew I wouldn't collect 100% all the time but I had felt reasonably sure that I'd be able to save at least $3,500 per month in the name of growth and progress. It wasn't working out that way. The high turnover rate, constant delinquencies, eviction costs, holding costs, maintenance, and damages done by tenants were eating up all my projected profit. I was devastated. All the efforts, all the dreams, all the hard work, and two years of hardcore, hands-on management were netting us only about $10,000 to $15,000 per year. That's not even close to the $42,000 I'd conservatively planned to make. Furthermore, these tenants were killing me emotionally. It just did not seem worth it. When you consider the time effort and risk and liability, it absolutely wasn't worth it!

This was a dark moment. So much working and dreaming, how did I miss the mark by so much? Completely demoralized, we agreed to sell everything. I put the properties up for sale, but no one who wanted to live in the low-income areas where I owned homes could qualify for a mortgage loan. Now I was in a panic. Was I going to get stuck with all these needy, nagging people for the rest of my life? I had to get out of my cocoon. I needed to rub shoulders with others who'd been in my shoes. What did they do?

Eventually, I spoke to someone who suggested I sell the homes and finance them myself. Reluctantly I decided that was the only way I could change my situation. The truth is, by now I was scared and a real "don't wanter" if you know what I mean? I really just wanted out. It's a stroke of luck that I could not sell the properties for cash because, if I could have I would have, and I'm sure I would've been done with real estate at that point. I had no idea what I was going to do if not real estate. I'd fall back into that *lost zone* again, and I hated that place in life.

I've learned that a lot of life's victories wait for me just beyond the storm. Success seems to loom just barely beyond the gut-wrenching struggle. I'd fallen apart in Mitchell Striping about a year and a half after it started, but the business opened right up in its second year. If I could've found a way to hold on I might have never seen that showroom floor or the Worcester, Massachusetts airport. In Mitchell Striping, life circumstances were pushing me out, even though I wanted to stay in. In real estate, life circumstances were holding me in, even though I wanted out. For whatever reason, the powers that be and real estate were not letting go of me. I was going to have to scratch and claw my way through this one. Just beyond the struggle I would win at the real estate game.

I started advertising the properties for sale with *owner financing*. I would finance a property to a buyer if they could come up with $3,000 down and pay a 10% annual interest rate. I found I could sell my homes for about $45,000 if I financed them for my buyers. They couldn't get a loan from a mortgage company but they could get a loan from me. On average I only had about $17,000 of debt on each house, so there was a good spread. I could arrange monthly mortgage payments that allowed me to clear about the same amount of cash flow I was trying to clear before with renters: $300 per month. This is how the numbers worked for me and my buyers.

$45,000 Sale Price
$ -3,000 Down Payment (Cash)
$42,000 Financed @ 10% for 180 months = $451 Principle & Interest (P&I)

$ 451 Principle & Interest (PI)
$ +150 Taxes & Insurance (TI)
$ 601 Total Monthly payment (PITI)

Below is what MY obligations on the property looked like.

$20,000 Purchase Price
$ -2,000 Down Payment
$18,000 Financed @ 7.5% for 360 months = $125/mo. Principle & Interest
(Financed by an Institutional Lender)

$ 125 My monthly Principle & Interest Payment (P&I)
$ +150 My Taxes and Insurance obligation (T&I)
$ 275 My Total obligations (PITI)

In this example, I was clearing about $326 per month between what my buyer owed me and what I owed the bank.

$ 601 The amount I collected from my Buyer
$ -275 The amount I owed for the property
$ 326 My potential profit per month on one house

Suddenly things began to look up. The people who wanted to live in my areas of town could not qualify for a loan, but they really wanted to own their homes. I found that plenty of them had enough for a down payment (especially around January 1st, income tax return time) and were willing to give up some hard-earned cash in the name of home ownership. Within about six months, I had sold all of the houses and, instead of dealing with tenants and phone calls, I was dealing with owners and very, very few phone calls.

Furthermore, when Tommi and I collected the mortgage payments, the money we collected was all ours. That was completely different than collecting rent. When we were collecting rent, we never knew if the money was really ours or not because we'd have to give the money up if an air conditioning unit broke or the water heater went bad, etc. Now that we were the lenders and not the landlords, all those maintenance costs were not our responsibility anymore. Tenants paid late, tore the place up and left. These new owners were paying on time, fixing the place up, and staying put! Not only that, I had collected an average of $3,000 down on 25 properties. Do the math! I had $75,000 in the bank; these down payments were nonrefundable! And that $7,500 I was supposed to clear in rental income was actually getting deposited now that I was collecting mortgage payments instead of rent. You read it correctly: The $7,500 was actually going into the bank account and staying there! Needless to say, I'd gone from devastation to elation in six months. Just on the other side of that dark moment came pay day. As if I wasn't on cloud nine already, what happened next really blew my mind.

CHAPTER 25
HIT IN THE HEAD WITH THE NOTE BUYER BAT!

• • •

People actually wanted to pay me cash TODAY for the payments due to me in the future!

I was going through the mail one day and noticed a lot of mail from note buyers. Apparently these note buyer guys spend time at the county courthouse looking through the recorded notes and deeds of trusts for individuals (as opposed to institutions) that have financed real estate for their buyers. The note buyers were offering to pay cash for the notes I'd created. I grabbed a file for one of my houses and called one of the note buyers. I'd sold this particular property for $38,000. I took $3,000 down and had financed the balance of $35,000 for 30 years at 10% interest. One note buyer offered to pay me $30,000 cash today for the $35,000 that was owed to me over time by the owner/occupant. I did some quick math in my head;

I owed $17,000 on the house

The note buyer had offered me $30,000 cash today

The difference between what I owed and what they wanted to pay me was $13,000

SOLD!

My mind was racing.

25 houses x $13,000 = $325,000

Let's not forget that I'd already collected $75,000 in down payments.

$325,000 + $75,000 = $400,000!

I felt like a thoroughbred horse running for the roses in the Kentucky Derby. Seven years of hard work, starting from zero, re-inventing myself, re-educating myself, transforming my mind over the miles and the hotels, through the mud, blood, sweat and tears. Never giving up was finally about to pay off. I had arrived. Finally, I had arrived!

I had read about these kinds of transactions but, as I said before, I am like a lot of people; I don't *get it* until I *live it*, or, maybe everyone else does *get it*, and I'm just a slow learner. When something smacks me upside the head is when I say to myself, "So that's what they were talking about in that book!"

While we're on the subject of note buying, one of the best companies in the business today is Colonial Funding Group. Eddie Speed is a good person and as honest as the day is long. If you're interested in creating notes and/or the business of buying and selling notes, you can download a free copy of Eddie's book, *Streetwise Seller Financing,* at **www.ColonialFundingGroup.com.** Eddie Speed and family have forgotten more about buying real estate lien notes than most of us will ever learn.

CHAPTER 26
DON'T JUMP TRACK

• • •

Dance with the one who brought you to the ball.

As you might imagine, so many things started happening once the cash flow and money side of things started falling into place. Our little kingdom and everything inside our meager moat were paid for. We could have done a lot of fun stuff with that money, but we realized that keeping our personal expenses the same (low) was what allowed us to expand our income-making horizons in the first place. Keeping our overhead low and not having to live off our investments is what generated the time necessary to get beyond the storm and break through to the sunshine of success. With the new money we'd made, we could have purchased a bigger home or finished our own home over night. We could have run out and bought matching BMW's, bought a boat or a timeshare. We could've done so many things. Instead, we kept our eye on the ball. We stayed focused and tried not to get overly excited and lose our discipline.

We were so excited about our new found success, but we did not want to change the formula for fear we'd mess up a perfect recipe. We kept our wits about us. We celebrated with a five-day, all-inclusive vacation to Playa Del Carmen, Mexico (about $2,000 total expense, including round-trip tickets from San Antonio, Texas, hotel, food and drinks). I love going to Mexico because a little bit of money can get you a long, long way, especially back then. For the money we'd made it was a frugal but a completely relaxing and enjoyable choice. While on that vacation, Tommi and I sipped our margaritas on the sunset beaches and dreamed about where our new found success might take us. We committed to stay with the concepts that had carried us this far. We weren't going to change a lot of things: We were going to dance with the one who'd brought us to the ball.

CHAPTER 27
MAILBOX MONEY

• • •

If you've never had someone send you money on a monthly basis, try it this year. I think you'll like it!

About this time, late in 1991, Tommi and I purchased our first storage facility. It was a very small complex with only nine units. However, they were located directly in front of the entrance to a popular public park on the lake. This started the first step into what would become a main profit center for years to come. Over the years we would steadily increase the number of units every chance we got. By 2007, we were approaching 1,000 units in 16 locations around the lake where we live. I'd buy them or build them, and Tommi would take it from there. Managing that many people is a full time job, and she took to it like a duck to water. Tommi had been responsible for other peoples' businesses all of her life, but now she was becoming an integral part of managing her own destiny, our destiny.

Sometimes I'd find deals on storage units when I wasn't in a position to buy them myself. When that happened, I'd call on my father and suggest he buy them. He was looking for retirement income, and the deals I found usually cash flowed better than most other traditional (conservative) investments. It was important to me that we buy as many of the existing units as we could, before the competition bought them. At least the units would still be in the family. I had a hunch as to who'd end up owning them one day.

There was a time when we didn't have so many storage units. I came home and announced that I was hot on the heels of another storage facility. Tommi got upset with me and asked when I was going to stop buying more units. "When is enough *enough*?" At the time we only had about 40 or 50 units and certainly not enough to live off of. I told her I would stop when we could wake up on a Monday morning, make the deposits and then ask ourselves, "What would we like to do for the rest of the day?"

She didn't look too impressed with my ambition, but I felt it was something we could achieve, and I told her, "Look, Honey, one of these days your job is going to be as simple as going to the mailbox and making the deposits." She was not convinced my plan was even a remote possibility. I took note of her position and over the months and years, I kept buying and/or expanding our storage facilities. Yeah, it caused some conflict between her and me.

The truth is, with the exception of my parents, my wife has had to change more than anyone in this world to accommodate me. She did not dream my dreams before she met me, nor did she wish for the life we've become so fortunate enough to have. Her needs were and still are, simple. Even so, she never abandoned me in my aspirations or visions, even when she did not understand them or me. As much as I have taken her beyond her bounds, she has kept me grounded, for I could have foolishly gone beyond the pull of gravity and never returned. I am eternally and forever grateful for her unconditional love and perseverance. I've pushed her in directions she'd never have looked towards. My time with her has been priceless. I'm hopeful that she will always think her time with me has been worth it. As you might imagine, life with me has not been easy.

"OPPOSITES ATTRACT"

Written by Mitch Stephen and Billy O'Rourke

Betty's got a little silk in the way she walks
Bobby's gotta little gravel in the way he talks
He likes his saddles worn, she likes Cadillacs
They're in love, can't see nothin' wrong with that

And there's no cowboy, could ever turn her head
He is her "King", just a little rough around the edge

CHORUS:
Opposites attract
Nothin' like a push, to pull you back
We love the dif'rences, baby that's a fact
'Cause opposites attract

Betty like's "Gone with the Wind"
Bobby like Merle on "TNN"
She keeps the bed he takes the couch
She cries on queue, Bobby sings his heart out

When those lights go down, he sneaks back in bed
It don't take long, Scarlett's back in love with Rhett

(REPEAT CHORUS)

And there ain't any "Queen", could ever turn his head
She is his "Cowgirl", just a little over dressed

(REPEAT CHORUS)

Listen: http://www.mitchstephen.com/opposites.asp?music=on
Sung by Kevin Hughes

www.MitchStephen.Com

One day I walked into the bedroom and found Tommi sitting on the edge of our bed with an obvious, exaggerated, pout for me to see. She had her best "sad face" on and her bottom lip was stuck waaay out. In my best baby talk I asked, "What's wrong little girl?"

She replied back in her little girl voice, "There's no money in the mailbox today."

I had waited a long time for this moment, "Oh little girl, don't worry. Do you remember a time when you didn't think it was possible to receive money in your mailbox? Now you're disappointed when there's not money in the mailbox everyday." My wife hates it when I remind her of things like that. But it's important that we, as investors, look back from time to time and recognize just how far we've come. Things don't happen overnight, and we tend not to recognize the subtle progress over the years. Tommi was the one helping to make that progress in the storage business but, because she never measures her life by money, she had not recognized how far the business had come financially.

A sunny day at one of our storage facilities

CHAPTER 28
CREDIT CARDS

• • •

It's not the cost of the money, it's the availability.

Up until late 1996 early 1997 in our house-buying career, we'd been functioning largely off credit cards and a few private lenders. It was not unusual for me, personally, to have over $150,000 to $200,000 of credit card debt on any given day. It sounds outrageous at first, but think about it. During that time, the credit card companies weren't holding the amount of potential unsecured credit you had available against you. If you had good credit you automatically got their best card and their best cash-advance limits. I collected about thirty-five to forty credit cards that had cash-advance limits of $10,000 to $30,000 each. I could literally have $300,000 to $450,000 on my kitchen table in a matter of days if that's what I wanted to do. Eventually, the credit card companies got tired of people who did just that and then left for Mexico for a life of leisure. While I recognized that potential immediately, it was never a consideration. I was searching for a legitimate way to earn a great living and be *free*, not to snatch a bag of money and then have to hide in Mexico.

I got over the stigma of credit card debt rather easily and with more vigor than most. Still, it was a bit of a hurdle. We are taught that debt is bad. The first step is to understand that not all debt is bad. There's *bad* debt and there is *good* debt. I distinguish the two by what I spend the money on. It's all right to have $200,000 in credit card debt if I've used the money to buy $400,000 worth of houses. It's okay to agree to $450 a month of credit card debt if what I buy with that money brings in $650 a month. In short, good debt religiously brings in more than the debt costs. Simple! I was entering into good debt. That is what I was doing, and that is why I had no problem sleeping at night.

I never co-mingled credit cards. If I used a particular card on a property, that card got taped to the inside cover of that property's file folder. I would only use that card for that specific property. When that card was maxed out, I'd grab another card and tape it to the inside of the file. It was important to keep these cards in their respective property files because, when I sold the property at the closing, I would walk out of the title company with the entire amount of the proceeds from the sale. Because I borrowed all the money for the property and repairs on a credit card, nothing would show up on the title as debt. There were no liens. When I'd get home after a sale, I'd ask my wife to get the credit cards out of the file and call for the pay-off balances. Our profit was the amount of money we had left over after we paid any and all of the credit cards taped inside the file folders. The rule was, we settled up with our credit card companies immediately upon selling a property. Good, bad, or ugly. We paid all the cards related to that property. No ifs, ands, or buts. No maybes, could've beens, or what ifs were acceptable. The appropriate cards got paid off upon closing!

These are some things I learned about credit cards that kept us profitable and out of trouble:

1. Use the credit card checks instead of walking into the bank with just the credit card. If you use the card, you'll be charged a percentage of the amount you borrow, say 3% to 5%. That can really add up when you are asking for $20,000–$30,000 or more. If you call ahead and have the cash-advance checks

mailed to you, you can write a check on the credit card account and pay as little as $0 to $50 per transaction, no matter how much the transaction is for.

2. Never hold your credit card bills. Pay the monthly payments the minute you get them. It seems that all credit card companies have built-in penalties that kick in when you are one second late on your payments. They are banking on the fact that most people fall into this trap. All those introductory rates of 6% - 3% - $0% for six months or for a year will skyrocket to 21% - 25% the second you are late one time. Some credit card companies seem to hold your payments until it's late and then enter your payment. That only had to happen once to me. From then on, I'd send my special rate card payments by certified, registered, return-receipt mail. That put a stop to that dookie!

If you get a company that insists you are late, don't fight them for long. Tell them you are going to do a balance transfer to another credit card if they don't re-instate the favorable rate. If they don't agree, then transfer the balance to another card immediately. If you have good credit, those introductory-rate credit cards are a dime a dozen and the perfect place to get the funds to repair your properties.

3. If you have a card balance that goes past that fantastic interest-rate time limit, simply transfer that balance to the next introductory rate of the day. It's work, but a very low interest rate is worth the effort. Even if you spend an hour transferring the balance, you'll get another six months to a year at a great rate!

CHAPTER 29
DOUBTING THOMAS

• • •

I believed in what I was doing, so I stuck to my guns.

If nothing else, the books I'd been reading had taught me one thing. There is no room for external doubt or negativity. You're either in or you're out. I had vowed to take control of my life and that meant everyone, and I mean everyone, had to decide if they were in or out!

If a person was having trouble deciding to support me or not, I would make the decision easy for them: They were out! It was easy this time around because this time I'd let everyone know the rules up front and especially my "wife to be" before my marriage proposal. I was headed down this uncertain path and I warned everyone, not to come if they did not want to follow me to wherever it might lead. I was prepared to be an island for the time it would take for me to mature. I was fortunate that my family supported me (as usual). If my family had not supported me, they would've had to get over it. I was prepared to wait and work for how ever long it took. And I absolutely believed in what I was doing.

This is the most common problem I see when new investors come onto the scene. Most of them have doubting spouses, and that, my friend, is a tough row to hoe. I know because I've lived it. I do not suggest going about it the way I did. I suppose a lot of women would have told me to stuff it where the sun doesn't shine. And I wouldn't have blamed them, really. I did not handle my situation with very much tact. There was little discussion about it. In my defense, I wasn't trying to be arrogant. I knew what I was capable of, but I couldn't tell anyone exactly how much I'd make or exactly how long it would take. That's just too gray for some black and white personalities. For me, the secret was to deal in margins so big that if I made a mistake I just made less than when I first penciled the plan on paper. Either way, I'd still be on the *plus* side! After the first five times, my lovely wife said, "No" to deals. I just stopped asking.

TOMMI: You bought a house without asking my opinion first?

ME: Yep.

TOMMI: Why didn't you ask me for my opinion?

ME: I already know your opinion. Your opinion is NO.

TOMMI: So, you are just going to buy them anyway?

ME: Yep.

Part of what made this difficult for Tommi was that I was doing my own thing without her consent. I understood her frustration. We were married so she did have a financial stake in what I was doing. The other part that made it difficult for her had to do with the disparity between our educations on the topic of real estate and entrepreneurialism in general. I'd been on the road reading and preparing myself for these moments for five years.

Even before that, I'd tried my hand at all types of businesses, and although they didn't work out that well, I had a handle on what I was good at and what I wasn't because of those ventures. Of course, we had talked about investing and everything that included before we got married, but I guess she never thought we (I) would really do it. I thought investing was what I was supposed to do! I guess Tommi never did mentally prepare. Suddenly, she was getting a crash course in being an entrepreneur and on real estate in real time with real money! It was overwhelming for her.

Racking up credit cards really freaked my wife out. Through a series of events, she slowly came to relax on the subject of credit card debt. The series of events went something like this.

I bought a house on a credit card.

I had a HUGE argument with my wife.

I sold it and we made money.

I bought another house on a credit card.

I had a big argument with my wife.

I sold it and we made money.

I bought another house on a credit card.

I had a small argument with my wife.

I sold it and we made money.

I bought another house on a credit card.

My wife asked me what I wanted special for dinner.

I sold it and we made money.

I bought another house on a credit card.

My wife bought us a nice five-day vacation.

I sold it and we made money.

I bought another house on a credit card.

My wife answered the door in lingerie.

Etc., etc., etc.

I'm not sure if Robert Frost would be all that impressed with the iambic pentameter of my little diddy above, but it is a part of the poetry of our life. It's not all that far from exactly what happened, really! The point is this: I had to drag my wife kicking and screaming into entrepreneurialism. It wasn't just the money or my credit at stake. Everything was on the line, including my relationship with my wife. Remember, at the beginning of this book, that day I hit rock bottom, traveling in that rickety, red van in the freezing cold for Spencer Engineering? Remember? Remember I said I was never going backwards again? Remember I vowed to eat beans and sleep on the floor by myself until I became financially independent? I remember saying it, and I meant it! No one was going to deprive me of my right to fail forward if that's what it took.

The reality of the situation was this: I was being met with pessimism even when I was succeeding, and I had a hard time handling that in a democratic fashion. Right or wrong I did what I thought I needed to do. I figured things would work out, but I was willing to live with whatever happened due to my actions. Fortunately, things worked out, but I took full responsibility, and I did not gamble with the money. I took calculated risks based on what I knew I could physically, mentally and economically do to profit from the properties I would purchase. Physically, I could change the aesthetics and engineering of the properties. Economically, I could offer owner financing and increase the volume of people who could potentially afford to buy my properties. Mentally, I would out market and out work anyone in the business.

CHAPTER 30
CREDIT CARD COUNSELING

• • •

Laughter is truly the best medicine.

The disparity between our logic got so bad that Tommi ended up taking us to counseling. We landed in the office of the marriage counselor of *Dr. Love*. (Yes, I've made up that name because I can't remember his real name.) We showed up at our appointment and were there for about an hour and a half. The good doctor asked Tommi about her childhood. She explained to him how she'd lost her father when she was five years old and her mother when she was twenty-one. About the same time she lost her mother, her first husband left. Imagine being a young woman with two babies…no husband and no parents. Her second marriage had resulted in yet another man defecting. By then, I was wondering why she has anything to do with men at all.

Now, my wife is *not* a whiner by any means. To her credit, she's always picked herself up and done very well on her own. I wasn't there but, from everything I've heard and seen, I have no doubt that she handled those adversities of her life with strength and dignity. She'd been raising two very well-behaved children, had her own home and was perfectly at peace, until she met me. Neither one of us had calculated the personality differences we were headed for. The first two years of our marriage I was gone ninety days at a time but I had a stable job, and that worked for her just fine. The checks came in and the bills got paid, and we missed each other and honeymooned every time we met. We'd talk on the phone and I'd send a check home every week, for several years.

One day, everything changed. I arrived home from off the road, entered our home, slammed the door shut, and shouted, "Honey, I'm Home!" and never left for my job on the road again.

The doctor started to point out to me how my investing habits could really be stressful for someone like Tommi who had spent an entire lifetime trying to hold a nest together. I did understand it. It made perfect sense to me. But we were married now and what was I supposed to do? Get a job at Wal-Mart so she wouldn't be uncomfortable?

We got around to my side of the story and how she compared my investing to gambling. To me, I was not gambling in any sense of the word. After all, I had proof of what houses were worth before I paid half price for them. The doctor grilled me on my tactics and my due diligence techniques. He was really pulling the entire business model out of me. I caught the paradigm shift in the conversation: Instead of him counseling us, I began counseling the good doctor on how to improve his financial situation. What happened next really got Tommi upset. It seems that Dr. Love had some money saved up in a self-directed IRA, and he wanted to invest it with me. When Tommi finally figured out I was counseling the counselor and that the counselor wanted to invest with me, she was steaming hot! Unfortunately, the session was over in short order.

As we got onto the elevator to go down to our car, I just couldn't help but see the humor in the situation. My wife had taken me to a marriage counselor to prove I was gambling with our money and it ended with the doctor wanting to invest his money with me. With a straight face and a calm, compassionate demeanor, I looked at

Tommi and said, "Sweetheart, if I'd have known counseling was going to work out so well, I'd have signed up a long time ago."

Even Tommi couldn't hide from the humor of the situation. By the time the elevator doors opened, we were in the full throws of laughter. In between bursts, I'd say things like, "I wonder how many marriage counselors there are in this town?" or "Honey, are there any other issues we can work on together?" I nearly shattered a blood vessel in my forehead. My apology didn't help us catch our breath either. "Sweetie Pie, I'm sorry…I'm so screwed up that even the *doctors* want to invest with me!"

Tommi had arranged the session to prove I was gambling. She learned, maybe, just maybe, I was calculating. I learned I needed to start talking to more doctors about investing with me. The truth of the matter is, if Tommi hadn't given the doctor such a hard time, he would probably still be investing his money with us today. All in all, the Doc did a wonderful job of getting us on the healing path. Laughter really is the best medicine.

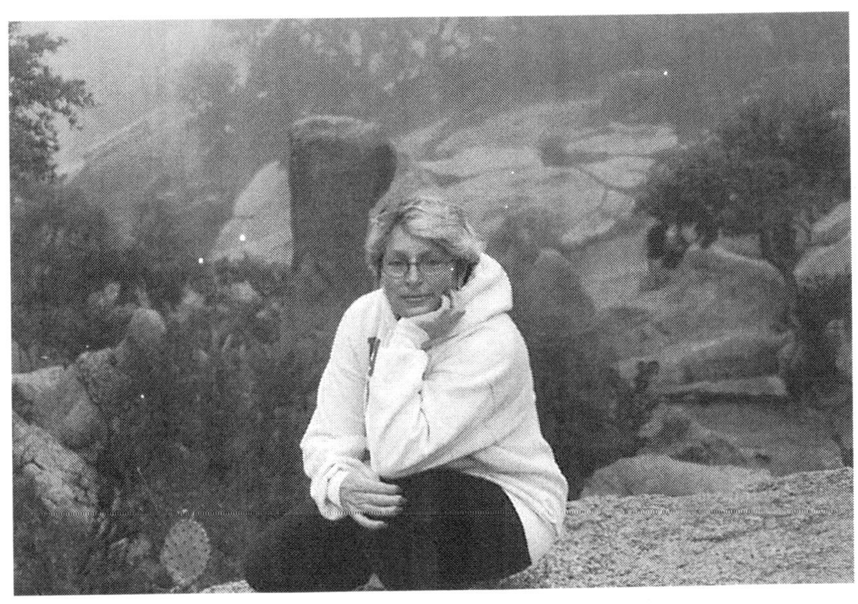

Tommi Stephen at Enchanted Rock near Fredricksburg, TX

CHAPTER 31
MEETING SAM HOMBRE

• • •

Some people say having a partner is the worst thing you can do. I think some people are just bad partner pickers.

I'd been going through the classifieds one day looking for properties. That routine is always followed by a stint of driving from one property to the next. In my real estate career, I've traveled an average of 55,000 miles per year. While it is true I live twenty-eight miles from town, I attribute much of my success to being out and about. For me, deals aren't made from behind a desk. They are made in the field. I don't think twice about jumping into my truck and driving to wherever I need to be. Personally, I don't calculate miles per gallon or the price of gas. It's never been on my tally sheet. The price of gas and the wear and tear on my vehicle are not significant, given the amount of money I can produce by finding a good deal.

Today, the gurus call it driving for dollars but back then we just called it working. I've had wanna-be investors decline to jump into their vehicles and meet me at a property because it was close to that five o'clock traffic time or because they'd just gotten home. I always hang up the phone in dismay. Traffic, *Smaffic*! I'm buying a house today. NEXT!

Everybody wants to go to heaven
Nobody wants to die!

One day I was answering an advertisement that touted a great deal on a house. I met a young, energetic man at the property and we began to talk real estate. I don't remember if I purchased that house from Sam Hombre or not, but I do remember this: We started talking and it didn't end for four years. He asked me what I was doing to make money in real estate. I told him that I was buying houses on my credit cards, fixing them up, and then reselling them. I asked him what he was doing, and he told me he had limited funds, so he was tying properties up on a contract and then selling his position in the contracts to people like me who had the resources or ingenuity to buy them quickly with cash. I immediately recognized Sam's modus operandi as a personal revelation and vice versa.

That was the start of a relationship that covered hundreds of deals and the entire south, east and west side of San Antonio and beyond. Sam and I still reminisce when we travel together downtown. Every street evokes an image of some little house we used to own. More often than not we remember the ones that caused us the greatest heartburn. Our efforts combined, it's almost impossible to find a street on which we've not paid a property tax.

CHAPTER 32
SIGNS OF TRYING

• • •

If you're going to make a mistake, make it going full speed!

During the late 1990's my brother Kleat was struggling. The cycle between his "regular self" to "manic" to "depression" and back again, was getting shorter and shorter. The manic state is a high or a wired state usually followed by a long time of sleep and/or depression. Typically, in his manic state, Kleat would go long periods of time without sleeping, sometimes days. To compound the situation he would get off into things that didn't serve him well. He'd finally crash and then wake up sometimes days later. After a season of waking up to things "not so fun to face" I tried to convince him to focus on something positive in his manic state instead of something negative. That way, when he woke up, he would have opportunity waiting at his door instead of the trouble. I was almost sure I'd not gotten through to him but I'd soon be proven wrong.

It was getting harder and harder for Kleat to function and, in an effort to sustain him financially, I'd pay him half the profit derived from any property purchased from plastic signs he'd put up around the city. These signs were not so popular in some parts of town but in the poorer areas where we bought most of our houses, plastic signs were the least of the worries and the signs tend to get little resistance. Over time, you get a sense for where "bandit" signs will be tolerated and where they won't, and that's important because you definitely don't want the "sign police" on your trail. It sounds reasonable enough, right? Well, apparently all the minutia of sign placement leaves the thought process when you slip into a manic state.

I got a call from Kleat early one morning. He was alive and vibrant and swelling with enthusiasm. I was pretty impressed being that it was 6:00 a.m. in the morning. He was telling me, with all the excitement a person can muster, that he had done what I'd suggested. He'd gotten into a manic state and instead of doing something negative he had done something positive…really, really positive! I was happy to hear him excited about something for a change. I perked up.

ME: "So what did you do?"
KLEAT: "You know how I get into this manic state and I can't sleep?
ME: Yeah.
KLEAT: Well about 3 days ago my manic started coming on so I made up my mind I was going to do something positive until I crashed, just like you talked to me about.
ME: That's great! What did you do?
KLEAT: I've been up for 3 days straight and haven't done anything but put up signs… for 3 days and nights—straight!"
ME: Man, Kleat, that's great! How many signs do you think you put up?
KLEAT: Over 650!
ME: (I'm thinking, HOLY COW! But I was trying to not show it over the phone.) Over 650?

KLEAT: Yeah, Mitch. We've got signs everywhere now! Everywhere! You can't believe how easy it is to put up signs in the middle of the night. At 3:00 a.m. and 4:00 a.m. in the morning, there's nobody anywhere and you can just park any place you want and put up signs like there's no tomorrow!
ME: Man, that's great Kleat! (The same two words still on my mind…HOLY COW!)
KLEAT: I'm getting ready to crash now. I'm finally getting tired. I'll call you in a day or so when I wake up. I know we're gonna buy some houses from this. There's no way it won't work, Mitch!
ME: Good job, Kleat! You go get some sleep now. You get some nice peaceful rest and don't worry about anything. Good things will be waiting for you when you wake up.

I had my doubts about things being good but he needed to rest. I wanted him to sleep with a smile on his face for a change. Whatever was going to happen was going to happen. The act had already been committed. We would just have to deal with it as it comes. Over the next few hours my phone calls started picking up and by noon I was answering the phone like the fire department on the 4th of July in a drought year. Most callers were potential sellers but every now and then an investor I knew would call and leave a message saying something to the affect of, "Mitch, how many signs did you put up? or "Man, you're crazy!" or something a bit more sarcastic like, "Hey Mitch, have you ever thought about putting on a SIGN seminar?" That's when I knew for sure this was out of control. I was afraid to get into my truck and drive into town. I could just picture it: a sign on every corner. It all added up to one thing; we were going to get pounded by the sign police. It was inevitable.

Sure enough, I received a call from a rather prominent part of town (actually a township inside San Antonio) called Castle Hills. Apparently Kleat had put a sign on the front and back of every telephone poll in that particular little township. To make matters worse, he had put them so high that they couldn't reach them easily. The powers that be were not happy to say the least. I was out of town so instead of trying to explain it over the phone, my Father cowboyed-up and went to the city offices to meet with the sign police in person on my behalf. After explaining our unique situation the official lightened up and instead of fining us some horrendous amount of money per sign, they allowed us some time to get them down. When the task of removing the signs from that area of town got underway Dad said it was unbelievable; there were signs everywhere, just like Kleat had said.

The number of signs in Castle Hills proper only accounted for a fraction of the actual number of signs Kleat had put out. The vast majority of signs stayed out and surprisingly enough we never got a single call from any other city officials. In the days and weeks, even months that followed, I drove the city of San Antonio in amazement. I drove through the city as part of my daily work routine and I can tell you, without a doubt, that 650 signs scattered about the city in 3 non-stop days is a tremendous and undeniable feat.

Although the day was emotionally tough, looking back it all worked out and it was definitely worth the stress. In a short period of time we had bought about 13 properties from those signs. In the long run we ended up buying well over 30 properties. We would buy houses from those sings for months and months to come. It went a long, long way to providing for both our families and given Kleat's medical issues we all needed every penny. Deep down I harbored the idea that if Kleat had some personal success things would change for the better. I thought if Kleat could make some money and get some confidence that this "Depression Phase" would pass. I was way off.

CHAPTER 33
THE GRAND SLAM OF REAL ESTATE INVESTING

• • •

I love selling properties before I actually own them.

When Sam and I tried to function out of our own pockets, our deal flow could get clogged up in hurry. We were just starting our investment careers, and we had a lot to learn. In those days, there were plenty of deals and not a lot of people out there chasing them. Since we were always short on cash, given the volume of deals we could buy, we had to get inventive. We learned to recognize scenarios that allowed us to profit with little or no money out of our pockets.

Investing with little or no money can be done. The secret is to gain a position on the property with very little money down and then pre-sell the property or sell your *position in the contract* before you have to actually *buy* the property. As I mentioned before, Sam was doing just that in his first days as an investor. He was trying to sell me his position in a contract when I met him. There are many variations of the example I'm about to give, but suffice it to say that nothing-down deals can be done. When you do a nothing-down deal, you are going to substitute work, time and knowledge for money. Like everything else, you just need the expertise and the ambition to do it.

First things first: Almost every transaction starts with an earnest-money contract (purchase contract). We need this contract *first* because we always want to buy title insurance when we spend our money on real estate. It is really nice to know that the person selling you the property is actually the owner, right? It's also nice to know that if you do buy a property from someone who does not own it, you'll have a way to get your money back. Title companies sell insurance that guarantees the buyer(s) that the title is good and that all parties with an interest in the property being sold are of record and being dealt with accordingly. That legal work takes time. When you have cash, that time can be a hindrance, but when you're working on a shoestring, that time can be of great benefit. You'll need that time to get a jump on finding your buyer. The more time you get before you have to close, the longer you'll have to find your buyer.

The minute you have a contract signed by both parties (you, the *Buyer* and them, the *Seller*), you have a position on the property. You have limited, legal control over the property for a certain amount of time. You haven't purchased the property yet, but you do have the right to purchase that property at an agreed-to price under the guidelines provided in your purchase contract. That contract is personal property and as with most personal property, you can sell it or your position in it.

HITTING A SINGLE

A single happens when you gain a position on real estate and then sell that position before you have to come up with the money to actually buy it!

One way to hit a single is called wholesaling. That's when you get a property under contract and then sell the contract for a modest fee. Here's an example.

> ***You get a property under contract for $50,000 by putting up $500 and getting the purchase contract signed. The property is valued at $80,000. You have thirty days to close. Before***

your thirty days are over, you sell your position to another investor for $50,000 +$5,000 + the $500 you put up on the purchase contract. In less than thirty days, you've made a deal to get back your $500 and receive an additional $5,000 at closing. Not bad for a guy who only had $500 to invest!

HITTING A HOME RUN

You could hit a home run on that same property by selling it to an end user. You get that same $80,000 property under contract for $50,000 using your $500 for earnest money, then sell the property to an end user (someone who wants to live in the house or otherwise improve the property for *themselves*). By selling to an end user you make way more money because you sell the property for the retail price. This is much trickier because your buyer is going to have to come up with $80,000 cash in less than thirty days. But I've seen it done–and the payoff is much larger, e.g., $30,000 minus some closing costs.

Finding a buyer who has the resources and the enthusiasm to buy a property for retail that fast is very difficult. It's further complicated because of the time pressures. If your buyer needs more time to close (which happens a lot), you are going to have to close your deal ahead of your buyer, or you're going to have to ask your seller for an extension, or you are going to lose your deal. Be on the lookout for a *home run* buyer but don't hold your breath.

HITTING A GRAND SLAM!

You can't hit a grand slam without getting your bases loaded. Sam and I would get a house under contract, find a buyer who needed our owner financing (pre-selling the home before actually buying it), and then get a note buyer to buy the payments we were about to create, *all on the same day*! No, we wouldn't find all of these pieces of the puzzle on the same day, but, we'd consummate all of them on the same day. Everything happens on one closing date.

Get a contract to buy the house.

Get a contract to sell the house with seller financing.

Get a contract to sell the note.

Then, consummate all of these contracts on the same day.

(In the correct order of course)

The note buyer would bring the money to buy the payments we were creating by financing our buyer. The note buyers wouldn't pay us the full amount we were owed, but typically they'd paid us anywhere from 83% to 97% of what we were owed, and that was good enough. The cool part was this: Since all of this happened at the same table on the same day and virtually at the same time, the money we used to *buy the house* came from the *note buyer*. We didn't have to bring any money to closing! I personally saw this happen fifteen or twenty time in 1996 alone.

As I said, you have to get your bases loaded to hit a grand slam. There are a few factors that come into play if you're going to sell a property within minutes of buying it.

1. The property must be livable and sellable the day you put it under contract.
2. You must have access to the inside of the property so you can show it.
3. You must have enough time on your purchase contract to find a buyer before *you* have to actually buy it.

4. You must make your sale to your Buyer contingent on *your* purchase of the property. The wording in your agreement with your buyer is crucial. You would NOT say, "This sale is contingent on the ability of the Seller to buy the property before it can be sold." You SHOULD say, "This contract is contingent upon the Seller's ability to provide clear title to the Buyer."
5. The property must appraise for at least the amount *you* are selling it for. Otherwise, your note buyer might kill the deal.

Of course, not every deal can be a grand slam. The stars and the moon have to line up just right for a grand slam to work, and that doesn't happen every day. More often than not, we had to have some money to buy the house already lined up incase any piece of the puzzle went south. If things didn't go just right we were prepared to close with those backup funds and collect some payments on the houses before we could sell the note. If we had to close the sale with backup funds we'd have to wait for our eventual profit but we'd make a little more for our time. As you might imagine, a *seasoned note* (a note where *several* payments have already been collected) is worth a lot more than a *pristine note* (a note where *no* payments have been collected yet). The longer we season a note, the more it is potentially worth. In short, the note buyers are willing to pay more if they can look at the history of the payer. Is the note proving to be a steady source of income or a shaky source of income? It's all common sense really. Note buyers pay more for notes that have a verifiable record of good pay history.

The numbers in the example below are low by today's standards. You can't buy many houses at 1996 prices these days. In 1997, Sam and I would buy and sell about 65 more houses. With a little more confidence and a little more money saved from our success, we were able to buy more properties that needed to be fixed up. We were also able to hold onto our notes a little longer before we sold them, so we could get a higher price for them. This is very close to what most of our deals looked like in the mid- to-late-'90's.

Buy a house for $30,000.

Find a buyer willing to pay $55,000 with $3,000 down.

Finance the $52,000 balance at 10% for 30 years.

Principle & Interest (P&I) = $456.34 / mo.

Take an application on the potential buyer.

Write up a deal sheet describing the terms of the sale.

Get the property appraised at $55,000 or better.

Fax all of the above to several note buyers and have them bid to buy the income stream.

When we'd receive an acceptable bid, we'd call our buyer and tell them they were approved.

When selling a house with owner financing, the main objective is to get the *buyer* into the office to sign a purchase agreement, complete an application, and give a down payment.

As previously mentioned, make sure the sales agreement with your buyer is contingent upon your ability to purchase the property. Also, if the note buyer(s) turns your buyer down or do not offer an amount you are happy with, return *all of the down payment* to your rejected buyer. Furthermore, we always return the credit application fees if the potential buyer had been honest about their credit worthiness and we were not able to get them a home.

Once you have an accepted buyer, schedule a simultaneous closing at the title company. You sell the property to your buyer with *seller financing* (creating a note), and then sell that note to the note buyer on the same day at the same closing table.

In those days, note buyers were offering about 83% of the note balance for notes that were *pristine* (no payments made yet) or for buyers that had extremely bad credit. In the example above, our owner-financed buyer owed us a balance of $52,000 the day of closing. $52,000 was the balance we were selling for 83%.

In the note sale above, the note buyer would pay us 83% of the $52,000…$43,160. Remember, we'd also collected a $3,000 down payment from our buyer as well. So, the total income was $46,160.

We'd borrowed $30,000, from private investors to acquire the property. After the title company subtracted what we owed on the property, we would walk out of closing with the difference of $16,160 (minus some closing costs, say, $1,160 for easy math).

$ 46,160 Income from the Note Buyer

$ -1,160 Closing Costs

$ -30,000 Money borrowed from Private Investors to acquire the property

$ 15, 000 Total Profit before taxes

Sam and I almost never put up more than $10 for earnest money.

That is a profit of roughly $15,000 using a ten dollar bill!

The annual rate of return, by the numbers, is off the charts.

$15,000 divided by $10 = 150,000% annual Return on Investment (ROI)

The calculation above is an *annual* rate of return. Many times we'd do this in thirty days or less.

In reality, any *nothing down* deal (and I consider $10 to be nothing) is a bit skewed when factoring in the work and time it took to get it done. I'm sure we all agree that time is money. That being said, I've worked a lot harder for $8.00 an hour digging ditches. I had found my niche!

CHAPTER 34
THE REUNION

• • •

Whether we like it or not we plant many seeds as we travel along. It amazes me where weeds can grow.

By the end of 1996, Sam and I had purchased and sold exactly 45 properties. Not bad for working on a shoestring. Sam Hombre and I were on fire, financially, emotionally, and with dreams of financial independence. At the time, we could find more houses than we could actually purchase. We would end up buying and selling about 65 homes in 1997 but, with a little help from an old friend, we were about to explode our horizons.

If we'd had more seminars under our belts, we'd have literally made an additional fortune collecting deeds or contracts and wholesaling what we couldn't handle directly. Instead, we passed on a lot of houses. During that time, the seminar scene had hardly hit our radar screens. Tapes and books and hours and hours of conversations had gotten us this far. That wasn't such a bad deal. I shudder to think what a difference a few seminars would've made but, then again, we were barely able to handle the revelations we were having in our own cocoon on a daily basis. Living in your own information vacuum is a double-edged sword. You stay focused, but some really great, *simple* concepts never occur to you.

We were starting to get a reputation around town and other investors were starting to knock on our door. A line was starting to form. Soon we'd form a strategy to take on more of them. The biggest problem was funding all of the deals. For now, we were running largely on credit cards, about forty credit cards to the best of my recollection.

I walked into International Bank of Commerce (IBC) one sunny day to get some money off my credit cards. I needed $20,000 to purchase the property and $10,000 to rehab the property. At the end of the remodel, the home would be worth about $55,000 owner financed. Once inside, I arrived at the teller station and requested $10,000 cash advances on each of three credit cards for a total of $30,000. The teller disappeared shortly after my request and took an exceptionally long time before she returned. Upon her arrival, I was invited back behind the teller's station to "walk on the carpet." The teller handed me the phone. Apparently, the Vice President of the bank wanted to speak with me.

IBC VICE PRESIDENT: Mr. Stephen, your request is a bit unusual so I'd like to verify who you are if you don't mind.

ME: I appreciate your concerns and actually commend you for taking the time to do so.

IBC VICE PRESIDENT: Do you mind if I ask you a few questions to verify who you are?

ME: What would you like know?

IBC VICE PRESIDENT: Well Mr. Stephen, who did you play football for?

ME: (I'm smiling and thinking, "Oh boy, who in the heck is this?) The John Marshall Fighting Rams!

IBD VICE PRESIDENT: What position did you play?

ME: (I'm really amused now) Tailback!

IBC VICE PRESIDENT: Who was the best quarterback you ever had?

ME: Steve Edlund? Who the heck made you vice president of a bank?

EDLUND: Who made me vice president of a bank? I'm wondering who in the heck gave Mitch Stephen thirty thousand dollars worth of unsecured credit cards!

I had inadvertently met up with an old teammate, high school quarterback, Steve Edlund. It's been happening since high schools were invented: You hang out with a group of people for four years. Learn, grow, compete, build a strong friendship and then, on the day after graduation, everyone heads out in a million different directions. You never really see them much anymore. Life just happens. It happened to me and some 2.5 decades later I headed out to attend my 25th year class reunion. It took me about fifteen minutes to get to the place where we were all going to meet that night. It was nice to see the old gang again and we all had a really good time. Then, when the evening was over, I jumped in my truck and headed back to the house. It took me twenty-five years to get home.

"THEE REUNION"

Written by Mitch Stephen

Me and my friends, will make the reunion
To dance thee old dances, to all thee old songs
And shout "hallelujah," for the good times remembered
And find where the kings and the queens have all gone
I spy a cheerleader's put on some weight
But I've gained a few pounds since my playin' days
And the ones I thought not, are now not what I thought
And alive with a beautiful glow

CHORUS:
"Hail to thee our alma mater," "HAIL TO THEE," we sang
Will soon be sung, by the sons and the daughters
And they'll heed no warning, of the words we might say
...to "live out everyday"
'Cause the class year reunion, we thought never would come
Is suddenly under way

BRIDGE:
Why the flags and why the banners
And why do we keep coming back?
We love the torture of a good of a good old langsyne

Now the songs have been sung, and the night danced away
The wallet sized pictures, are all back in place
Before we go, Shall we raise one last toast
"To the fallen along the way"

MODIFIED CHORUS:
Who sang, "Hail to thee our alma mater," "HAIL TO THEE" they sang
Soon be sung, by their sons and their daughters
And we'll heed no warning, of the words from their graves
... To "live out everyday"
'Cause the grandest reunion, we think never will come
Is already on its way .... It's already well on its way

Listen: http://www.mitchstephen.com/thee.asp?music=on
Sung by Kevin Hughes

www.MitchStephen.com

CHAPTER 35
THE BANK CALLS

• • •

You want to loan me how much?

It had been fifteen years since we'd seen each other or even talked to each other. That day at the bank, Steve and I had a great laugh over the phone and reconnected somewhat. The last thing Steve Edlund said before he hung up the phone got me fired up.

EDLUND: What are you using this money for?

ME: I'm buying a house with it.

EDLUND: So it's a down payment for a house?

ME: No, I'm buying a house for $20,000 and using another $10,000 to fix it up!

EDLUND: Well, I hope you know what the heck you're doing.

I thought to myself, "I'll show him if I know what I'm doing alright." And with that I walked out of the bank with my $30,000 cashier's check.

A few hours later, I bought that house, and within a few weeks I had it cleaned up and sold. This particular house turned around rather quickly. The day I sold that house, I got a nice, chunky check. I decided to let Mr. *Vice President* Edlund see just how I was doing.

I took the closing statement from the day I bought the house and wrote the word **PURCHASE** at the top in big, bold, black marker and then I moved down the page and circled the purchase price on the bottom line—**$20,000**. Next I took the statement where I'd sold the property and wrote the word **SOLD** at the top of it and circled the sales price of **$55,000**. To complete my mission, I faxed both the buying and selling statements to the first IBC location I found in the phone book. The fax cover sheet read; TO: STEVE EDLUND. I figured if he was *vice president,* it'd get to him one way or the other. Now I know I did *not* make all the money in between these two numbers. I had repair costs, holding costs, etc., but suffice it to say, I made plenty in the middle in a very short period of time. I'd let Steve guess at just how much.

Somewhere along the way, I gave my assistant instructions to send a fax to Edlund every time we sold a property. I went on about my life never thinking much about the bank after that. Then, one day, I received a call on my cell phone. It was Steve Edlund of IBC bank. I answered the phone:

ME: This is Mitch.
STEVE: Hey Mitch, the bank wants to talk to you.
ME: What's wrong?
STEVE: Nothin's wrong. The bank wants to talk with you.
ME: Did a check bounce? What's wrong?

Banks never wanted to talk to Mitch Stephen unless there was a problem. The last time the bank called I got to meet an FBI agent. Remember?

STEVE: They want to talk to you about loaning you money. You could use some money, right?

ME: Yeah, I could use some more money to buy houses, I guess.

STEVE: How much do you need?

ME: I don't know, Steve, $20,000…maybe 30,000. I'm willing to start slow.

I think I've mentioned this before. I'm a bit naïve sometimes, to say the least.

STEVE: $20,000 or $30,000? I figure you need more than that. I've seen you sell at least ten to fifteen houses in the past 30 days. How much are you paying for the average house?

ME: I guess I'm paying about $30,000 to $40,000 each at the end of the day.

STEVE: So you need a half-million-dollar line of credit, right? Could you use a half million?

ME: I'll be there in ten minutes.

Shortly after that phone call, I had a $245,000 line of credit. It wasn't the half million we'd talked about, but it was still great to be given a little more of the reins so we could run a little harder. As it turns out, not getting the $500,000 turned out to be a blessing in disguise. It all has to do with meeting a guy named Carlos Balido, but we'll talk about that later.

Given our propensity and the climate for finding deals, Sam and I blew past the $245K credit limit in a matter of days. I called Steve and tried to get IBC to increase the limit again to $500K but to no avail. I thought the bank would be impressed with our immediate and decisive use of their money but I was completely wrong about that. Banks in general move slowly, especially when you're young in a particular business and burn through credit lines fast. Figuring we might be able to get large sums of capital to invest much quicker in the private sector, Steve called again. This time he had a different plan.

Steve said he could introduce me to some very successful businessmen who were not so risk adverse. The down side is I'd probably be paying way more for the money. We discussed the pros and cons as they applied to the house business and agreed, if we were holding the properties for short periods of time, the interest rate was a non-issue compared to the money that could be made. Remember, "It is not always the cost of the money that counts. It's the *availability*."

CHAPTER 36
KEEPING RELATIONS:

• • •

There is a time for business and a time for pleasure. People with passion for what they do, get them both done at the same time.

Back in the day I'd never have guessed that Steve would give me my first line of credit and introduce me to people that would become my life long partners. I am very grateful for all the help he and IBC have given me and my family. In 2003, Steve became chief executive officer of International Bank of Commerce in San Antonio, Texas. Today, we both mitigate different battles, but it's still fun to be teammates of sorts again.

For many years, it has been a privilege to deer hunt on the IBC ranch. Every season I've been invited to go, and it's always an exciting trip. The bank has a first-class operation down there near Laredo, Texas, and a bunch of really fine businessmen gather there every November and December to have some fun. Believe me when I say, *"I am honored to be in the same camp with some of these guys."* We are treated like kings, and the trophy bucks on that land can make your jaw drop to the ground. If you're a hunter, you know exactly what I'm talking about. You don't get to hunt a place like that as a guest very often.

Once I was hunting with Steve and a couple of other bank customers when we spotted a huge buck. I lowered my rifle down on the deer immediately and had the sites of my 270 perfectly set. I was steady and ready. The mammoth buck was frozen in a spectacular broad side pose and looking right at us. Only 150 yards away, it was a *sure kill*. I was waiting for Steve to age the deer and tell me *yes* or *no*. It was probably just a few seconds that Steve stood gazing through his binoculars, but it seemed like forever. Finally Steve made the call, "No, he's too young."

I remained in my position, with the cross hairs of my scope nailed to the shoulder of the world-class deer. "Look again," I said. I was still frozen to my gun, cheek still stuck to the stock of my rifle, eye peering down the scope and finger on the trigger.

Steve took a very short time to reply, "No, he's too young. It is obvious." Still fixed like stone, I asked, "Steve, what happens if I pull the trigger and kill this deer, *right now?*"

Steve said, 'I'll be looking for a new bank to work for tomorrow.'

I released the breath I'd been holding and took in a deeper breath, the cross hairs of my scope still on the shoulder of the deer, "So what's the down side, Steve?"

There was a slight chuckle from Steve and the other two hunters that ended when they heard the safety on my rifle click forward into the *fire* position. Steve said, "If you shoot that deer I'm calling all your notes due."

After making Steve sweat for about ten seconds, I gave up my position on the deer. "What do you mean you're gonna call all my notes due? You said if I shot that deer you'd be fired! How can you call my notes due if you're *fired*?"

We laughed and joked and generally had a good time over the whole situation. But one thing is for sure, Steve Edlund doesn't know just how close he came to working for another bank that day.

Me enjoying another bountiful hunt at the IBC Lease in Aguilares, TX near Laredo

CHAPTER 37
THE REAL COST OF MONEY

• • •

It amazes me the number of investors that will walk away with $0 because they don't want to share the wealth.

Let's say you could buy a house for $50,000 and sell it in less than sixty days for $75,000, but you don't have the money to do so. Now let's say that a friend of yours hears about the deal and offers to loan you the money at 21% interest annually. Here's how the math looks.

$50,000 x 21% = $10,500 annually if you have the money out for 12 months (but you're only going to have the money out for 2 months.)
$10,500 / 12 = $875 per month
$875 x 2 months (60 days) = $1,750

So when the math is all said and done you are going to have to pay $1,750 of your profit to your private lender if you are going to take advantage of this great deal you've found. The scenario gets real simple and the main question even simpler.

If you don't borrow the money at 21% you will lose the deal and the $25,000 potential profit. If you borrow the money at 21% you won't make $25,000 but you will make $23,250. The question is:

Do I want to make $0 or do I want to make $23,250?

(in 60 days or less)

It baffles me to no end the number of people that will make $0 because they just cannot stand the thought of spreading the wealth around just a little. Even worse are investors who agree with the rationalization above but lose the deal because they messed around too long, trying to find a different investor offering a lower interest rate. A few things come to mind when I think about investors who are slow to catch on. It's really not all that hard a concept to grasp.

Any percentage of something is better than 100% of nothing.

You can't go broke making a profit.

If you are a new investor I hope the two sentences in bold above are perfectly clear. The problem is that so many young investors treat each deal as if they will never find another deal. A seasoned investor knows without a doubt, today's deal is not the last deal!

Make some money and move on down the road. Try it a few times and maybe one day you'll have the money in the bank to make that 100% you've been dreaming of all your life.

The best deals in the world usually have some kind of imminent deadline. As investors, we are able to make great deals by finding the money and consummating those deals before the imminent deadline passes. *Banks* are generally too slow. *Private Lenders* are usually the fastest, but they are going to charge you more. Get over it and get the deal done. You can't make great deals on houses in slow motion.

If you pay as agreed, your private lenders will become your friends, believe me! Don't be surprised when your private lenders start bringing you deals.

CHAPTER 38
PARTNERING UP

• • •

The dollars come and go but the knowledge is yours forever. If you capture the knowledge, there will always be more dollars ahead of you.

If you thought 21% was expensive, you're going to hate this idea. There is another way to buy that $50,000 home that's worth $75,000 when you don't have the money. Offer to split the deal with a seasoned investor who has the money. Instead of making $23,250 you'll only make $11,625 (Half). If you are young in the business and really smart, you'll go this route. Here's why:

1. If you're young in business that $23,250 just might be a daydream. When a seasoned investor looks at your deal and decides to partner with you, you really *do* have a deal. You are going to make some money!
2. You have absolutely no risk of losing any of your own money or your credit.
3. If you work well with this seasoned investor, you are going to be on the fast track. Do what they tell you to do. You will learn a ton in the process. Learn to think like they think. Learn *why* they think as they do. This is an opportunity to hitch a ride on an educational rocket!
4. Your network is going to expand over night. The seasoned investor's network gets added to your network. Let's do the math. You have zero connections. The seasoned investor has

> hundreds of connections. Working with a seasoned investor puts you in contact with hundreds of "connections." It's a no brainer!

The learning curve eats up most novice investors before they get started. They get burned on their first few deals, and they are out of the game for life.

I've had more partners than anyone I've ever met. If I've had one partner, I've had a hundred (probably more). Many of my partners are still my partners, and I've done literally hundreds of deals with some of them individually. Could I have gone on my own and made 100% instead of 50%? The answer is YES. So why would I partner? The answer is simple on the surface but hard to own.

In the beginning, it had to do with delayed gratification. I was exchanging potential dollars for their knowledge. The dollars would come and go but the knowledge was mine forever. Later, I found that I simply enjoyed the camaraderie and the allegiances and more than that, I grow when I am around other thinkers. I found that when I was partnered up with trusted allies I could participate in more deals because I'd have more help in more areas of expertise. Last but not least, if I was a good partner, all my other partners would eventually bring me in on deals I would have never found or been invited to otherwise...and that is where I'd make up the money I'd given away to them in the first place. I knew that if I was a good partner I'd make my money back in spades and still get the benefit of their knowledge.

It all starts to overlap into this big network/database connections/resources experience type of mesh. Maybe I'm in a deal on an apartment complex with someone and we run into a CPA/tax question. I call up a CPA I'm in partnership with on a house and get the answer. He doesn't charge me because I'm his partner and because I've helped him with his questions or his needs in the recent past.

I would rather have 50% of twenty deals than 100% of ten.

Think about it; 50% of twenty or 100% of ten equals the same amount of money but the networking doubles if you choose to take 50% of twenty deals. And there are a lot more benefits than just that.

CONFIRMATION: Having a good partner who specializes in an area you don't know much about can confirm something you were sensing. You may think you have a great deal, but getting your suspicions confirmed by an expert in the field can give you confidence in your abilities. Making them your partner can give you a support system as well as generate the personal nerve to proceed when you might have otherwise quit the deal. Very few of us are willing to take our own money and jump into a completely new endeavor.

LIMIT YOUR RISK: Taking on a partner can limit your risk in at least two ways. First, if your new partner brings all or part of the money to the table, you've hedged your bet in the monetary department. Second, another pair of eyes, an extra set of legs, two more ears, and an additional brain never hurt any deal. In fact, I can credit many of my best paychecks to the creative and thoughtful actions of my partners without whom I'd have never seen the pot of gold at the end of the rainbow.

THEIR KNOWLEDGE BECOMES YOUR KNOWLEDGE: We don't learn anything in a vacuum. I find that if I shut up and listen, I'll learn everything the other investors know. I'll learn the way they rationalize and why. I'll learn what has worked for them and what hasn't and why. I'll learn their philosophy of business and of life and why. I can take it or I can leave it. I can add into my life what I believe in, and I can leave out the parts I don't believe in. But I grow when I'm around others, not when I'm by myself.

Make no mistake about it. This is a two-way street. You must give if you are going to receive. You'll never have a worthy relationship with a successful investor if you don't participate full on. By *full on* I mean you have to be willing to share your good experiences and your bad experiences. Talking about your bad experiences or your losses makes you human. It makes you real. An investor who never tells me about a bad experience is a user.

You also have to be willing to share your network. You cannot be selfish with your connections or your experiences. Don't think for a minute that a savvy investor won't recognize someone who is pumping them for information and giving nothing back in return. May I suggest: Give first and give abundantly. If the person you are giving to is not reciprocating, quietly stop giving away anything useful. Don't cut off the relationship, just cut off the flow of good information until they change their ways. Don't worry one minute about the knowledge you've already dispensed. Look at it like this: You've planted a seed that'll have a chance to bloom some other day. The reality is, it's more about growing than it is about money. Grow enough and money will never be your problem.

THEIR SPECIALTY BECOMES YOUR INCOME STREAM: There are so many different ways to make money in real estate that you need to know different investors in different specialized areas. For example, I have never purchased a large apartment complex on my own. However, if I run across one that seems to be a good deal, I can pick up the phone and team up with investors in town who are experts in that field. I can partner with them or I can simply wholesale the deal to them. Either way, I've got an outlet to make some money from a deal I might have otherwise passed on. The list of niches seems to be endless. Here are a few off the top of my head.

Single Family Residences: Buy & Sell / Lease / Owner Finance / Wholesale

Multi-Family Residences: Buy & Sell / Lease / Owner Finance / Wholesale

Apartments: Buy & Sell / Lease / Condo Conversions / Wholesale

Residential Lots: Buy & Sell / Land—developed or undeveloped

Commercial Lots: Buy & Sell / Land—developed or undeveloped

Mobile home Lots: Buy & Sell / Lease / Owner Finance / Mobile Home Parks / Rent

There are also niches that investors specialize in when looking for deals on real estate:

Tax Auctiosns / Foreclosures / Pre-Foreclosures / Wholesaler / Owner financing /
Frustrated Landlords / Note Buyers / Note Sellers / Private Lenders / Mortgage Brokers / Money Brokers / Bank REO Departments

This list can be as lengthy as the yellow pages! Finding someone in a particular field is not difficult. Finding someone who is reputable in a particular field is always difficult. I figure if there can be good and bad priests, there can be good and bad anything and everything. Honesty and integrity are hard to find in any field. A solid recommendation can help you avoid the stupid tax.

CHAPTER 39
PRIVATE MONEY (PART I)

• • •

It takes some effort to find private money.
Once you find the right private lenders, life gets really good.

My little trip to the marriage counselor had opened my eyes. I put together a plan to find *private lenders* and started knocking on doors. I'd also been working with Steve Edlund at IBC to get more private lenders. He suggested I see a man in town who was infamous for his skill at buying and selling cars with owner financing. I took Steve's lead and met with Mr. Carman (yes, the name has been changed to protect the innocent), and we got along great. Our businesses were not all that different except for a few points.

My core asset (real estate) generally appreciated in value.

His core assets (automobiles) generally decreased in value.

My core asset was attached to the ground.

His core asset could be driven off to anywhere USA

(or transferred abroad for that matter).

Mr. Carman really liked my real estate angle and everything was looking up until he invited his attorney in to assess the viability of our partnership. Within about five minutes everything good had gone to hell in a hand basket. This attorney presented more ways for Mr. Carman to lose his butt in real estate then I ever knew existed. I'm surprised I didn't quit real estate myself. I was young and it happened so fast I could hardly defend myself. All I know is that Mr. Carman's attorney cost me a relationship I'd probably still have today. He also cost his client, Mr. Carman, a great business partner that day- ME! Don't get me wrong. Mr. Carman didn't need me to be a success. He was already a success when I met him and he is even more successful as I write this chapter. Please also understand; I'm sure that Mr. Carman's attorney is great at some thing he does for Mr. Carman or Mr. Carman wouldn't have sought his advice. There are times you absolutely need an attorney, and there are things you absolutely need an attorney for. But may I suggest that attorneys are for drawing up documents that lay out the ground rules for a relationship. Attorneys are not for deciding whether or not a relationship is going to be profitable, or if the partnership is going to be a good match.

Okay, so I lost a potential private lender because an attorney decided the real estate business wasn't for him and, therefore, not for his client. So what? NEXT.

I turned the pages of defeat quickly and reported the lackluster news to Steve. He referred me to another potential investor named Carlos Balido. Mr. Balido was, and still is, a very interesting man. His story reads like a contemplative novel. Check out the chapters in this man's book:

Born in Cuba.

As a teenager, he flees to the U.S. for political asylum when Fidel Castro takes over the country, and it becomes a communist regime.

He volunteers to secretly train as a Freedom Fighter, unofficially sponsored by then President Nixon, the CIA, and underground USA military factions.

He leaves the safety of the USA to fight Castro in Cuba and to free his country.

In 1961, Carlos is captured by Cuban forces in the confrontation known in history as "The Bay Of Pigs Invasion." Carlos and his comrades are sentenced to prison as traitors to their country. We all know who the real traitors were—Fidel Castro, for turning Communist and John F. Kennedy for dropping off the Freedom Fighters and then calling off the air support they'd been promised.

After 2.5 years of torture and great suffering, 200 surviving prisoners are freed, in large part, due to the efforts of Amnesty International. Carlos Balido's life is valued at one John Deere tractor and /or some medical supplies.

Carlos and his comrades are returned to the U.S. They are war heroes in the Cuban/USA community. He begins his life in America with nothing but the shirt on his back.

In 1983, Carlos Balido is arguably the largest distributor of Latin Music in the USA. He sells his company to a worldwide concern.

I have heard Carlos say it a thousand times, "*What a country!*" After the betrayal he has experienced, I don't know how he ever forgave this country.

> **ME**: How did you ever forgive the U.S. for what they did to you and your countrymen?
> **CARLOS**: There is a big difference between the men (presidents) that come and go and the country itself. Take Cuba for example: I love that country and my countrymen even though I hate the dictatorship that currently rules and ruins that land. Today, my allegiance is to the United States. I may

> agree or disagree with the president of the day. That is part of what makes this country what it is. But no matter who is in office, the United States of America is still the greatest country in the world. No other place in the world provides for opportunity the way America does. As long as countries are run by mankind I doubt there will ever be a perfect country. But the United States of America is the only place in the world I could have lived the dream I've lived. What a country!

By the time I was introduced to Carlos, my relationship with Sam had escalated. We'd purchased forty-five houses in 1996 and another sixty-five in 1997. We had corporations, bank accounts, offices, and employees together. I invited Sam to join in the hunt for private money, and we went to see Carlos together. Carlos was like royalty to Sam and me. And his Cuban accent added to his mystique. He courted us for what seemed like forever over lunches, dinners, drinks...over and over. Much of the time we spoke about anything and everything except business. I was a little disconcerted about the direction of our conversations until I rationalized what Carlos was trying to accomplish. And what he was doing made perfect sense.

Carlos is a very fast study. He immediately understood the business model. He would loan the money for us to buy houses, fix them up (or not), sell them with owner financing, and then sell the notes. He'd loan us money at $2,000 per property and 18% interest. In the end we'd all make our money. The part Carlos didn't know was, "Who were Mitch and Sam?" The banter between the three of us was giving Carlos clues as to who we really were. He was spending time with us in an effort to answer one question: Who were we on the inside and could we be trusted?

One day I guess he'd heard enough, and singled me out for a meeting. The meeting didn't go as I thought it would. Seems Carlos didn't see a need for the business to involve three people. For him it was simple, he'd supply the money and I'd supply everything else. We'd split 50/50. The problem was, I was committed to my partner Sam. Sam and I had been brainstorming the ins and outs of this business and the possible relationship with a third party private lender. We were like men possessed. Sam and I were perfecting things that we were going to use this money for, and it didn't seem fair to me at all to cut Sam out. I struggled with it for a short while. I was struggling with how to tell Carlos, "No." The next day I called Carlos.

ME: Hey, Carlos, it's Mitch. Got a second?

CARLOS: Sure, have you made a decision?

ME: Yes, I have, but I'm sure you're not going to like it.

CARLOS: Tell me, what have you decided?

ME: I've decided that if Sam and I can't have a relationship with you as a team, then I'll have to decline your offer. I will not partner with you on my own.

CARLOS: I don't understand. This is a great opportunity for you. It is just business. Any businessman should understand. Surely Sam would understand.

ME: Well, you might be right. Sam might understand and then again, he might not. Either way, I don't think I would be being fair to Sam if I took your offer.

CARLOS: So, you are sure about your decision?

ME: Yes, Carlos I am sure. And I am sure I would not do it to you if you were my partner.

CARLOS: I understand you. There is something to be said for that. I wish you didn't feel so strongly but I accept your position.

By the end of the conversation I figured that was the end of that. I wasn't sure how I was going to explain this to Sam but the immediate challenge at hand was to get over the bad news myself. Luckily, I was in no hurry to speak with Sam about the day's events. The whole thing was awkward for me, and I really didn't even want to address it. I didn't want to make Sam feel bad about anything. I could've really gotten down about the whole situation but, instead, I did what I always do. I shouted out that one single word I put in my head for exactly situations like this one…NEXT!

A few days later I got a call from Carlos.

CARLOS: Hey Mitch, it's Carlos. Do you still feel the same way about your partner, Sam?
ME: Yes Sir, I do.
CARLOS: Then I guess I'll take you both. I want it understood, though: *You* are the one I will be looking to, good or bad. Do you have a problem with that?
ME: No Sir, I don't have any problem with that. How many houses do you want us to buy?
CARLOS: You can't buy enough houses.
ME: Okay, we'll turn on the after burners.

I called Sam and told him the good news! We had an open line of credit with no limit I was aware of. I never mentioned any of the other stuff that happened in the middle. I didn't see any reason to.

I only mention it in this book because the story says something about being loyal and true to your partners as well as to yourself. It says that people see and appreciate loyalty when it happens. The truth is everyone can appreciate loyalty, including Carlos. I've never regretted my decision to stick by Sam. I've never grown so much or come so far as in my time with Sam Hombre. Sam has been one of the best partners I've ever had in my life. Many years later, I will say the same thing about Carlos Balido, but that's a different story.

CHAPTER 40
PRIVATE MONEY (II)

• • •

Early in your career, you can't get enough private money.

I can't tell you how important it is to raise private money for investing. In the early days, I started with credit cards because they didn't require me to explain why I wanted their money. Credit card companies asked a lot of question upfront, but after you have those credit cards they never ask what you're going to buy with their money or why. Back then, they were not paying attention to the amount of credit cards you had acquired or even how much cash you were capable of snatching from those cards. Like everything else good, the idiots of the world figured out they could grab a bunch of unsecured money right before they went broke and run like hell. People with less integrity figured, if I'm going to file bankruptcy, a few more unpaid credit cards won't matter. The credit card companies got tired of that fast!

Although I'd acquired some substantial credit card lines and even some bank lines of credit, I recognized the need to raise private money. It is a slow process, but if you treat your private lenders well they start recommending you. They also make great references when you are courting a new, potential lender. I can also attest to the fact that the limit I start out borrowing from an individual is not the limit I end up with from them. It almost always grows.

My typical private lender is between the ages of sixty and eighty-five. They are not rich, but they have enough to live the lifestyle they are accustomed to. When stock markets get shaky, these seniors get real nervous. They can't afford to (or don't want to) start all over so late in life. At the same time, they can't afford to live off safer investments like CDs, because the return on their money is too low. They really get themselves into a pickle and worry about their future a lot! I offer private lenders the opportunity to have a little bit of both worlds: a relatively safe investment, backed by real estate (with real value) and a high rate of return that is very difficult for them to find. This is my typical investment opportunity for such investors.

The private investor will be given a first lien on any property they lend on.

The private investor's *maximum* investment in a property will never exceed 70% of the value of that property.

The private investor's actual collateral value (the value of the property) is determined by a third party, a licensed, certified MAI Appraiser.

They will be given a Mortgagee's Title Policy (Title Insurance) at the time of funding to insure their first lien position in the property.

Here is a simple example. Let's say I want to purchase a property valued at $100,000. (But remember, I don't buy things for what they are *valued* at. I buy properties for much less than they are valued at.) The property is valued at $100,000, but for this example let's say I can buy the property for $50,000, because it needs $20,000 in repairs. I go to my private lender and offer to give them a lien position in the property if they will loan me the $70,000 I need to buy and repair the property. In addition, I offer to pay my investor interest on their money. If they do not get paid back the $70,000 I owe them, then they get the $100,000 property from me.

This is only an example but I am still compelled to say, I have never given a house back to anyone. I have always succeeded in the original plan of borrowing and then paying back the money I borrowed, with interest! Nevertheless, we have to talk about what could happen and how my investors are reasonably protected.

Also understand that every deal is done one at a time, and every deal stands on its own. If a private lender wants to invest $500,000 with me, I will present the lender with *one deal at a time* until we have their $500,000 invested and making interest. No investor has ever just handed me $500,000. Because we get their money out one deal at a time, the actual investment may end up being $497,000 or $502,000. It's hard to hit the nail exactly on the head. Just for the record, we don't just automatically go to 70% of the value of the property. I think the average loan to value right now is less than 65%.

So what if Mitch Stephen dies, and you're a doctor who doesn't know anything about how to liquidate a house? I cover this in a report I give to all my private lenders before they invest, but in a nut shell, this is what I tell them to do.

If Mitch Stephen dies, do this: Take your first lien documents and a copy of your title insurance to the San Antonio Real Estate Investor Association (SAREIA) meeting. There you will find anywhere from 150 to 300 peopled gathered for the meeting and for the networking. Get to the meeting early. When they start the networking session get in line so that you may present your opportunity to the members. When it is your turn to speak, say this:

"I had lent the late Mr. Stephen some money on a property, God rest his soul. Now that he is no longer with us, I would like to get my money back out of this property. I've been told the property is worth $100,000. I want to get my $70,000 back in return for the deed. If you would like to own this $100,000 property for $70,000, please meet me in the lobby immediately."

Take your time getting to the lobby. There should be several fist-fights in or about that meeting spot to decide exactly *who* got there first! Eventually, someone will hand a cashier's check to you. You shouldn't worry if there's a little blood on the cashier's check, your bank will honor it.

This is a simplistic example because, truthfully, my family, my organization, and/or my estate are equipped to handle this situation legally in such fashion that you may never even know I've died unless you get an invitation to the funeral. I want you to understand *why* my private lenders feel safe with the collateral I provide them. Real estate is tangible. It has *real value*. It is not a certificate or a piece of paper like stocks or bonds. When things go wrong in real-estate related transactions you can usually roll up your sleeves, take some action, and make things better. When things go wrong in the stock market, you can only pray.

To this day, I still have (or could have back) every private lender I've ever borrowed money from. I don't have trouble very often. On days I have had troubles, my lender(s) never knew about it. They just get their checks in the mail like they've always gotten them. That being said, I've also taken steps to protect my private lenders even in the event of my absence. If you are an investor and would like to see what I give my private lenders you can review the entire "Special Report" on this subject in greater detail at: **www.Homes2Go.NET/PrivateLending**

CHAPTER 41
JUNIOR PARTNERS

• • •

When the word got out on the street that we were partnering 50/50,our business exploded.

Sam and I'd begun a journey of epic proportions in comparison to the life we'd lived before. In the last three quarters of 1996, as I've mentioned previously, we purchased 45 homes. In 1997, we purchased 65 homes. In 1998, with the help and financial backing of Carlos Balido, we purchased exactly 150 houses and sold 97 of them. On January 1, 1999, we had 53 houses *for sale* in our inventory.

In retrospect, we had something important going for us that we did not realize at the time. So much of our success was due to the framework of the deal that we had orchestrated with Carlos. Sam and I were working under an agreement that allowed us to borrow as much money as we legitimately needed to buy and remodel homes. The coup-de-grace was that the $2,000 up-front fee and the 18% annual interest accrued on the property in lieu of having to make monthly payments. Ask yourself this question: How many houses can you buy and maintain if you don't have to make monthly payments? As long as you can sell the properties in a reasonable length of time, the answer is, unlimited. That's exactly what Sam and I did.

And we did it over and over and over again, hundreds and hundreds of times!

Sam and I set up a program to burn through houses. As I mentioned before, the local investor community had been knocking at our door. We put the word out on the streets: We would put up all the money for the acquisition and rehab if you brought a property to the table at 50 to 60 cents on the dollar and agreed to do the work based on the advice of yours truly, Mitch and Sam.

Business exploded. It took everything we could muster as individuals and as families to hold it together. Every day there were more investors lined up outside our front door. There were more investors than we could conceive to deal with. It was a unique time in San Antonio history. The cat was out of the bag. After years of being a Mecca for a select few savvy investors in the know, San Antonio was now booming with entrepreneurs getting into the real estate game. Looking back, I'm almost sure we should've handled it differently but for better or worse, this is what we were offering.

1. Mitch & Sam will partner with investors that bring a deal at 50% to 60% on the dollar.
2. Mitch & Sam will put up the acquisition money and the rehab money.
3. Mitch & Sam will oversee the investment and bookkeeping. The partner will do all the legwork.
4. Mitch & Sam will split the profit 50/50 with the deal-finding partner.

We agreed that the properties would always be purchased in a land trust and the 100% beneficiary of the land trust would go to whoever put up the money (or borrowed the money). Everyone else due a portion of the proceeds would be dealt with on a handshake.

We always maintained 100% control. Some investors were leery at first and took a wait-and-see attitude. Others figured they had nothing to lose and jumped right in. As deals matured, we started to pay our Jr. Partners as agreed, and the word got around that we were honest. Before long, our business practices became accepted and everyone was comfortable. As I said, a line started to form at our front door and it was reputation driven.

While our Jr. Partners trusted us to pay them, they did not have to trust us on how much they got paid. Every investor's paycheck was accompanied with an exact accounting of every dollar that ran through the bank related to his or her project. The document was complete with check numbers, check dates, who got paid, and how much we paid them. If there was any doubt, the Jr. Partner was positively allowed to call for an independent audit of the books. In all the deals we did, an audit was never called for by any Jr. Partner. The deal was almost too good to be true for the Jr. Partners, and they knew it. They were making 50% profit with no overhead and no risk. As our overhead grew, we were forced to change the split to 60/40. That was hard for some of the original Jr. Partners to accept.

We had solved one problem for sure. We weren't out looking for houses any more! We had deals coming at us from every corner of the city. We had good partners, and we had bad partners come out of the situation. Some of the partners were borderline lunatics. Since our partnerships were structured one deal at a time, it was easy to get out of a bad relationship. Simply sell the deals you had with that Jr. Partner, and stop getting into any new deals with him or her. Luckily, the good far out-weighed the bad, and we reached levels of income that exceeded our wildest expectations at the time. Our biggest month yielded the closing of 18 deals. The Jr. Partners held 50% and Sam and I held 25% each. I remember the month clearly.

My 25% was worth over $80,000! If the money was over the top for us, the stress levels were off the charts. Just imagine 150 purchases and nearly 100 sales. That's 250 closings either coming or going in one year. If you take out the 52 weekends, you end up having 1.7 closings per working day in 1998. I don't care who you are, that is a lot of closings for a privately held company! For two boys just out of a job, it should've been crushing. We survived with the help of our spouses and my daughter, Shannon. We had two other employees at the time as well.

Surprisingly enough, in that same year (1998) Sam and I took more vacations than either of us had taken in our lives. The truth is, the daily stress of managing the volume took its toll, and quick! The routine went something like this: Sam would leave for four or five days to Mexico. When he got back, we'd hang out for a week or so to get caught up and on the same page. Then I'd take off for four or five days. It was more of a survival tactic than a luxury, really. The good news was that both of us trusted the other implicitly and, better yet, the trust wasn't unfounded. We rotated in and out of town like two migrating birds. I took eight vacations that year, but I'm not sure I ever really got rested.

As 1999 rolled around, Sam and I started to question ourselves. The volume was impressive to the banks and the lenders, but was it really worth it? Large sums of the money we'd hoped to make on paper were being lost out the back doors. Some of our partners and all of our contractors were getting one over on us on a daily basis. After a self-imposed audit, we found that we were suffering an average loss of $800 per closing simply due to lack of document review alone. I'm not proud of this, but I guess I'm building the argument that volume is *not* necessarily the best way to go, if you can't watch over it. In addition, all the different personalities were hard to juggle and it was impossible to make everyone happy no matter how much money they were making. In retrospect, we should have been cherry picking our deal: Those properties that simply needed cosmetic work and not a total overhaul. We should have been doing less and making more. We could've been choosing projects with larger margins and managing them much better. Our financial statement and our quality of life would have been greatly improved.

CHAPTER 42
NEEDLE IN A HAYSTACK

• • •

Volume vs. Vigilance

One afternoon my brother, Kleat, came to me excited about an abandoned house he had his eye on. He said he was trying to locate the owner, and he'd get back to me when he had more information. My brother had given a glowing report about the house he was stalking, and it was in an area we'd always been successful in. I was curious, so I made a mental note of the address and headed out that way. Once in front of the home, I knew we wanted it if we could get it for the right price.

Kleat's a consummate house finder and had gone through the usual routine to find the current owners. Usually you can find out everything you need to know just by talking to the neighbors, but not this time. Nobody in the neighborhood seemed to know anything about the current owners.

When Kleat told me he was having trouble, I sat down at the computer to do a little research of my own. I was in shock when I found the owners. It was US! Apparently Sam and I had owned the property for six months and it wasn't on our inventory board. The advantage of *not* having to make monthly payments had worked against us in this situation. Somehow, somewhere this file had fallen in a crack and, because we weren't missing any monthly payments to the lender. (Because we didn't have to make "monthly payments") no one was complaining.

This was about the last straw in the "I want volume" quest for houses. When you live in a town of over one million people, and you start trying to buy houses you already own, you need to reconsider what you're doing. Our system was broken. We began to slow down that day. I mean, what were the odds that we'd find out about this missing house in our inventory like that? I often wonder how long we would've owned that property before we found out it wasn't on our inventory sheet anywhere. It could have been a very long, long time. Sometimes you just figure the angels are watching out for you.

CHAPTER 43
BLACK TUESDAY

• • •

I remember reading somewhere that markets have cycles.

Sam and I chugged along for awhile, cutting back on the volume and cherry picking the best deals. We were definitely downsizing. During the year 2000, we also began to move in different directions individually. I was getting into more and more boat and mini storages, and Sam was moving into multi-family properties and small apartment complexes. Then one day, about June of 2001, the largest note buyer in the country (and my guess, the largest in the world) closed its doors. Sam and I call it Black Tuesday. The day that Associates (previously a division of Ford Motor Credit) closed its doors, business as we knew it ceased to exist. Our company didn't sell directly to Associates, but we were still going to feel their closing 100%. No matter who you dealt with in the note buying community, one thing became crystal clear: Eventually all the notes ended up at Associates. When Citibank bought Associates they didn't much appreciate the $30 billion in notes from the secondary market (as opposed to notes they originated) so they shut that division down.

News in the real-estate investment community was doom and gloom and for good reason. I heard Citibank gave about 1,400 employees of Associates their walking papers on that Tuesday…and on that Tuesday, the ultimate destination for every note in the country died in an instant. An untold number of people and companies across the country went broke overnight.

We were in fear for our financial life. The cheese had been moved, moved so far away that not a mouse in the land could smell where it was hidden. Sam and I had used the exact business model for over 400 deals in a row; buy, fix, owner finance, and sell the note. At the time, I had about 50 vacant houses of my own for sale and Sam had even more. The bulk of them were financed by Carlos Balido or the doctor. Many other properties were financed by retired people who absolutely could not survive a financial loss with much dignity. Our houses were never going to be worth nothing, but at the time it was easy to think catastrophically. Over the years, all these *private lenders* had become good friends. Just the thought of letting them down could put me into a panic. Millions of dollars worth of houses were racking up interest, and our end game unequivocally crushed. All the years of seminars, all the creative thinking and now, I could not come up with *anything* to solve my problems. I was drawing a complete blank.

Eventually, I'd come to the conclusion that there's always a way out. It may not be as good as the original plan but there's always a way out…and I was going to find it. But not even that thought occurred to me for a few days, and those days were some of the darkest days of my entire business life to date. It is one thing to have nothing and get bad news. It is quite a different thing to be exceeding your dreams, have everyone counting on you, and then have your business dry up over night. Losing my money is one thing, losing someone else's money is another. The only way to save the business was to get people into the houses and then hold steady. So that's what Sam and I did. We put making the bigger money on hold while we mitigated our empty houses, stopped the bleeding, and protected our lenders.

By now, Sam and I weren't daily business partners. We'd phased out the office and had divided up what was left of the house inventory. We had grown more and more independent of each other in a good, successful kind of way. We simply didn't need to hold hands like before, when we were both new and scared in the business. We were then, and still are now, great friends. We've hardly ever had a disagreement in over 400 transactions together.

It is easy to have good partners during good times. You learn the value of your partners during the bad times.

Sam had been a great partner even when there were bumps in the road…even when there were creators in the road…even when the road ended. At this point in the note buying collapse, we were both functioning solo from our respective homes, and we still shared the private money lenders we'd acquired when we were in business together. (We share those same investors to this day.) So it was no surprise at all that we came back together as a brain consortium when the business got tough.

CHAPTER 44
LIFE HAPPENS

• • •

Sometimes…it just takes time.

The investor news was bad, the emails were worse, and the phone calls were devastating. Everyone I talked to was trying to prop themselves up. No one was screaming or crying (out loud), and everyone was trying to say that things would get better. I could tell by the end of those conversations that most of them were capsizing quickly.

Sam and I were the exceptions. We'd done well by our profits and reinvested almost every dime we'd made during the good times. Yeah, we took some vacations but vacations in Mexico can be cheaper than staying at home. During the good times, Sam had put his money into multi-family properties and houses, and I'd put everything I'd made into boat and mini storages and houses. We'd invested well and that was our saving grace. We had very good cash flow from the money we'd saved from the house business. Even so, everything was changing. If we didn't handle this right we'd go under too. I had trouble on two fronts. My brother's battle with depression was reaching critical mass, and the investor real estate market was reaching a critical mess.

Kleat was becoming more and more despondent and when we'd talk to him he was empty. This problem was not new but it had been progressively getting worse. After ten years of fighting, his illness was beginning to win big. We could not reach him with our words or with all the love in our hearts. His ability to feel loved seemed all but erased. Our lament for him was never ending and never winning. It was as if my brother was losing his ability to feel love. I struggled during the day and, at night I would turn inward.

"LET SOMEBODY LOVE YOU"

Written by Mitch Stephen & Billy O'Rourke

The world would be a better place
A smile would always light your face
If you let somebody love you
And when you're scared and lost alone
You'd have a light to guide you home
If you let somebody love you

Chorus:
If you let somebody love you, need you
And you let somebody hold you, reach you
Then the purest thought appears
It's the reason we're all here
And you wonder why, it took so long …
To let somebody love you

Bridge:
We're young then old and then we're gone
A part of you just might live on
If you let somebody love you
Oh let somebody love you

The world would be a better place
A smile would always light your face
Let somebody love you
Let somebody love you
Oh let somebody love you
Let somebody love you

Listen: http://www.mitchstephen.com/letsomebody.asp?music=on
Sung by Billy O'Rourke

Bill Green Music Publishing
www.MitchStephen.com

Kleat was suffering from severe depression and asking for permission to leave this earthly place, but none of us would give him that permission. In the beginning the depression came and went, so it was difficult to know when he was ok and when he wasn't. And there were tons of pills and doctors…and bills for all of them. I was trying desperately to get him in touch with a **Dr. Laura Marangell** at the Baylor School of Medicine. **Dr. Marangell** was experimenting with new procedures that were producing testimony of cured depression in a high percentage of patients. Nevertheless, I missed my mark, and I was unable to get Kleat involved in the new procedures. As a family, we were trying everything we knew but we kept hitting brick walls. I hold nothing against the doctors. It was the system. I hope Dr. Marangell keeps going in her endeavor.

We knew this was bad, but by now, we could not see just how bad it really was. Over the years there had been so many crisis that loved ones around the victim get numb. The disease wears on everyone and slips up on them slowly. It progresses so slow that you become tolerant. Over the years you become tolerant of things you would never tolerate in the beginning. Yes, we had doctors, yes we had therapists, yes we had pills, and yes we had tried so many things. Kleat had been fighting for over ten years. It was getting worse, and he was getting tired. We were all getting tired, all of our families. We were all losing our grip. We were all fighting economically, fighting emotionally. Everyone was fighting for one more breath. Speaking to my family about my less than stellar business situation was not an option. With Kleat's life at stake, the topic of my business held no weight…and rightfully so. I would have to handle that problem on my own.

It is very easy to second guess what we might have done. The most predominant thing people have said about this situation is, "Well, they have medicine for that condition now." Do me a favor, out of the kindness of your heart: *Please* don't ever say that to me.

Just guess what happens when you give powerful pills to a mentally unstable person...just take a guess! I'd wake up on fire from head to toe, sensing how imminent my brother's deadline was. No matter what we tried, we all felt helpless to stop this thing. Anyone who has been there knows exactly what I'm talking about. I respectfully state, the rest of you are ill equipped. I promise you, you are ill equipped. Just take my word for it. I pray you never understand what I'm talking about.

If the days were bad, the nights were horrible. I'd wake up in a pool of sweat. My side of the bed would be literally drenched. I tried to hide my fear, but my wife knew I was in a bad place. Other than telling her I'd wet the bed, what could I say? No exaggeration, my side of the bed was soaked. Finally, after about a week of thinking every catastrophic thing imaginable, I decided I'd had enough. I was not going to go down this way. If I was going down, I was going down swinging. I had to take control of my mind. If I believed I was going under business wise, I was as good as sunk. If I believed I could not help my brother, then I couldn't help him. I woke up one morning and shoved myself in front of the mirror in our master bathroom. There I chewed my own butt like I've never had it chewed before, by anyone.

"Listen here Mitch Stephen, you are a good man. You are a strong man. You are a smart man...and you will beat these situations. You are going to stop this panic. You are going to put a smile on your face and keep it there for as long as you can every day and you are going to start winning, NOW! You are going to reach Dr. Marangell, and you are going to come up with a plan to solve the problems of these 50 houses and protect your lenders. You have, or you will find, or you will be given everything you need. You will figure it out...all of it!"

I put my face inches from the mirror and looked directly into my own eyes and yelled it at myself—screamed it at myself—over and over again in whatever order it came to me. Teeth gritted, spit flying, and tears rolling. I was compassionate to my inner spirit but irreverent in my resolve to see action. I ended my rant by consoling myself in a whisper, ***"Mitch, if you commit to do the very best you can do, you can relieve yourself of any fear, guilt, or embarrassment."*** In that moment, I purged my fear.

I committed to do my very best concerning these situations and not to think about *failure*. Everything else in life got put on hold indefinitely. Now that I was not paralyzed with fear I was able to focus and get some things done. A lot of things got better. Then, some twenty days after I learned my business was in peril, we lost my little brother, Kleat. He committed suicide on June 20, 2001. He was 38 years old, and I was 40. It was surreal. It would take a few weeks just to get off my knees. Not to get over it, you understand, but just to get off my knees.

CHAPTER 45
LOSING KLEAT

• • •

I can never find the right words, but I'll try.

During my entire career, I extended every opportunity to my brother, Kleat. I don't really know where to start or where to end on this subject but I will confide in you. My brother was bi-polar/manic-depressive (at least that is what they called it then). His suicide ended the hardest time period I have ever experienced in my life. I worked with Kleat after his career as a Marine. I got him on at Spencer Engineering, and we worked together and saw much of the world together. He also worked with me during the first five years of my real estate career. As a person used to *fixing things,* helplessly watching my brother's decline was gut wrenching. I loved him. The decisions not to abandon him cost relationships and partnerships. His condition also pressed every family member to the brink of all out war with each other concerning the issues and the choices of what to do and how to handle his imminent decline.

If they would have told our family that my brother could be cured by taking off our shoes and walking west into the sun until we arrive from the east and back to our shoes, every one of us would have started walking, and we would have finished the task. It wasn't even that simple. The happiest and the saddest day of my life happened on the day he died. I was so happy for him that his troubled journey had ended. I was so inconsolably sad for my parents that it took a long time for me to feel my own sense of loss.

His death brought me to a place where I truly got lost myself. I buried myself in work but, for the life of me, I don't remember what I did that year. I thank my family and my God that I did not turn to drugs or alcohol during that time. I now understand how that can happen to people. All I know is this: I went to work to keep from endlessly thinking about it. I am sorry to say the final years of Kleat's life were not very pretty. If we let those days be what he is remembered for, then I'm afraid it is an ugly picture. Those of us who knew Kleat for a long time knew a much different Kleat. I would like to say something here and now as a reminder of that fact and especially for the benefit of his daughter, Shelby Stephen, who was eight when her father died.

When he was healthy, Kleat Stephen was one of the most beautiful men on the planet and absolutely worth knowing—funny, strong, handsome, caring, creative—and Lord how he could make you laugh.

Personally, I look forward to meeting him again in the great beyond. There I will tell him how sorry I am for not fully understanding sometimes. Stupid *me* thought a good income and a worthwhile career was all he needed to get back on track. I put pressures on him that I am sure did not help him. I was a fool and I've prayed for his forgiveness. It simply took too long for me to recognize his brand of depression. If there were things the family should've done, those things were not presented to us in a form or fashion that we could recognize during that time. Still, it is an empty thought. We lost him.

Maybe the hard and rough and ugly times arrive by design. Maybe they serve to round our own hard and rough and ugly edges. I don't know about your life, but it seems to be working that way in my life. Like it or not, life is polishing me. Life is rounding me. I suspect life is polishing and rounding all of us. My brother's passing has rounded me in many ways.

I'm humbled.

Time has grown more important.

I see pain where I never saw it before.

I am very slow to judge others these days.

I understand the huge power of my spoken word.

I am softer than before and I strive to be softer still.

I recognize and appreciate the struggle of others.

I am more forgiving than I have ever been.

I find myself saying things like,

"But by the grace of God
There go I."

Kleat Stephen

CHAPTER 46
KEEP ON KEEPIN' ON

• • •

We really have no choice in the matter.

In our personal endeavors to become a success at whatever it is we choose, life is going to happen. We never figure in the monumental obstacles of regular life when we write our goals.

THIS YEAR'S GOALS

Buy twenty properties.

Build fifty more mini-storage units.

Survive the death of my brother.

And then…

We never write goals like that.

I believe we all have the right to live this life with all the happiness we can muster. How we handle an unpleasant part of life is a matter of personal choice. If I may respectfully evoke, moving on is not a lack of respect for the deceased or an act of selfishness on our part. Moving forward does not mean that we have forgotten them or that we somehow don't love them anymore. I feel, in some ways, we owe it to them to move on. In fact, I believe the ones we've loved and lost would want us to live our lives to the fullest. Actually, we have very few choices in the matter.

I chose to bury myself in work when my brother died. You may choose a different way to deal with life's arrows. As I learned to live beyond catastrophe in my own life, I hoped to heal and emerge with good things on my horizon and not an addiction or another set of mountains to overcome. We should strive to find healthy ways to deal with the unpleasant parts of life. Hopefully, when we come to terms, find that peaceful place, and check back into life, opportunities will await us instead of more problems.

Kleat four years and Mitch six years

Kleat in Little League baseball – Diamond Bar, CA.

CHAPTER 47
STANDING UP

• • •

It's OK to get knocked down. It's not OK to stay down.

I was fighting to find a place to start over from. I was in survival mode, running on pure instinct. And from what I'd learned all those years from reading books, I needed to take care of myself, my family, my parents, and my lenders. I decided that the forces against me were too strong for me to handle alone, so I vowed to start listening to positive tapes and CDs, 24/7. I joined the gym and worked my muscles so hard I couldn't feel the hole in my heart. I committed to work my days as hard as I'd ever worked. I'd be serving my investors well, and I wouldn't have the time nor the energy to think about the ugly things. Like the days of Mitchell Striping, I was about to go in over my head again, but this time I gave myself permission and the absolute right to have a peaceful night's rest, every night. I did not want to repeat what had happened to me in Mitchell Striping.

I had about fifty house of my own to mitigate, alone. Sam had his own huge inventory, as well. Although we weren't officially in business together, we had endless conversations about how to handle the debacle of the note-buying business. We came up with a plan to handle the situation and to protect both our private and institutional lenders—the lenders we had together and the lenders we had cultivated on our own outside our partnership. Protecting our lenders was paramount, no matter what happened to *us*.

As it turns out, the answers to our problems were really pretty simple. In fact, the new plan was easier than the old plan. Before things went to hell in a hand basket Sam and I operated under the **Old Plan**:

Buy a house.

Sell the house with owner financing.

Sell the note.

The **New Plan** was almost the same.

We had houses.

We sold them with owner financing.

We collected the payments.

Like before, the payments we were to receive from our buyer always exceeded what we owed our lenders. The only difference in the Old Plan and the New Plan was that we weren't going to be able to liquidate the notes in return for a pocket full of fast cash today. Maybe tomorrow or on another day we could, but not today.

It was a ton of work, but in less than four months, I had fifty buyers living in and paying for my fifty houses. On paper I'd averaged about $250 profit per house after I paid the taxes, the insurance, and my lenders. The formula was 50 houses x $250 = $12,500 per month. That's a long way from filing bankruptcy! In addition, my storage units had grown to around 800 units, and they were cash flowing like crazy. At this point, I know a lot of you are wondering, "How does all this happen in such a relatively short period of time?" All I can say is, that Tommi, Shannon, Jason, and I worked very hard during very trying times.

Finally, with the bulk of my work done and my lenders now safe, I could relax. The grief I'd been running from could finally catch up with me. In the calm of my new situation I could finally settle down and cry all the tears I needed to. Months after my personal loss, I could finally reconcile with my emotions. During that time of reconciliation, I forgave any injustice I might have conceived. I forgave every doctor and every therapist. I forgave every friend or business relation who could not understand. I forgave myself, and I forgave my brother Kleat. The truth is, my brother fought longer and harder than I could have ever imagined myself being able to endure. He loved his wife, Tina, and his daughter, Shelby, as much or more than any man who ever loved his own. I know this because he spoke of it often, very often. It says to me that his affliction was overpowering and overwhelming. I am so proud of the fight that my brother put forth. As if he ever needed my forgiveness, I forgave my brother for taking his own life.

From left to right: Jason, Shannon, Tommi, and me

"I'LL FORGIVE YOU"

Written by Mitch Stephen and Billy O'Rourke

If it's your decision I can't stop you
If you wanna leave I'll let go
But deep inside the fire won't die
'Cause lovin' you is all I've ever known
But if that's what you really want ...

CHORUS:
I can cry tears, I can build walls
I can pretend, this didn't happen at all
And I can live life without a regret
And I'll forgive you ...but I'll never forget

I will always know that blue's your favorite color
"Always On My Mind" 's your favorite song
It'd be easier if I could not remember
But I'll never find a way to turn it off
So what else can I do but sing on

(REPEAT CHORUS)

(In loving memory of Kleat Stephen)
Listen: http://www.mitchstephen.com/illforgive.asp?music=on
Sung by Billy O'Rourke

Bill Green Music Publishing
www.MitchStephen.com

"FORGIVEN"

(1 Cross, 3 Nails, Forgiven)

Written by Mitch Stephen& Bobby Flores

Have you ever thought about
The way that life might be without
That single ray of light
To save us when we've fallen from
That straight and narrow path we're on
And leave us no doubt
A band of angels waits for you
In a house with many rooms
...and they wanted you to know

CHORUS:
Know matter what you've done, You will be washed
No sin will overcome, His cleansing cloth
No soldier gone astray, Has ever lost his way
If he believes in... One cross, Three nails, Forgiven

So when my time on earth is done
And they blow the horns and bang the drums
I won't be afraid
That peaceful rest is my reward
Virtues lost or virtues forged
For I have been saved
And all the souls that love me
Will be waiting in the light
And in the blink of an eye

MODIFIED CHORUS:
No mater what I've done, I will be washed
No sin will overcome, His cleansing cloth
No soldier gone astray, Has ever lost his way
If he believes in...
No angry words in vein, Will stain my lips
These steps across the grain, His love forgives
That sword of pain I swung, Will all but be undone
Because I believe in... One cross, Three nails, Forgiven

(In loving memory of Kleat Stephen)
Listen: http://www.mitchstephen.com/illforgive.asp?music=on
Sung by Kevin Hughes

www.MitchStephen.com

The year 2001 was proving to be very challenging. The note business died and my business theories were in question. My brother died and my entire reason for living was in question. Then, on September 11, the Twin Towers fell. For the first time in the history of the United States, we'd been successfully attacked on our own soil. Now, even the freedom and the financial stability of my country was in question. I have never been faced with so many fears at the same time, one piled upon the other. To have all this happen in the first nine months of one year was inconceivable to me. I started to change my war cry from **Next!** to **What Next?**

If there's anything I've learned, it's this: Very little happens on my time frame, and *everything* changes. Yes, we've all heard it before but, eventually, you take the lesson as your own. When times are good, we better save some for a rainy day. When times are bad, well, sometimes it's everything we can do to just hold our ground and let time pass. So that's what I did for a year or so. I just held on—with all my might.

CHAPTER 48
WHEEL ESTATE

• • •

Roll with the changes.

By 2003, I'd been isolated from the invigorating input of other thinkers for a few years. My emotional struggles due to the death of my brother had sent me into a cocoon of sorts, and over time it was starting to paralyze me. I find that the more I'm alone, the dumber I get. My life in real estate had always been about rubbing shoulders with others. When I was the most successful, I'd played strongly off the emotions and enthusiasms of others. Now, with everything that'd happened, I found myself isolated and out of the loop (self-imposed). I was fighting my own brand of depression but, because of all I'd read and all that I knew from that reading, I recognized the need to take control of my mind yet again. I made a plan to go to some high-powered seminars and to get back in touch with the part of me that could hear an inspirational speaker and get inspired. Two seminars later I was on fire with new energy and ideas.

The hardest thing an entrepreneur will ever do...
is to find one good idea and finish.

Because of all the seminars being held all over the nation, there was a huge explosion of investors coming onto the real estate scene. It was getting tougher and tougher to find deals. Once upon a time, you could get into the classifieds and buy a house a day, or five, if you had the money—and all of them would make you $20,000 a pop. In 1986, when Sam and I bought 150 properties, we were doing just that because we had the money or the lenders. At this time in life, I had all the financing I needed, but it was getting harder and harder to find an outstanding deal. Luckily, I had a good reputation, and people brought me deals and I'd partner with many of them. A lot of those partners lived hand to mouth, which caused me to make some marginal decisions. I'm simply too nice for my own financial good sometimes. Those few marginal decisions didn't sink me but they did slow my financial improvement efforts. In short, I could have made more money if I were more hard nosed. With the market saturated, I was looking for a different angle. I'd find it in the most unlikely place.

In the early 2000s, the mobile home industry went through catastrophic changes. The politicians got together to add yet another taxing entity to their arsenals and decided that the mobile home industry needed to be regulated in the name of consumer protection. In their infinite wisdom, they passed a law that made it illegal to finance *the land* and *the home* separately. This made it impossible for most of the wanna-be mobile home owners to qualify for a loan. Before the law, a consumer could purchase the vacant land with owner financing (which wouldn't hit their credit report) and then finance the mobile home through an institutional lender. When the new law went into effect, those same buyers couldn't qualify for the total value of the land plus the home. So the Texas manufactured home industry hit the skids. Overnight, companies went bankrupt, and soon there were an estimated 70,000 repossessed homes sitting on foreclosure lots around the state.

It was 2003 when I learned that I could pick up a 1998-to-2001, three-bedroom, two-bath, 16' x 76', manufactured home (in real decent condition) for an incredibly low price. In fact, if you could buy in quantity, you could own those manufactured homes for as little as $6,000 per unit. Now, I'm no genius, but I know a good deal when I see one. I wasn't ready to jump to a new venue, but again, opportunity knocked, and I got in the jumping mood.

I had absolutely resolved to be around creative thinkers to get my juices flowing again. Sam Hombre was enjoying semi-retirement and was busy traveling. Other trustworthy investors I knew wanted partners to do all the work, while they supplied the money and knowledge and enjoyed a life of more leisure. This manufactured home endeavor was going to be pure work, and I needed a working partner. One morning I woke up and I knew exactly whom I wanted for a partner. We'd been talking about teaming up for some time. Maybe now was the time. I called my trusted financier and friend, Carlos Balido.

It took a bit of convincing to get Carlos over the stigma of mobile homes. At first, he would have nothing to do with the idea. I finally got him to agree to partner with me on one mobile home for $6,000. This particular home was already set up in a park. People who live in parks don't own the land their homes sit on. They own their homes but they rent their lots.

I managed to convince Carlos to partner up with me on *one* mobile home. As it turned out, we found a buyer for that home in just a few days. We sold the home for $21,000. We agreed to take $3,000 down and finance the $18,000 balance at 12.75% for seventy-five months. This made the monthly principle and interest payment about $350 + $50 for taxes and insurance + $250 for the park lot rent. The new buyer's total monthly payment to live in that home, in that park, was $650 per month. We completed the transaction and everyone was happy! The buyer was happy, the park was happy, and Carlos and I were happy.

The tipping point in the partnership of Carlos Balido and Mitch Stephen happened on the day we delivered the keys to those new buyers. We had just arrived in the park and pulled up to the home in my truck. Carlos was in the passenger seat and the young couple was standing just outside the passenger-side window, in front of their "new" used home. Carlos exited the truck and approached the new owners. But before he could hand the keys to the young man, the wife smothered Carlos with a hug…a big, long hug! I was sitting behind the wheel of my truck looking out the side window at Carlos' back. I could see the lady's face over his shoulder as she embraced him. She was crying. For an instant I thought to myself, "Oh no, what's wrong?" But she was smiling and crying. I'd seen this many times in my career. It is one of the most rewarding moments that can happen in anyone's business. It is always a good day when your customer cries tears of joy when the deal is consummated. The couple didn't have good credit, and I suppose they thought they'd never be able to own a place of their very own. Obviously, they felt very grateful that we'd taken a chance on them. It was a very compelling scene.

After Carlos delivered the keys and got back into the truck, he stared out the window towards the couple, who were waving us goodbye. As we pulled away from the curb, they retreated into their home.

CARLOS: Did you see that? They cried when I gave them the keys. Even *I* started to cry!

I stopped and put the truck in reverse. I proceeded to back up to our previous parking spot.

ME: Yeah, I saw it.

CARLOS: What are you doing?

ME: I want you to think about something tonight. I want you to look out the window at that home. I want you to look at that home and think about the couple who cried with joy when you handed them the keys. I want you to be my partner in this business.

He sat perfectly still and stared out the widow for quite some time. I waited for him to speak first.

CARLOS: Okay…Let's do it.

CHAPTER 49
JUMPING IN WITH BOTH FEET

• • •

A leap of faith.

In July 2003, we formed a corporation. By the end of July we'd obtained a million dollar credit line to buy manufactured homes. Within sixty days, we'd purchased 140 homes. We were buying houses like the wind: ten, fifteen, even twenty at a time. That never happened to me with stick-built houses. Every day we were talking to banks and lenders and trying to get great deals on their repossessed inventory. That sounds real exciting right? Well, it really is, and it was, until we looked up one morning and realized, wow, we have 140 vacancies!

For the next 18 months we worked like madmen, seven days a week, 14 to 16 hours a day. We were fighting some pretty impossible odds, and if we didn't get the job done we'd be sunk. I'm sure there should have been some sleepless nights, but we were so tired from working that we actually slept very well. On that note, I'll say that this work wasn't like the work of digging a ditch. It was the work of passion. When you work with passion, the hours don't seem like drudgery. When I say we worked 14 to 16 hours a day, it's not like we counted the hours or that we even felt the hours (until it was time to go to sleep). It's just something you do when you are enthralled with the potential outcome of an endeavor. We were helping people get into homes and we were building a business at the same time. It was a win-win situation.

Eighteen months later, all the houses were occupied with paying customers, some current and some behind, but nothing left to sell on that day. It was a landmark day. That being done, we immediately began to replace the problem customers with responsible customers. Needless to say, the days of being 100% occupied didn't last long, but being 100% occupied was a victorious moment nonetheless. It had always been our goal to sell these properties *once* and be done with it, but life is not that simple.

As I've said before, life happens. It happens to your customers as well as to you. There were plenty of good people to whom good and bad things happened: death, births, marriage, divorce, illness, promotions, transfers…you name it, it happens. We were forced to sell some of those homes more than once—but make no mistake about it, we never planned nor wanted to take anyone's home back. More often than not, they simply returned the properties to us.

For those who think taking back houses and reselling them is a business, let me tell you, taking a house back is always a losing proposition. Many of the gurus try to glamorize the upside of taking properties back but, in reality, it's almost always a lose-lose proposition. They lose and you lose. We always tried to manage the situation by giving the benefit of the doubt to ailing buyers. We'd try everything from extra payment plans to adding their past-due balances to the end of their amortization. We even wiped the slate clean for some people so they could start over again and not be behind anymore. Usually, these plans would fail for reasons beyond our control, no matter how hard we tried.

Through the years 2003 to 2007, we did have our fair share of great payer/occupants. I set out on a path to sell those notes that were paying us well, but the market in general said that *mobile home only* notes weren't worth the paper they were written on. I knew better. After all, people sell accounts receivables on cars, furniture, home improvements, and a multitude of less worthy commodities. If investors would buy the notes on those types of things, why on earth wouldn't a note on a manufactured *home* (key word *home*) be worth buying? I've always had this theory: If you can sleep in it, shower in it, go to the bathroom in it, store your food in it, raise your children in it, keep your pets in it, eat in it, store your clothes in it, keep your furniture and computer in it, air condition it, heat it, watch TV in it, and make love to your spouse in it, it's worth something! And *something* is a far cry from *nothing*!

Some folks would argue that manufactured homes are a clandestine port of refuge. Manufactured homes are listed as depreciating assets. I wonder if the wood in a manufactured home rots faster than the wood in a regular house? Seems to me manufactured homes are made out of the same material most houses are made out of. You know, if you don't fix the roof or occasionally paint the exterior of a million-dollar home, it's not going to last very long either. A banker once asked me, "How long do you think these manufactured homes will last?"

To which I answered, "They last as long as you choose to take care of them…Just like *your* house."

Manufactured homes will last as long as your $1,000,000 house, if you take care of them. If your expensive house has a roof leak and you don't take care of the problem, then your expensive house will not be worth a dime in short order. Manufactured homes are no different. If you don't paint the house when its time, the house will rot. It's true for manufactured homes and it's true for million-dollar homes. The only factor in their longevity is the care they're given, not their physical components.

At the time of this writing, I receive payments on mobile homes that are more than thirty years old. These homes have been cared for by people who place a priority on caring for them.

I say that manufactured homes are the last bastion of affordable housing left on the planet. There is a need for this type of affordable housing, and it will never end. The longer we go into the future, the more affordable housing will be needed. If you want to get into the minutia of the financial upsides, manufactured homes generally decrease in taxable value, due to their *personal property* categorization. This is a plus for the owners who keep them up and enjoy the extra living space, given the price they've paid. The book value indicates that manufactured homes go down in value every year, and so the taxes go down every year until they are virtually zero. But I can attest that their values do go up, given the right circumstances. The main problem with the value of older mobile homes is the difficulty in getting them financed. If you change that and provide a way for the manufactured home to be financed, you change that dynamic. The value placed on them by the consumers goes up, no doubt about it!

I've learned a lot about mobile homes—manufactured homes—in my days of buying and selling real estate. I've learned that there's a segment of the population that values the extra space for a lower price and less taxation than traditional, site-built homes. Investors who can afford to finance manufactured homes and take their profits over time can accomplish some great things.

They can provide affordable housing to those who need and value it.

They can create a viable business for themselves.

By the end of 2007, Carlos and I had created a business that put a plus sign in everyone's column. We helped families obtain affordable housing. We helped park owners fill their spaces. We employed carpet layers, sheet rockers, painters, AC/Heat contractors, carpenters, roofers, and a host of other companies along the way. In the process, we had organized a profitable business for ourselves. Win-win situations are what this country—and any business—is all about.

In 2004, I set out on a quest to find people who understood that dynamic about manufactured homes. I was searching for a thin slice of pie, but I will conclude this segment with an astounding fact: Carlos and I were able to liquidate about 60% of our notes to pay off 98% of our company's debt, leaving us with over sixty homes virtually free and clear! How did this happen? Well, when you're looking for a needle in a haystack, you have to cast a wide net. I used the World Wide Web, the *Internet*, to find the note buyers we needed.

CHAPTER 50
INTERNET MARKETING

• • •

Networking at lightning speed.

When I talk with excitement about using the Internet, maybe you should get excited too! I use the Internet to find houses, sell houses, find private money (lenders), find contractors, note buyers, insurance, you name it—and I can find it on the Internet. In the case where I sold our manufacture home notes, I simply posted some notes for sale on the 'net and let the interested parties search for *me*. And they did!

In my real estate career, I use the computer religiously to get what I want: everything from buyers, sellers, private money lenders, contractors, etc. I send a message to my network and ask them for what I need. Imagine being able to send a message to 8,000 realtors in your town and ask them if they've listed a property with foundation problems? For a person who knows how to handle foundation problems, the responses are invaluable. Imagine being able to hit 1,800 investors in town and ask them if they can recommend a good roofer because yours just fell off a roof and broke his leg (just kidding). What if you wanted to wholesale a property because you simply had too much on your plate to take on another project? Do you think you could sell a true wholesale deal by noon if you had the email addresses of 1,800 hundred local investors?

I could talk to you about using the Internet for days. I'm constantly amazed at how many deaf ears my enthusiasm can fall on. I have created a website to do just that kind of networking: Find buyers and sellers for houses, manufactured homes, and lien notes. If you're interested in hearing more about what I've learned on the subject of Internet marketing for real estate (and it works the same for manufactured homes and notes) you can go to:

http://www.Homes2Go.NET/FreeVideo

In all fairness, let me warn you in advance. I sell *investor websites.* That being said, you can learn a lot on the topic in my hour-plus PowerPoint Presentation (above), even if you don't decide to buy anything. Fair enough?

CHAPTER 51
25TH ANNUAL TEJANO MUSIC AWARDS

• • •

And the winner is…

I've been writing music for over 30 years. I like to think I'm going to get good at it any day now. Apparently, a few people thought my co-writer and I got good at it in March of 2005.

My phone rang, and a friend on the other end of the line asked if I was going to the Tejano Music Awards this year. I laughed and asked, "Why in the heck would you ask me that question?" He informed me that our song, "Who's That Gringo," had been nominated for an award. I didn't believe him at first. "Yeah, right…like I'm gonna fall for that." He assured me that it was the truth, and when we hung up I immediately got on the computer to verify the nomination. My friend was not pulling my leg. It was right there on the Tejano Music Awards website. "Who's That Gringo," performed by David Lee Garza y Los Musicales was nominated for **Tejano Crossover Song of the Year** at the 25th Annual Tejano Music Awards.

The event was going to be held in Eagle Pass, Texas, in three days. That wasn't much lead time. I was pondering if I could go or not when I received a call from my mother. When I told her what had just happened, that was all the notification she needed. She had the limo reserved and the sequined dress ordered before I could hang up the phone. I kept downplaying the whole thing because honestly, I'd never heard of the event—and the last time I was on the Kickapoo Nation Indian Reservation at the gambling casino, it wasn't all that impressive. It'd been a long time ago, but I recalled the place as being sort of like a triple-wide mobile home with slot machines inside. Not all that cool! Mom didn't care. I guess we were headed to Eagle Pass and that's all there was to it!

On the day of the event, we loaded into my F-350 four-door truck and headed south. I was driving with my wife and my Mom and Dad in tow. When we arrived, there were no hotel rooms available. "Wow, this must be a big deal," Dad surmised. After searching for sometime for a place to stay, I began to think the event was bigger than I'd estimated. Everywhere we looked, the Tejano bands had lavish buses with their names painted on the sides. Every hotel was booked. Finally, we got a room due to a cancellation and some lucky timing.

We all unpacked and got ready for the event. When everyone was lookin' good and smellin' good we headed to the Indian Reservation. When we got there it was quite a surprise. While I'd been away, the Kickapoo Indians had greatly improved their casino facilities, and the newest addition was a large, beautiful convention center. There was a very long line wrapping around the event center, and we were all impressed. Dad kept looking at me with this grin that said, "What in the world has my boy done now?"

Mom kept saying, "You're gonna win, you're gonna win." My wife didn't know what to think and wouldn't let go of my arm. I was getting excited about the whole situation but, honestly, the thought of winning never crossed my mind one iota. Then I realized we didn't have any tickets. It took a little doing but we finally found four tickets together in the nosebleed section. You know…waaay up there!

The place was packed, and the event was just like the Hollywood award shows. Everyone dressed to the nines, a suave and debonair master of ceremony, beautiful women in sparkling gowns escorting all the nominees on and off the stage, a huge jumbotron overhead so even those of us in the nosebleed section could see the reactions of the winners up close. They really had it going on! Suddenly, the category for *Crossover Song of the Year* came up. My wife and mother reached for my hand.

MASTER OF CEREMONIES (MC): The nominees for *Crossover Song of the Year* are:
"My Woman My Lover My Friend" performed by ***Jimmy Gonzalez Y Groupo Mazz!***

There was some light but steady applause.

MC: *"Amor, Familia Y Respecto*" featuring ***Fat Joe!*** Performed by ***K1!***
Again, there was some polite applause.

MC: *"Quemar* (R&B "Ushers Song Burn") performed by ***Maz Ambicion!***
Some pretty good applause.

MC: ***"Takin' on the World"*** performed by ***Stefani Montiel!***
Again, some light applause. And then it was our turn…

MC: ***"Who's That Gringo,"*** performed by ***Billy O'Rourke and David Lee Garza Y Los Musicales!***

The crowd went crazy! I could hardly believe the response. It was truly overwhelming, and it made a statement. I leaned forward in my seat and looked down the row at my family, "Is this really gonna happen?"

DAD: Sure feels like it Mitch.
MC: And the winner is..."Who's That Gringo," written by Billy O'Rourke and Mitch Stephen, recorded by David Lee Garza y Los Musicales!

The place lit up, the song began to play, and everyone started singing along. I couldn't believe my ears. The entire convention center knew the words to our little song. Many danced in the aisles, and everyone clapped in unison to the beat. I was jumping up and down with my hands held high over my head in victory, "Yes – Yes – Yes!" and my family smothered me with celebratory hugs. The music faded down and out as Billy and the group came on stage to accept the award. Multiple Grammy award-winner and group patriarch, David Lee, graciously allowed Billy out front to be speak for the group.

BILLY: Wow, what an honor... Who'd ever thought this would happen? I'd like to thank all the fans of Tejano music and my co-writer Mitch Stephen. I heard that Mitch was here. Does anyone know where he is? Mitch, are you out there?

Billy put his hand under the brim of his cowboy hat to shield his eyes as he intently searched for me beyond the glaring stage lights. Other spotlights began to pan across the crowd looking for me, so I stood up and yelled at the top of my lungs towards the stage that seemed to be a million miles away. "HEY BILLY!"

When the spotlights found me, I shouted, "There's *two* gringos here tonight!" I was relieved to hear everyone laugh. They invited me to come down but it was too far.

The group accepted their trophy, said some more thank yous and were escorted back stage. Momma was crying. Dad was shaking his head, "You son of a gun," and my wife was looking at me in amazement, smiling a smile that begged the question, "How in the heck did you pull this stunt off?"

I was higher than a kite. My feet didn't touch the ground for at least two weeks. I was so proud to be associated with Billy and David Lee and the band, Los Musicales. Finally, after years and years of writing, someone handed us a little glass trophy and a royalty check and said, "Not bad, boys. Not bad."

That night in Eagle Pass is one of my favorite recollections, and I can't talk about it or write about it without smiling. If you're interested in my music you can find much of my life's work in that department at **www.MitchStephen.Com.** Be sure to listen to **"Who's That Gringo."**

"WHO'S THAT GRINGO"

Written by Mitch Stephen & Billy O'Rourke

Everywhere I go people ask me
Tell us are you brown or are you white
I tell 'em I'm a white boy from West Texas
They shake their heads and can't believe their eyes

They see me jammin' with The Poteet Posse
Standin' right there next to David Lee
But it never fails to happen, I'll see somebody laughin'
The second that I take the mic. and sing

CHORUS:
Hey David who's that gringo, Standin' up there on the stage
Did you hear that singin' gringo, and that Ramone Ayala song he sang
Did you see that playin' gringo, does he play the Bajosexto
If he's white on the outside, his heart must be refried
Who's that gringo on the stage

I remember our reunion show in Houston
60,000 came to see us play
It was Ram, Emilio and Papa Tony
There was Marcos, Oscar G and we had "Jay"

They brought the house lights down
The place went crazy
It's the greatest feeling that I've ever known
But you could feel the tension, when somebody yelled the question
That echoed through the Houston Astrodome

(REPEAT CHORUS)

Now somewhere down the road when we're in Heaven
And the angels open up those pearly gates
They'll say, "Here's Los Musicales" …but I'll be the one that's nervous
'Cause I sure hope the good Lord doesn't say

(REPEAT CHORUS)

Listen: http://www.mitchstephen.com/whosthatgringo.asp?music=on
Sung by Billy O'Rourke

Publishers; Bill Green Music / David Lee Garza – DLG Records - BMI
www.MitchStephen.com

"Who's That Gringo" being performed live at the 25th Anniversary Tejano Music Awards by David Lee Garza y Los Musicales. David Lee is in the white hat to the left and co-writer Billy O'Rourke is in the white hat to the right 3.15.2005

CHAPTER 52
MILE STONES

• • •

One day I needed to retrieve a particular document from our file storage unit. I tried hard to pawn off that task on my wife, Tommi, or our daughter, Shannon, but the stars and moon weren't lining up just right. Seems they were either too busy or too far away to justify my delegating that task to either one of them. I eventually came to the conclusion I'd have to go there myself.

Forever, it seems the office staff would bundle up all the files at the end of each year and send them off to this storage place. I've been charged with micro-managing certain things but when it came to this annual ritual, I'd never been involved in organizing or shipping the files. I was wondering if I'd even be able to find the folder I needed to get into.

I arrived at my destination and took the key out of my pocket. I removed the lock, bent down, grabbed the handle to the storage door and lifted it open. I looked into the storage, and there they were…hundreds and hundreds of files. They were stacked along three walls of the storage from the bottom to the top. The containers we labeled 1996, 1997, 1998 and so on, and they went through to the year 2007. I stood there in shock at first and then amazement. I entered the unit gazing at all the Tupperware file containers, remembering bits and pieces from each year, all the work and effort, all the fun and the hardships.

I opened a container and counted the number of house files it contained. In my head, I took the number of files in the one container and multiplied by the number of containers. I concluded that the number I'd arrived at was wrong—simply not possible. I recounted the number of containers lining the walls of the storage. This time, before I did my calculation, I went to my truck and found a calculator. I did the math a second time. "No way" I thought. "Is it possible I'd had my head down, working so hard, that I actually bought that many?"

I remembered my conversation with Ken D'Angelo back when I was young in the business. I'd started out to become a landlord and to own some rental houses. I ended up *owner financing houses* and then *selling the notes*. Eleven years after my humble beginning I was standing in a storage unit looking at all the files.

And looking back at me…my life and 1,000 houses.

CHAPTER 53
MORE STORIES FROM MY LIFE & 1,000 HOUSES

• • •

When I began *My Life & 1,000 Houses* I actually started out to simply document some of the funny or strange things that had happened to me in my career. As the stories started to fall into place, I began to look back at all that had happened and what it had taken for me to get to that point in the first place. As you well know by now, I haven't become the world's richest man or received the Nobel Peace Prize. I don't have my own TV show, and I'm not famous by a long shot. But I did accomplish the one thing I wanted to do the most. I became financially independent. In the circles I travel in, the question of the day is; "how do I become financially free." In my book everyone should ask that question of themselves at some time or another but most don't. Most don't think they can become financially independent.

I'm really not comfortable telling anyone how they should go about doing anything much less how to become "financially free." However, I knew I wouldn't mind telling you how *I* became financially free. And if that helps someone find their own path to financial freedom, then I am delighted. The first half of this book has been dedicated to just that; a chronological explanation of how *I* eventually figured out how to become financially free.

The second half of this book is a little different. Each story stands on its own and there is no rhyme or reasons as to the order they are in. In the beginning I wasn't sure I'd even have enough stories to fill a book, but, as I traveled around and spoke with past and present business colleagues, I was surprised to find that almost all of them were able to recall a deal or a situation that was well worth writing about. It's been fun reliving those moments with my friends, and I've enjoyed the process of committing those stories to paper. I hope you enjoy reading about my adventures as much as I've enjoyed writing them. Now, in no particular order and with no further ado…more stories from My Life & 1,000 Houses.

STORY 1
THE GIFT

• • •

Sometimes, you just can't resist.

You are probably familiar with the saying, "The best things in life are free." That directly contradicts another well-known saying, "Nothing in life is free." Just as in life, real estate has its conflicting ideas.

When I started out on my real estate adventures, I never thought anyone would ever give me anything. One day it happened. Somebody wanted to give me something. This inevitably led me to many other sayings including, "risk equals reward," "time is money," and "if it sounds too good to be true, *it probably needs to be checked into!*" (I love self-employment. You get to make up your own sayings!) In the end, I'll let you decide. Was this a gift or theft of service?

One day a man, I'll call him Mr. Gonzales, wandered into my office insisting on giving me a mobile home. I say "insisting" because he only spoke Spanish, and it took quit awhile for someone in my office to figure out what he was trying to say. In Spanish, Mr. Gonzales kept saying, "I want to give you my mobile home." We kept looking at each other saying, "That can't be right, ask him again." He kept repeating the same thing until we finally decided, without a doubt, Mr. Gonzales wanted to *give* us his mobile home. Don't get me wrong. I firmly believe that too-good-to-be-true real estate deals happen every day because I make a living finding them. I just wasn't real sure about my ability to interpret the Spanish.

Luckily, my long time partner and friend arrived, in his usual timely fashion, to lend his expertise. Señor Samuel Hombre, God bless him, is fluent in Spanish. With the language barrier gone, we proceeded to delve into this intriguing prospect.

Apparently, Mr. Gonzales was quite distraught over the fact that his ex-son-in-law was living in his mobile home and had forgotten to pay his rent for the past six months. I've seen this plenty of times. A family member/landlord wants to avoid evicting another family member, so they sell the property out from under the no-good, freeloading relative and leave the dirty work of evicting them to professionals like us.

In this case, the mobile home was *free and clear* so that part wasn't causing Mr. Gonzales any financial stress. The problem was that the lot rent, which he had signed for during better family relations, was costing him $150.00 per month. He wanted to walk away from the entire arrangement, but he was a man of his word and he didn't want any bad marks against his good name. It didn't take long to comprehend that he wanted to give us the mobile home and his ex-son-in-law if we would take over the lot payment.

Sam and I only had a million things to do that day but since we were so intrigued about the idea of someone giving us something we decided to go take a look at the mobile home. Besides, we favored a little hole-in-the-wall restaurant near that part of town, and it was getting to be lunchtime.

On the drive over to the mobile home park, Sam and I mused over exactly what we were going to find. We sarcastically fantasized about the beautiful, modern triple-wide we were about to inherit. We jokingly wondered if it would have a marble entrance or if it had its own private pool with a white gazebo. We ended up in stitches trying to convince each other that Donald Trump started out this way. Most of all, we laughed about all the important things we were not doing simply because we wanted to get something for FREE. Sam and I tend to laugh a lot about how glamorous people think our lives are. If they only knew!

As we pulled up to the address, reality started to set in. There was a moment of silence as we gazed at our potential acquisition. It looked like a new foil-wrapped suppository to the 100th power. This can't be it. Where's the pool and the gazebo? Dang, someone stole the marble entrance and the white picket fence! Little did we know, the worst was yet to come.

Not sure if the ex-son-in-law was inside, we gingerly walked around the 1968, hail-damaged, aluminum-clad residence on wheels. We found the front door incapable of being shut and, therefore, wide open. I called into the structure, "Anybody home? Hello." Convinced no one could be living in this contraption, we stepped in. There was no one in there at that time, but it was obvious to us that somebody *was* living in this thing.

I don't know if we were both holding our breath when we entered or if the wind somehow changed direction, but all at once Sam and I began to gasp at the smell. It was horrible! We looked at each other with wide eyes and proceeded to pull the necks of our shirts up over our noses. "Man, where is that stench coming from?" We stretched our necks as we looked around the corner and down the hall towards the back room. The abundance of swarming flies made me briefly wonder if someone might be dead. Fortunately that was not the case.

Inside the home, there was no electricity and no carpet. It was clear as fog that the person living here had been using the facilities even though there was no water. After a very brief inspection of the bathroom, we found that the toilet had been long since filled beyond capacity and the inhabitant had been using the tub instead for quit some time. I'll never know how people live like that but it happens more often than you might think. We exited.

"Well, how 'bout lunch, Sam?" I said chokingly, jokingly. I started laughing 'cause Sam was dusting himself off like the smell was somehow stuck to him. We decided to postpone lunch until we could put some time and distance between us and the filth we'd just witnessed. I had laughed at Sam dusting himself off, but the truth be known, I really wanted a shower.

On the drive back to the office we were perplexed about what to do. On one hand we had a chance to get this thing for FREE. On the other hand, *it was disgusting.* We came to the conclusion that this FREE thing could cost us some money given the fact that we would be obligating ourselves to the monthly lot rent of $150.00 per month. As it turned out we weren't going to be required to accept the rent obligation in writing. But we agreed that if we took the title, we'd have to remain true to our word and pay the lot rent, even if it hurt.

I love that about Sam. A deal is a deal, whether it's in writing or not. We have always agreed on that. The secret to keeping a good reputation and your integrity is to never let your mouth or your pen obligate you to something you can't physically, monetarily, or emotionally do.

Before a deal is made you need to always look at the worst-case scenario. If you can't find your way out of the worst possible turn of events with reputation and integrity intact, then you DON'T DO IT! If you can't find a respectful way to leave out the back door when the front door gets jammed, then you're locked in. You never want to get locked into a bad deal. Therefore, it's rather natural for me to check my back door options before I decide to walk into a deal. Let's look at the back door as it applies to this situation.

First of all, if we could not sell this beauty, we would have to pay the lot rent. If it became apparent that it was simply *not* going to sell, then we could be obligated for a long time. At that point, we would be locked into a bad deal, and that was just not acceptable! The only reason we were looking at this deal in the first place was because we would have no money in it—but that could change quickly. We came up with two back doors we felt comfortable with.

1. We could give the mobile home to someone else, provided we got the benefactor to replace Mr. Gonzales on the rental agreement with the park. (Remember, we'd have to protect Mr. Gonzales' good name. That was the deal). This was reasonable.
2. If we couldn't give this thing away, we could pay $1,000 to have the mobile home removed and taken to the dump. Then we could terminate the lease on the lot. Definitely doable!

Whether we did this deal or not, two things were agreed upon: we would not do one iota of work on the place and, more importantly, neither one of us was ever going to set foot in that place again. We made a pact.

With two viable back-door options in hand, we proceeded to the next, all-important question: How much would we lose if the deal completely failed? The worst option was obviously the second back door, where we would have to pay the $1,000 to have the mobile home carted off to the dump. Sam and I agreed that we wouldn't go longer than two months before deciding to cut our losses. That would mean two months worth of lot rent: $300. We also figured we'd have some advertising expense: $100 max. The answer to the all-important question: We could lose $1,400. Since we were going to do the deal as partners, we would each be responsible for $700 if the deal failed. Next question: Did we have the money to cover the loss? Yes. Last question: If we were to lose $700 each, would it kill us? No. Now that the risk had limits and the back doors were covered, it was time to start pondering the positive side of things.

Sam and I decided that the starting sales price would be $2,900 (overly optimistic we knew) and that we would accept the first offer no matter how low it was. We figured that the sale would probably go to a person already living in the park, and so we would put a sign on the mobile for the first four days. If the sign didn't produce any action, we would place an ad in the paper immediately to catch the weekend edition. As with most deals, time was going to be the enemy. The negative time clock would begin ticking the moment we accepted the title from Mr. Gonzales. Mr. Gonzales had just paid the rent for the next thirty days, and so we were off to a good start as far as the rent coming due. Feeling up to the challenge, we called Mr. Gonzales and made arrangements to pick up the title.

As I recall, the sign didn't produce much, so we had to place the newspaper ad.

Mobile home for sale, 2-1

$2,900 CASH, lot rent $150/Mo.

259 Hot Wells, Lot #110

737-XXXX

The classified ad began that Saturday and I soon got a call from "Mr. Hoboken." I'll call him Mr. Hoboken because, and I am totally serious when I say this, he was a hobo! A genuine, train-riding, just-the-shirt-on-his-back, one-town-to-the-next, sleep-wherever *hobo*! Imagine my inner thoughts during this phone conversation.

ME: Hello. This is Mitch!

MR. HOBOKEN: Hi, I'm calling about your ad in the paper. Are you the one selling the mobile home for $2,900?

My thoughts: (Please Lord, let this be my Buyer)

ME: Yes, I'm the owner. Have you seen the outside of the place?

MR. HOBOKEN: Yes, I saw it earlier today. Can I see the inside?

My thoughts: (He's motivated. Stock up 1 point)

ME: When do you want to see it?

MR. HOBOKEN: Well, I don't know, I don't have a car. When can you come pick me up?

My thoughts: (Stock just went down 10 points)

ME: You don't have a car? How did you get to the place to look at it?

My thoughts: (I'm wasting cellular air time)

MR. HOBOKEN: I had to take the bus but it's not dependable enough if I have to meet someone at a certain time.

My thoughts (He's considerate of my time. Stock back up 3 points)

ME: Where do you live?

MR. HOBOKEN: I live at the shelter downtown on So-N-So Street.

My thoughts: (WHAT?)

ME: I'm sorry, say that again please.

MR. HOBOKEN: I live at the shelter downtown on So-N-So Street.

My thoughts: (Stock crashes, reminiscent of 1932. Whatever his stock was up to, he's wiped out.)

ME: Well, I was asking $2,900 cash. Is that something you can do if you like the inside?

My thoughts: ("Like the inside?" That was stupid. Who in the heck could like the inside of a septic tank? Maybe I'd better hang in with this guy a bit longer. The buyer is *not* going to be the Queen of England, you know. Besides, who needs a home more than a homeless guy? Wake up, Mitch!)

MR: HOBOKEN: Yes, Sir. If I want the place, I have the *cash*, but you might have to take me to Frost Bank, if you don't mind.

My thoughts: (He has a bank account at *Frost?* Stock up 30 points! He's polite, too. Give him another 10 points.)

ME: I'll be right over.

My thoughts: (I hope this guy isn't a schizophrenic axe murderer. Is my life insurance paid up?)

ME: (yelling to the secretary) Anyone seen my car keys?

My thoughts: (But Sam, he said he had a *Frost Bank account!*)

As I piled into my truck I was really thinking, "If this works out, it'll make a great story for a book." So I'm off to the homeless shelter to pick up Mr. Hoboken. It was destiny, I tell you!

As I pulled up to the shelter he spotted me. With custom stenciled signs on my truck doors that boldly read "Cash4Houses.NET," I'm not hard to recognize. And wow! This guy belonged on the cover of *Homeless Magazine!* I mean he looked more like a homeless person than anyone I'd ever seen, the homeless spokesperson if you will. He had long gray hair down past his shoulders and a ZZ Top-style, extra-long gray beard that tapered down to a point right about belt-buckle level. His beard was on the whiter side of gray except for the brownish area around his mouth where, obviously, the tar from many a pack of cigarettes had left their mark. Sporting several tattoos and a pack of Camels rolled up in his t-shirt sleeve, he opened the door to my truck and hopped in. Carefully, I monitored my first breath with him in the seat next to me. I noted that he was a very clean homeless person. I was both thankful and encouraged.

On the drive across town I learned a lot about Mr. Hoboken. He sounded very intelligent as he told me about himself and his travels. He said he had jumped a train from Corpus Christi, Texas, to get to San Antonio (that was my first concrete clue he was a hobo). He said he was prone to seizures, and therefore he chose not to drive. I don't remember what he said his occupation used to be, but it was something professional, an engineer or something like that. This guy seemed so smart and articulate; I finally had to ask him, with all due respect, "How is a guy like you homeless?"

He went on to explain that he once had it all: The job, the house, the family, the car, etc. And then it all changed. I don't remember everything he said, but I do remember him saying that the only way he knew to be free was to be rid of all possessions. I still think about that statement from time to time and it scares the living heck out of me. "*The only way to be free is to be rid of all possessions.*" Haunting isn't it? I think he might be right.

After satisfying but a fraction of my curiosity, I was parked in front of the mobile home. I snapped back into sales mode. "Well, there she is! Ain't she a beauty?" I said, intently watching his face awaiting his reaction.

If he'd begun to laugh, then I'd have laughed with him (playing my enthusiasm off as sarcasm). However, his face showed more of an expression of agreement, so I continued with sincerity, "She doesn't look like much now, but I bet you can put quite a shine on her. All this place needs is someone like you to bring out its full potential."

It's not that I was trying to manipulate Mr. Hoboken. In fact, I like to think I was doing the opposite. I was putting him on the spot. I was going to see what he was made of. When I said, "Ain't she a beauty," I was just cutting to the chase. Did *he* see any potential? If he couldn't see the potential of the outside, I wasn't about to let him go inside. When Mr. Hoboken didn't disagree with "ain't she a beauty," I knew he had a vision of what the place could be—and I *never, never ever* discourage a person with a vision. No amount of salesmanship was going to make this ugly duckling a swan. It was just too big of a mess. Mr. Hoboken was homeless, not blind. But it did have potential. I knew it. Sam knew it. Shoot, if we hadn't thought the place had potential then we wouldn't have taken ownership of it. I know I've had some fun talking about what a dump this place was, but here's the bottom line: The challenge was not to con some poor soul into buying a dump. The challenge was to find a person who could see the potential of that poor neglected mobile home.

Keeping true to the pact that Sam and I had made, I didn't enter the meager residence but let Mr. Hoboken venture inside alone. No salesmanship was going to help me on the inside either. After what seemed like an eternity, Mr. Hoboken emerged from the shanty. The moment of truth was upon me. This was it.

Expressionless, he made his way toward my truck where I was. I had already decided to hold my tongue and let him initiate conversation. Then he spoke. "Well, I could fix it, I suppose, but I'd like to make you an offer if you wouldn't be offended." I assured him I wouldn't be offended (as you can imagine, I was already delighted that he was not condemning the place). "I think $1,800 would be a fair price. Could you part with it for $1,800?"

I didn't want to sound too eager so I stood silent and gazed at the ground while I scratched my head, pretending to struggle with the offer. I knew immediately that I wanted to accept the offer, but I also knew that he'd feel much better about his purchase if he felt like he had haggled me down. Not wanting to run him off, I gingerly pointed out that his offer was about 35% less than what I was asking. "Could you meet me half way, say, $2,400?" I asked.

He stuck to his guns. "$1,800 is a fair price," he said firmly.

"When could you get me the money?" I asked.

Then Mr. Hoboken said that if I would take him to Frost Bank, he could give it to me right there.

I made a concerted effort to reluctantly give in. "Well, I really don't have time for this, and I guess I wouldn't have to drive over here anymore, so I'll agree to the $1,800 if you'll make this month's lot rent payment of $150." With that we shook on it, and as far as I was concerned the deal was cast in stone.

On the trek to the bank I was eager to satisfy more of my curiosity. I was genuine in my inquiries, and Mr. Hoboken seemed happy to tell me more about his life. He told me that he traveled around the countryside buying little places just like the one he was about to purchase from me. He'd eventually catch a ride to the local flea market and gather his tools and supplies and repair the place. Upon completion, he'd put it up for sale at a profit. When the places sold, he'd pick another town somewhere off in the distance and do it all over again. That's why he had left Corpus Christi. He had purchased a mobile there for $4,500, and eventually he sold it for $12,000 cash. He estimated his profit to be about $6,000 including his living expenses. WHAT A COUNTRY! Even a hobo can enjoy the fruits of entrepreneurship. I'll say it again, WHAT A COUNTRY!

At the bank, Mr. Hoboken insisted I come with him to the teller's counter. When it was our turn, he told the teller that he wanted to know what his balance was and that he wanted to make a cash withdrawal. Upon locating his balance on the computer, the teller looked pensive as she asked how he would like the balance presented. She was very professional, and I quickly came to the conclusion that she wasn't sure if I was supposed to hear the balance. I offered to excuse myself, but Mr. Hoboken refused. He told her to write the number on a piece of paper. She did as he requested and, consistent with her professionalism, folded it in half to ensure his privacy. He looked pleased as he read the numbers. Then he placed the paper on the counter and slid it over in front of me so I could see it. Mr. Hoboken's balance was $60,000 and change. Shall I say it again? WHAT A COUNTRY! This guy was starting to amaze me.

After getting the cashiers check for the $1,800, I drove Mr. Hoboken over to the office where I gave him the title to the mobile home. Then, I drove him back to the shelter. Before he left the truck, I made him promise not to be late on the lot rent, and he assured me that it would be paid on time. I believed him.

As we said goodbye, he invited me to come by some time and visit. Regretfully, it was several months before I decided to stop by. When I did, I was pleasantly surprised at how nice the place looked. I knocked on the door only to find that Mr. Hoboken had moved on. I didn't have the nerve to ask the new residents how much the place had sold for, but whatever the price I'm sure my hobo friend had made a profit. I was sad that I missed him but happy for his success. Congratulations Mr. Hoboken, wherever you are.

In the end, Sam and I made a profit of $850 apiece. Not a lot of money on the surface but look at it this way: I probably spent more time typing this little story than I did doing the actual deal. As I recall, it was seven days from start to finish but in actual man-hours I bet we didn't spend eight hours on this deal. That's over $100 each per hour. Another way to look at it is like this: We ended up investing $100 in advertising to make $1,800. Talk about your cash-on-cash return on investment!

Income divided by Investment = Rate of Return
$1,800 divided by $100 = 1800% Rate of Return

1800% is an *annual* rate of return (as if it took a year to make this money). This was done in seven days! Generally a *rate of return* is figured annually. Anyone care to do that math? You would start by finding out how many times 7 days divides into 365 days. Needless to say, most calculators won't have enough decimal places to handle the annual rate of return.

At any rate, I chose to tell this story because the principles apply to big deals as well. Assessing your risk, finding your back doors, pre-qualifying *but not prejudging*, and making the buyer feel that he's earned his price are all part of making a deal work. Besides, some people might like to hear that it doesn't take a stack of cash to make a decent profit in the house business. Everybody I know started out very small. Small deals can give a person the confidence and the cash they need to eventually start doing bigger deals. Today, Sam and I would pass on this deal or maybe we'd make one or two phone calls and wholesale the opportunity to an eager "Jr. Investor" for a few hundred bucks.

Last but not least, it's apparent that we all make a living by solving other people's problems. Think about that. It's no different in real estate. If you're waiting for someone to give you a perfectly good property for no reason at all, you're going to be waiting a long time to do your first deal—probably forever.

STORY 2
TOO MUCH MOJO

• • •

Sometimes you just need to move away from stuff that stinks.

Several years ago, a small group of us met at a coffee shop on a Saturday morning. Jack Word, Sam Hombre, and I were shooting the breeze over coffee when my phone rang. It was a realtor who needed to sell a particular house *that day!* Now, as I recall, I wasn't really in the mood to look at a home so early on a Saturday morning, but the realtor was giving off all the signs an investor looks for when searching for a deal. Removing the phone slightly from my ear, I asked the group if they'd like to go see the house the realtor was desperate to sell. Everyone agreed, so I wrote down the directions on a napkin and, after a few more sips of coffee, we piled into Jack's "Good Times" van and headed south.

As we pulled up to the house, we could see some commotion. People were streaming in and out. Apparently they were moving all the contents of the house to the curb. It looked like an eviction but that didn't make sense. It was Saturday and FE&Ds (Forceful Entry and Detainers) happen during the week, *not* on the weekends. I don't know if anyone else caught it, but I also noticed that all the people hauling the contents out of the house were wearing latex rubber gloves, the kind you'd see a surgeon put on before an operation.

Once inside, I knew it was going to be one of those houses. You know, the kind where the person who lived there (or used to live there) never threw anything away. Ever. The place was filled to the brim with heaps of stuff: everything from magazine and newspapers to childhood trophies and coffee mug collections. The only reason we could navigate the home at all was in large part due to the huge volume of junk already taken to the curb. The formal name for this condition is disposophobia (the fear of disposing of things), and it's commonly known as compulsive hoarding. It's more prevalent than you might think. The more I know about mental illness in this world, the more I thank God for my disposition.

Soon, the realtor, who had called me less than an hour before, greeted us. We maneuvered our way through the door and into the foyer, dodging the diligent worker ants coming and going as they attempted to empty the house. The realtor was pleasant, and we all introduced ourselves. With the formalities out of the way, we began our guided tour.

We followed behind the realtor in single file as she led us down the hall to one end of the house. There she took us inside the far bedroom and described the size and showed us some evidence of settling problems, etc. Nothing much to tell that we couldn't see with our own eyes, until she said, "One last thing. As you know, I am a licensed realtor and I am required by the law to disclose certain things. There was a violent murder committed in this room two years ago."

Then she asked if we were still interested in seeing the rest of the home. The three of us looked around at each other and shrugged, as if to say, "Yes."

With that confirmation, she exited the room and we followed her down the hall to the next room. Nothing much to say about this room either except, "A violent murder was committed in this room also. One year ago. Do you still wish to see more of the home?"

I asked the group, "Does that bother anyone?"

Everyone said something to the effect of "No, let's keep looking."

So we headed off towards the other end of the home. I'd fallen behind and instead of going around the kitchen via the living room, I opted to take a shortcut through the kitchen in an effort to catch up to the herd. I was just about half way across the kitchen when I noticed I was walking on thick, quilted moving blankets. I stopped in the middle of the blankets and looked down at them beneath my feet wondering why on earth they were there. My first instinct was that someone was hiding something, like a cracked slab or some other evidence of settling they didn't want us to see. I bent down and pulled one of the seamed corners back and found the blankets were laid over the top of a brownish, mud-like substance. I actually thought it was mud coming up through a crack in the slab, maybe forced up by water from a broken water pipe or something like that. I pulled the rug all the way back and the mud got thicker and wider with every foot of the floor I revealed. I called out, "Hey guys! Come here!"

Within a few seconds, my comrades appeared at the entrance of the kitchen. I asked, "Someone turn on the light." The light came on and I was searching intently for a crack in the slab. We were all standing there in the kitchen looking down at this mud when the realtor showed up.

She sounded a little frustrated, "I was going to get to this room next but, since you're here, I must tell you that a murder was committed here last night. A young man was stabbed repeatedly. It was supposed to be cleaned up before I got here but it wasn't. I put the blankets down to cover the blood until we could have it cleaned up."

So let's review. There had been a murder two years before and then a murder last year, and yet another murder committed LAST NIGHT! And that stuff I thought was mud was blood! I asked the question before the realtor had a chance to ask it, "You guys still want to see the rest of the house?"

Jack said, "Well, there are only two rooms left to see. We're here, so we might as well see the rest of the place." We all agreed and headed towards the last two rooms. I'm thinking to myself, "Why miss the chance to see where the next murders are bound to happen!" We finished the viewing and quietly headed for the door.

We'd exited the home and were standing in the front yard when the realtor prompted us for an offer. She wanted to sell the home that day and felt sure that the seller (the landlord) would be very, very reasonable on this property. I asked the realtor in front of everyone if we might have a little time alone to discuss our options. She graciously excused herself and we proceeded to Jack's van for some private discussion.

I was making my way around the van to the passenger's side reflecting on the situation: All of us had done hundreds of deals. All of us had purchased homes that people had died in before. We had all purchased homes after natural deaths had occurred in them. I knew most of us had purchased properties even after suicides had been committed inside them. I was trying to rationalize making a deal.

Once we all piled into the van, Jack started up the engine, cracked the driver-side window, and lit a cigarette. Exhaling his first draw of smoke out the window, he broke the silence inside the van, "Well, what do ya'll wanna do?"

We all looked at around at each other, none of us wanting to be the first to speak. When I'd had enough lingering, I offered up my opinion, "Well, I'll tell you what I think. I think we put this van in gear and GET THE HECK OUTTA HERE!"

A unanimous "AMEN, BROTHER," came from all the other passengers in unison.

Jack pulled the gearshift down into drive, and Sam said, "What about the realtor?"

Jack said in a nervous laugh, "What about the realtor?"

Sam started to laugh, "Shouldn't we at least say goodbye?"

And with that Jack rolled down his window and shouted "GOODBYE!" to the realtor and proceeded to burn rubber all the way out of the subdivision.

I felt a little bad about leaving that poor realtor standing on the front porch waiting for us.

I called her later and apologized. The truth is, even though we all held ourselves out as consummate professionals, we couldn't wait another second to get out of there. There was just too much mojo.

STORY 3
SO, WHAT CAN A DOLLAR BUY?

• • •

Never let a deal die on your side of the desk.

Some of the best deals seem to happen almost by accident. "Pure luck," some people would say.

Personally, I believe in the old adage, "The harder I work, the luckier I get." At any rate, I wasn't looking for this kind of deal when it appeared.

I was traveling in the car with a realtor friend of mine. We went to look at a house that was for sale but, upon our arrival, we found that the property had been put under contract some time earlier. On the drive back we were consoling ourselves with the old "win some, lose some" routine when I glanced out the passenger side window and saw the smallest "FOR SALE" sign I'd ever seen on a commercial building. One of those tiny black and florescent orange For Sale signs you'd buy at a hardware store.

As we passed the advertisement, I asked my realtor friend if he would turn around because I was curious as to what price that building was selling for. (I am constantly checking prices, even when I think things are probably going to be too expensive. I just like to see which properties go for what price.) I wasn't looking for a commercial building, but one thing stood out as unusual. As I mentioned, it was the smallest sign I'd ever seen on a commercial building. Either someone really didn't want to sell this building (thus the price would be high), or someone didn't have much enthusiasm for this building (which could mean a chance for a possible bargain). The small, hardware-store sign was Hint # 1.

I called the number on the little sign and to my surprise a lady answered, "Schertz Bank." The receptionist connected me to the lady in charge, and I explained to her that I was standing in front of the building on Main Street, and that I wanted to know the asking price. She said, "I'll be right there," and hung up on me before I could explain to her that I was probably not that interested, just curious.

The realtor and I were scratching our heads, wondering how long we'd have to wait, when she appeared from around the corner. "Wow," I said. "That was fast! I don't see a Superwoman cape, so obviously your office isn't far away."

Meanwhile I took note that she was overly eager to show this property—Hint # 2. She introduced herself as she was unlocking the door. All I really wanted to do was get a price but, now that we were here and now that I had two hints, I was wondering if there was a deal to be made. So I started in with my usual questions.

How many square feet is this building? 3,800 square feet.

How long has the bank owned the building? Nine months.

What did this building used to be? An English-style pub. Before that, it was a bank.

Is there anything wrong with the building? Nothing, except it has only eight parking spaces.

Does the kitchen equipment stay with the building? Everything in here is yours if you buy the building.

How is the a/c and heat? It was replaced by the previous owner and should be fine.

How much do you want for the building? $100,000.00

Upon hearing the sales price, my realtor friend immediately started in on the banker, stating that the property was not worth that kind of money. He went on to point out many of the weak points of the building, including the lack of parking spaces, the location, etc. He was really letting her have it! Feeling a bit uncomfortable, I wandered off into other areas of the building as if I were still checking the place out, all the while tuned into the ongoing debate in the other room.

I personally don't try to beat someone up in the negotiating process, but I know others that are very successful with that style. For now, I was content to let the realtor punch on the banker for a while. I listened intently from the other rooms to see if his brash approach could make some headway. It didn't take long before I was sure it wasn't going to work, so I meandered back into the room and took over the conversation. I just love coming into negotiations as the good guy. I prefer the "kill'em with kindness" approach.

ME: Ma'am, I'm a professional investor, but I usually deal in residential properties. I am really out of my league when it comes to commercial real estate. I was thinking that if I could get the property for say, $40,000 to $50,000, I might be a *cash buyer*. Would the bank consider such an offer or would it be a waste of your valuable time?

BANKER: Oh no, the bank could not accept such a low offer.

ME: Well, let me ask you this. What price does the bank have to get for this building and not lose money?

My thoughts: (I was expecting her to give me the old, "You'll have to make us an offer" song and dance.)

BANKER: $78,000.00.

(HINT #3: They really just want out!)

ME: That's still more than I would be willing to write a check for. Would the bank be willing to finance the building for me?

BANKER: Yes, that's possible, but you'd have to have good credit and put a down payment of 20% cash. Also, the sales price would probably have to be closer to the original asking price of $100,000 if we financed it. The $78,000 would be a cash price.

My thoughts: (These are the exact problems that had been working against the sale of the building for the past nine months.)

Now, there was no way I was buying this building at that time for $78,000, bank financed or otherwise. I truly was out of my league when it came to commercial real estate, no joke, unless the opportunity came at a no-brainer price. That wasn't a sales pitch. Furthermore, I had just tried my best cash offer to no avail. Just when I was about to say, "Thank you very much," and leave, I remembered the golden rule of investing: Never let a deal die on your side of the table. Always leave *them* with an offer *you* can live with.

ME: Ma'am, I think we're not really close enough on the price to strike a deal today, *but* I just might have an idea that could make everybody happy in the end. I don't normally think of banks as being "open minded," but you have impressed me as someone who could put a good idea into motion. Would you like to hear it?

BANKER: I'm open. Let's hear it.

ME: First of all, I would like you to understand two things: Number one, I feel almost certain that I can sell your building faster than any realtor or the bank.

BANKER: How can you sell it faster than us?

ME: Because I'm going to ask twice as much as the bank!

BANKER: Well, that certainly won't make it sell faster.

ME: You're absolutely right. Raising the price wouldn't normally make anything sell faster. *But*…after I raise the price, I'm going to offer it for sale with a $0.00 down payment, a thirty-year term, 10.50% fixed interest – and perfect credit not necessary. Now what do you think?

BANKER: Interesting.

ME: Can the bank offer such terms?

BANKER: No, the bank would be cut to shreds by our regulators. We absolutely would not be able to offer any of those terms. *Zero* down, fixed interest rate for thirty years, less than perfect credit? Not in a million years.

ME: That's why I think I can sell it before a realtor or the bank. I'm going to give terms and, just as you've acknowledged, terms can override price. I'll provide the terms necessary to sell this building if the bank will allow me to advertise those terms and show the property. By giving me an option to purchase the building at $78,000 cash, I can do all those things legally and without a license.

BANKER: I can see where your phone would ring off the wall when you ask for zero down payment, but aren't you just begging for a buyer whom you'll eventually have to foreclose on?

ME: No, because I'm going to demand that the buyer invest a substantial amount of money into the improvement of this building (my collateral) in lieu of a down payment. I figure that the buyer will have to spend $15,000 to $20,000 to get this building up to speed. I'll need to approve his remodeling plans in advance, but the building has some obvious needs. Once my buyer spends money on the improvements, he will be *vested*, and my collateral will be worth a substantially higher value.

BANKER: I can see how your strategy could work quite effectively if you find the right person.

ME: Yes. It can be an effective strategy, but remember, when I find a potential buyer at my terms ($150,000 at10.50% fixed interest for thirty years with a monthly P&I payment of approx. $1,372.12), I'm going to have to write a check for $78,000. I'm probably not going to take the first person who walks in the door. I make a living by finding good people who have learned from their mistakes in the past. Good, hardworking people who, unfortunately, the banks can't take a chance on because of their past credit problems. I'm also looking for a buyer with the monetary means to make the necessary improvements to the building. When I find that buyer, I'll exercise the option to purchase the building for $78,000 cash.

BANKER: What kind of option are you going to propose exactly?

ME: That brings me to the second thing I wanted you to understand. I won't impede your current position. That is to say, the bank will continue to carry the property on its books, and if the bank finds a buyer first, then I'll give way to the success of that sale. I'd like to propose that the bank give me the *option* to purchase this building for $78,000.00, so that I may go to work in an effort to move the property off of the bank's books.

BANKER: How much will you pay us for such an option?

ME: Well, considering the fact that I haven't taken away any of the bank's rights to sell the building on their own, not very much. How about this: I'll give you a token $1.00 for the option to purchase your building for $78,000.00. If you sell the building before I exercise my option to buy the building, well, we'll still part as friends. The bank has nothing to lose and everything to gain. I'll pay $1.00 and all my own advertising expenses for the right to solve the bank's problem and sell this building.

BANKER: Would you please type up your proposal and fax it to my office? I'd like to present this idea to the board at our next meeting.

I went home and did just that. Yes, I did just that and then…I promptly forgot about it. I'd rather have my teeth pulled than to hang my hopes on the outcome of a bank board meeting. I'm sorry if that seems a bit crass, but thus far in my career I'd never had much luck dealing with the board of anything. I just figured I'd type up the agreement in the form of a *letter of intent* simply as a courtesy to the lady banker who gave me her time, and then I'd forget about it because nothing was going to ever happen. It would be lost in "banker limbo," never to be seen or heard of again.

TWO MONTHS LATER:

My cellular phone rings like it does about seventy-five times per day.

ME: Thiiiis iiiis Mitch! (I say it like a modified version of Ed McMahon's *Tonight Show*, "Heeere's Johnny!"

BANKER: Hi Mitch. It's Beverly. The bank wants to accept your proposal.

ME: Beverly? Bank? Help me out a little bit will you, Beverly…I'm sorry, I'm lost. I don't know what we're talking about.

BANKER: It's Beverly, with Schertz Bank. We have that building for sale on Main Street. The bank wants to give you the *option* to buy the building for $78,000, remember?

ME: Oh Beverly! Yes…Schertz Bank. Now I remember. So they want to give me the option?

BANKER: Yes, we finally got everyone to the look over your proposal. All I need to do is get you a copy of the signed agreement and collect that $1.00 from you (She laughed at the one dollar part). When can you come to the bank and pick up the keys?

ME: I'll be right over!

BANKER: Don't forget to bring that $1.00.

She really thought that was funny! I laughed about it too…all the way to the bank, literally.

At that moment, I took notice that a small miracle had just taken place. A bank had given me an option on a $100,000 building for the grand total price of $1.00. I wasted no time in turning my truck in the appropriate direction. I was about to control a piece of real estate with a few pieces of paper and $1.00. That is *way* better than ownership!

After signing and exchanging the paperwork at the bank, I strolled over to the building. I took the opportunity to get some duplicate keys at the adjoining hardware store. During the process, I noticed an elderly woman counting inventory. To my surprise, I found out she was the owner of the store. I approached her and introduced myself as her new neighbor and that I was offering the building next to her for sale, owner financed. She never stopped counting her inventory. She never looked up at me, but she did manage to ask me how much I would be asking for the building. I barely got out the words "one-hundred, fifty-thousand dollars" out of my mouth when she abruptly cut me off.

Looking at me for the first time she said in disgust, "You don't have a Chinaman's chance in hell." I love it when people say things like that to me. Really, I love it! I paid for the keys, bid her good day, and left. On my way out, I noticed a copier with a sign that touted "5 cents per copy."

I had my keys and was heading to my truck for a lock box and a sign so I could begin the process of selling this little jewel. There was only one problem. I didn't have any signs in my truck because I'd used them all. I could've gone back to the hardware store and bought a sign but I made my up mind that there was only one reason worth going back into that place—and getting a sign wasn't it. I struggled with how to solve the sign dilemma without having to leave and then come all the way back.

After digging around the bed of my truck, I found a half full bottle of white shoe polish. Perfect! I unlocked the front door of the vacant building and went upstairs to find a prominent window to "shoe polish," one that faced directly down Main Street. As if that weren't good enough, I took note that, from the second floor window, I was looking directly down toward a stop light at a substantial intersection. I caught myself guessing at how many people would be reading my "Poor Boy" For Sale sign the next morning. Having a sign in a high-traffic area is worth something, but having a sign with traffic held captive at an intersection by a little red light…BINGO!

The second floor window was about the size of a regular sliding glass door. There I began to write.

4 SALE

Owner Finance

0 Down, $1,372.12 / month

210-805-XXX

Simple enough, right? Wrong! You see, I was writing on the inside of the window, and people were going to be reading this little diddy on the outside of the window. That meant that I had to write the entire thing backwards. Now, for a guy who can't draw a stick person, this is no easy task. In fact, looking backwards (pun intended), it was the most challenging event of the entire transaction. Oh me, oh my, the problems of dealing with commercial real estate.

The next day I was going to have a big 4' x 8' sign made up. I was going to put an ad in the classifieds. I was going to do so many things. Instead, my phone rang, and I began the process of selling the property to a couple who'd read the makeshift for sale sign scribed in the window.

Ironically, despite having very good credit, these prospective buyers had tried unsuccessfully to purchase the building from the bank earlier that year. They knew that the building had been for sale by the bank for $100,000. I was initially worried about that, given the fact that I was now offering the building for $150,000. My doubts started to subside when I learned *why* they were unable to consummate a deal with the bank. Let's review the reason the bank couldn't approve these buyers.

1. The buyers were both self employed with less than two years in business.
2. The bank wanted the buyers to put $20,000 down (20% of $100,000).

3. The bank wanted the buyers to accept a floating interest rate, very dangerous.
4. The bank would only amortize the loan balance of $80,000 for ten years, making the payments roughly $1,000 per month. The current payment amount was not a problem but, again, the floating interest rate gave the buyers cause for great concern. A good deal today could be a terrible deal tomorrow if the interest rate floated too high.
5. After putting the required $20,000 down, the buyers would be left with no money to remodel the space or for initial start-up costs.

In the end, the bank was doing a great job in protecting its own interests, but it left the buyer with little opportunity to actually purchase the building. Now let's look at the deal I was able to structure for the buyers.

After talking to the buyers, I was able to determine their current financial status and what their goals were. The husband had recently retired from the military with a life-long retirement income of $1,500 per month. He had started a septic tank installation business that had been doing reasonably well the past year and a half. The wife was operating her own bookkeeping business that provided a reasonable income. Both of them were working out of their home, which they were purchasing. I was happy to hear that they did in fact have $20,000 in savings to invest in this new venture, but they needed it to fix the building. (Remember: The bank wanted the $20,000 for a down payment, thus, leaving them nothing for repairs.) After pulling their credit, I learned that they had very respectable credit scores of around 720.

To put credit scores into perspective, I consider a perfect score to be 800. I routinely owner finance houses to buyers with credit scores as low as 500. In my opinion, credit scores are highly subjective. Scores can be driven down by an abundance of available credit even when it's unused. It can also be driven down by medical debts, which are not typically elected for. If you've ever been hit with an incorrect charge off by a credit reporting company, you will no doubt agree with me when I say that libelous remarks on your credit report are difficult to get removed no matter how easy they say it is to get them corrected. (Don't even get me onto *that* subject!) In my travels, I've found that some good scores are undeserving—and some bad scores are undeserving. All that being said; an undeserving *bad credit score* is much easier to come by than an undeserving *good credit score*. In this case, it was my opinion that the 720 credit score was a fair assessment of my buyer's credit.

In my conversations with the buyers, I asked them how much money they figured to spend on the building for it to meet their needs. They estimated that it would take $20,000 to update the building and get a certificate of occupancy. They also told me that they would need two months to complete the remodeling process.

I presented the buyers with the following terms.

Sale Price $150,000
Down Pmt $ -0-
Loan Balance $150,000 @10.50% fixed for 30 years with a 10 year balloon.
Monthly Principle & Interest = $1,372.12

I also created a side note for $20,000 (making the total price $170,000), which I promised to release once they had a certificate of occupancy (commonly referred to as a "c of o"). I estimated it would take about that much to get a c of o. This side note was, in essence, a form of insurance. If the buyers really didn't intend to remodel the building, then this would kill the deal immediately. If they were sincere about their intentions to remodel the building, then this temporary side note wouldn't faze them. When I presented them with this little catch, the buyers didn't flinch one iota. I knew, at that moment, their intentions were sincere. As I said before, I estimated a $20,000 expense to get the building up to Code. I didn't care how much *they* actually spent. If they were smart enough to get a c of o by spending only $10,000 dollars, I'd still release the $20,000 side note.

I met the buyers at the building. We discussed the improvements they intended to do, and then we signed the earnest money contract. After my buyers left, I walked over to the hardware store. It'd been only three days since my last visit. There was no one tending the sales counter, so I rang the small chrome service bell. "Who is it?" The gruff voice from the back was oh sooo familiar.

I replied loudly in an effort to be heard from the distance, "A Chinaman from Hell."

When the owner arrived at the cash register I asked her if I could get some copies made. She held out her hand and I handed her my signed contract. The sales price on the front page was unmistakable – $150,000.

Sales Price: $150,000

Copies: $0.05 each

The look on her face: Priceless!

SOLD IT! NOW I HAVE TO BUY IT

I extremely limited my risk by securing an option to purchase the building. The option allowed me not only to freeze the purchase price but also to gain legitimate access and the right to sell the property. As luck would have it, I have found a great buyer in just a few days. Now, things were getting exciting. Once you get the pieces to come together, you have to take action if a good idea is going to transform into a good paycheck. In the beginning, I didn't want this building for $78,000. Now, with an approved buyer in hand, I was pulling out all the stops to make the purchase.

Have you ever laughed at those nothing-down real estate infomercials on late night TV? Well, I'm here to tell you, buying real estate with none of your own money isn't a fantasy. At the risk of sounding like an infomercial, I'm here to tell you: This happens every day. It's a frame of mind. No, not everyone is up to the task, but everyone *could* do it theoretically. Once you realize that you can make a deal on real estate without money, you have *no* price-range limit. You can buy any level of real estate if your deal-structuring skills are up to the task. I'm often asked, "What price-range properties do I seek to purchase?" To that I like to reply, "The half-price range."

I'll buy the Empire State Building if I can get it under contract for half price." Do I have millions in the bank? No. Do I have the ability to borrow millions? Not today. So how am I going to actually buy the Empire State Building even if I do get it under contract for half price? Well, it's all quite simple. I'm going to fax Donald Trump a simple invitation that reads:

Dear Mr. Trump,

I recently secured a contact to purchase the Empire State Building for half of its actual value. Would you care to fly me to New York and buy me lunch?

Regards,
Mitch Stephen

Maybe he'll call or maybe he won't but you get the general idea. You don't have to have *the money* when you have *the contract*. Money gets real easy to find when you have a great deal under wraps. In the above situation, I would be more than willing to give Mr. Trump half the profit if he would be willing to put up the purchase money. If he drove a real hard bargain, I might have to settle for 25%. Maybe he's a real jerk and just offers me a measly *few million dollars* for my contract (at which time I might elect to fax a few other billionaires before I give in to such a petty offer). As long as I have a solid contract, I'm in control.

A few good ideas to live by if you're not laden with cash:

1. 50% of something is better than 100% of nothing.
2. 50% of ten deals with ten partners is much better than 100% of five deals by yourself.
   (To feel this way you have to value network, expertise, and accelerated learning).
3. You can never go broke making a profit.

Back to reality. I'd obtained an option to purchase a building for $78,000 and now I had an acceptable, willing and able buyer under contract to purchase the same building for $150,000. I needed to find $78,000 to buy the property before I could sell it. I started my quest for the purchase money at my local bank where I have a good reputation. I explained my situation to my banker, and he agreed to loan me 85% of the purchase price ($66,300), which meant that I still needed to come up with the other 15% ($11,700) plus closing costs of approximately $2,000.

No, I did not fax Mr. Trump but I did find an investor to put up the $13,700 for the down payment. My investor would receive a 33.333% of the potential profit in return for his risk.

OVERVIEW:

This is how the deal went down.

1. I obtained an option to purchase a building for $78,000 cash plus closing costs for $1.00.
2. I sold the property in advance with the following terms:

$150,000 Sale Price
$0 Down Payment
$150,000 Owner Financed @ 10.50% for thirty years with a ten-year balloon
Monthly Principle & Interest payments = $1,372.12 with a ten-year balloon

3. I gave a local investor 33.333% of the deal for putting up the $13,700 down payment necessary to borrow the purchase money.

END RESULT

We elected to pay the bank $1,300 per month towards our $66,300.00 debt on the building ($78,000 - $11,700 = $66,300). At $1,300 per month, we would pay off the debt to the bank in roughly seven years. This would leave us $72.12 in our account each month for seven years for bookkeeping expenses. Our buyers owed thirty years worth of payments at $1,372.12 with a ten-year balloon, so in years eight, nine, and ten, we would receive $1,372.12 a month *free and clear!* At year eleven, the buyers would have to pay off the balance (the ten-year balloon), which would be $137,263.76. Let's look at the potential profit to be made on this deal.

For seven years we would profit $72.12 per month
7 years X 12 months X $72.12 = +$ 6,058.08
Years 8, 9, 10 we receive the entire payment of $1,372.12
(Because we no longer have a payment to the Bank)
3 years X 12 months X $1,372.12 = +$ 16,465.44
At the end of 10 years the Buyer has agreed to cash us out.
("10 year Balloon" means they pay off the balance due at ten years)
The balance due at the end of 10 years = +$137,263.76

THE TOTAL INCOME OVER TEN YEARS
$159,787.28

Less 33.33% to my investor
<$53,261.89>

TOTAL NET INVESTMENT INCOME TO ME
$106,525.39

Not too shabby for an investment of $1.00 and a few hours of work!

Some people might say that it was foolish to give away 33.333% to the investor for a mere $11,700, but at the time, I had other investments at hand that required my cash. As I stated previously, I was really out of my league dealing with commercial properties, and this particular investor was an expert in that field. I consulted with him regularly during the strategies and negotiations of this transaction. It's absolutely safe to say that I chose this investor for economic reasons as well as for his knowledge. Besides, it's a perfect example of how to make a deal when you *don't* have any cash personally.

THE MORAL OF THE INVESTMENT STORY:

- Don't worry about the purchase money when you have a solid contract at a prime price.
- Ask for an "option" if you want or need to have the deal sold *before* you buy it.
- If you have to take on a cash partner, try to get one who's an expert in what you're trying to purchase.

STORY 4
GAMBLING OR INVESTING?

• • •

Taking advantage of a calculated risk is NOT gambling.

One time I found a four-plex in the central part of town that, apparently, I just couldn't live without. I was investigating the viability of owning the place and had learned some interesting things about the owner of the property, and the overall situation. The seller, David Heirman (yes, I changed his name, too), had inherited this little jewel when his father had passed away. Typical of second-generation heirs, the poor young man just didn't know how to handle the place. It was bad enough that the four-plex was in a rough section of town, but David's situation was even worse. He was also the heir to a tall, wiry thug residing in one of the units who had appointed himself "chief rent collector" and was doing just that: collecting all of the rent and keeping it! It was obvious that this thug had intimidated the new owner so badly that he just wanted out. We call these kinds of sellers *don't wanters*. And Mr. Heirman was a *don't wanter* of the first degree!

Mr. Heirman wanted $70,000 for the place. I did some quick math.

4 units x $650 Rent = $2,600 /month

Now I'm no genius, but right off the bat there seemed to be some cash flow in this deal, and if there was anything I needed more than anything else, it was cash flow!

Mr. Heirman was *not* flexible on his price. He knew he was giving the place away, and I couldn't really argue with him. I did, however, get him to agree to carry the note for me. My problem was he wanted $20,000 as a down payment. I was in no position whatsoever to give the man $20,000 cash for one simple reason—I didn't have $20,000. I went home thinking I wasn't going to be able to buy the place without taking on a money partner, but then I decided to make an offer that suited me before I just gave up. At worst, all he could say was "No," right? I decided to make him an offer that included his asking price of $70,000 but with $0 down payment. Furthermore, I was going to ask for eight months before I had to start making payments. It was a long shot but I put my heart and soul into selling the idea.

First, I rationalized to the seller that I needed to keep my $20,000 so I could do all of the necessary repairs. I couldn't afford to give him $20,000 down payment plus pay for repairs. I reckoned that was easy enough to understand.

Second, I had to explain why I couldn't make payments for eight months. Easy enough, I couldn't afford to pay for the evictions and the taxes and the insurance while I was spending $20,000 and working for free to fix up his collateral. I was going to have to run out all of the tenants because they were all in the way of my remodel. The four-plex would have $0 income for some time.

Heirman was teetering on saying, "Yes," when I pulled out the big guns and pushed him over the top. Once he had agreed that everything I had to do was necessary and that the time and expense calculations were accurate, I simply hit him with one last question.

If I don't do it

YOU are going to have to do it . . .

RIGHT?

That was the straw that broke the landlord's back! The last thing in the world he wanted was to deal with this property and the chief rent collector/thug. I had pointed out the time, money, and effort it was going to take, and it was more than he could imagine doing himself. We signed documents shortly after that. The deal read something like this:

$70,000 Sale Price
$0 Down Payment
$70,000 Finance Amount
10% Annual Interest
240 Monthly Installments
$675.52 Principle & Interest
Amortization & 1st payment to begin in eight months

The minute I got control of the four-plex I went to work. I moved out two tenants right away and began my remodel. I still had a problem. The chief rent collector I inherited when I purchased the property was not paying and *not moving*. He'd already threatened my other tenants about paying the rent to him and that is part of the reason the first two tenants were easy to move. The thug's name was Darby, and we were about to meet for the first time.

It was July in San Antonio and temperatures were reaching well over 100 degrees every day. I pulled up in front of Darby's unit. He was obviously inside taking full advantage of the window-unit air conditioner as it was churning for all it was worth. On the way to the front door I picked up a baseball bat I saw lying in the front yard. Then, I decided to pick up a basketball, too, so I looked more like a "Good Samaritan" than a threat. I knocked on the door with a big friendly smile on my face. Darby answered the door. I stuck out my hand.

ME: Hi Darby. My name is Mitch. I just recently purchased the building and I've stopped by to introduce myself and to make sure everything is working right. I found this stuff in your front yard. May I come in? How is the AC working?

Darby let me in and I made sure to set the basketball and the baseball bat down near the AC unit.

DARBY: AC works fine, man.

ME: Are you sure? Seems to me it has major problems.

DARBY: What's wrong with it?

ME: Don't worry, I can fix it.

Then I reached over and took hold of baseball bat. Raising it up over my head Darby started backing up. Then I brought it down with all the force I could muster. WHAM! I smashed the bat into the perfectly blowing, freezing, cold, window unit.

DARBY: Dude, what are you doing?

ME: I'm fixing this AC unit, Darby!

WHAM! I struck the AC unit again with the bat.

DARBY: Dude, you ain't fixin' nothin'!

WHAM! I struck it again, and the unit began to fail.

ME: Darby, I *am* fixing it! (WHAM!) See how it's starting to run correctly? See? (WHAM!)

DARBY: Man, you crazy!

ME: See Darby? It's running perfect. It's perfect! Now it runs just like you pay!

DARBY: Man, when you leave here I'm gonna burn this bitch to the ground.

I picked up a lighter from off the coffee table and as I got to the door I pitched it to Darby.

ME: You don't have the guts Darby.

And with that I got into my truck and left. The whole drive home I kept looking in my rearview mirror praying for smoke. Unfortunately, I was right. Darby didn't have what it took to be an arsonist.

Darby also didn't have what it took to sleep in the 115-degree heat of his upstairs bedroom either. He was gone the next day.

I normally do everything by the book, notices, court dates, etc., but when it comes to drug dealers, pimps, thieves, and thugs, all bets are off. I've learned to recognize when lawless people can't afford to call the law on you. When a tenant can't call the law because they're wanted, the landlord can push limits. I've also learned to run criminal background checks on tenants before I commit to the time and expense of a formal eviction. Nine times out of ten, if they're really into the illegal stuff, these thugs have warrants or parole violations. Once I confirm they're wanted by the authorities, I just let the police pick them up, or sometimes, I'll stop by and warn the thugs that if they don't leave *tonight*, the police will be there in the morning to exercise their warrants. I have an abandonment clause in my leases that allows me to take possession and dispose of their possessions if the property is unattended for more than three days while behind on the rent. This makes for a very quick and affordable eviction! During the time I met Darby, I hadn't figured out that tactic yet. I probably could've saved myself a perfectly good window unit. I'm willing to bet Darby had warrants for his arrest.

I had the four-plex cleaned up and leased out way ahead of schedule. Within two months, I was 100% occupied with $2,600 worth of deposits and collecting that $2,600 per month in rent. The total rehab had only cost me $12,000. Come to find out, it really didn't need all that much. I had turned the place around much quicker and for far less than I'd originally proposed. (Who'd have guessed?) It was a good thing, too, because Tommi was about to find the credit card I had used to pay for everything.

I was taking a shower when I heard Tommi screaming bloody murder. She'd gotten to the mailbox before me and was opening the mail. Seems Wells Fargo showed a balance of $12,000 as our credit card balance. I tried to explain to her that I had six months before I had to make the first four-plex payment and that I was going to be collecting $2,600 per month for the next six months. Six months x $2,600 = $15,600 but she just wasn't up to doing math at that moment. All Tommi understood was that I'd put $12,000 on our credit cards without her permission. Before it was all over she had her bags packed and I was standing outside the door of her car.

ME: Tommi, you're being completely irrational about this and if you'll give me sixty seconds I'll explain exactly why.

Tommi looked down at her watch.

TOMMI: Okay. Ready. Set. GO!

ME: This isn't *gambling*, but *you* think it is. So I'm going to put this into terms you can understand. Pretend I'm at a poker table and I've placed a bet for $12,000 on the table. I've discarded two cards, and I'm due to draw my two new cards. And you're leaving *before* I get my cards! I mean, what if I win? You're going to be gone, and I think I'm going to win! At least wait to leave *after* I lose. Leave after I lose—not before! Watch what happens first!

Lucky for me, things went pretty much as planned. Within a reasonable amount of time I had the four-plex all fixed up and rented out. The money was coming in, and I had all the credit card debt paid off. Tommi had settled down, but she still wasn't thrilled with all of this investor stuff. I quietly put the place up for sale and had a contract to sell the property in no time at all. On the day of closing, I called my wife and asked if she could sign some papers at the title company. She figured I was buying more properties and it took a little work to get her to agree. I did not, however, tell her that I was selling the four-plex. Eventually she agreed to go sign papers.

I had told the closing agent of my plight and asked if I could slide in a document of my own for my wife to sign right before she received the proceeds check from the sale. The closing agent thought it was cute and agreed to pull the document out at the very last minute before handing over the check. Meanwhile, I found a trophy shop to make that document. I created a special, gold ribbon embossed, official certificate looking paper scribed with some very personal words for Tommi.

Tommi showed up at the closing. Her grimace slowly turned to a pleasant smile as she learned that we were *not* buying, we were selling. If there's one thing in the world Tommi knows, she knows how to find the bottom line. There, as plain as day, it read: $33,000 PROFIT! When Tommi had signed all of the papers, the closing agent excused herself as she went to get the check. Upon returning, the agent apologized and said that there was one more document that still needed to be signed. She slid my little "official" document across the table for Tommi to execute. The document read:

I, Tommi Stephen, do remember the day I had my bags packed.

I won't tell you exactly what Tommi said after reading this, but I will tell you that she left with the check, and she did *not* sign the document. Nevertheless, it was a very good day!

STORY 5
CHEAP LOTS – LOTS OF INCOME

• • •

There's always a way to make it work.

Recently, I made a great deal on about sixteen lots on the south side of San Antonio. I tend to take the Internet for granted, but when I think back about the best deals I ever made, I realize that most of them have come from the Internet in one form or another. Now I guess you could say it's that way because that's where I choose to focus my attentions. The truth of the matter is I've done about every kind of marketing that makes sense, and you just can't beat the Internet's bang for the buck. At any rate, this deal racked up about $108,000 in less than one year. I know for sure it never would have happened if it hadn't been for the World Wide Web.

A partner and I had been experiencing some success building little 1,200 square foot houses on scattered lots in and about the south side of San Antonio. I liked the little business and my partner so we decided to crank it up a notch or two. We decided to put out the word that we were looking to buy some lots. What is the first thing I do when I decide to "put out the word"? I go to my computer and send out a well-written message.

I've taken great care to collect an extremely large amount of email addresses pertaining to the real estate community in my market. Today, I have more than 8,000 realtors' email addresses and another 1,800 email addresses of real estate investors. All of them are actively involved in real estate in the San Antonio area where I live and work. Because I've learned to network through these email addresses I am reasonably famous in my town for doing what I do. I invest in real estate! It's the big fish in a small pond syndrome but that's what you need when you're searching for deals.

On this one particular day, I decided to hit my entire investor list first. I normally don't like to send out more than 250 emails at a time, but I was *really* eager to buy some lots and I'd freed up my time to do just that. I honed a message that looked like this:

ATTENTION INVESTORS

Mitch Stephen is looking for scattered lots to build small, affordable houses on. If you come across unwanted lots in the lesser parts of town, I am interested in speaking with you about them.

The lots must be at least 4,000 Sq. Ft.

The lots must be at least 50' wide.

I am ready to buy today!

Mitch Stephen

210-669-XXXX

Mitch@Homes2Go.NET

Within about five minutes, I had constructed the message and sent out an email to the 1,800 or so investors in San Antonio. Now, I'm going to take a little side step here and use this next paragraph to drive home a message to all of you out there.

Where else in the world can you hit hundreds, even thousands, of people in your direct market with a personal message within five minutes for virtually FREE? If you think I'm a bit over the top when I get excited about Internet marketing, well that's why! There's no other way to reach so many in an instant. So many of the investors I know out there are missing this opportunity completely.

Now, where were we? Oh yeah. I was trying to buy some lots.

With my email campaign delivered, I figured I'd have some lots in inventory within a week or so, and I was right. I didn't pick up as many as I'd hoped to, but I did have three on the hook right away. I was buying lots for $8,000 to $12,000 each. They were standard lots of the minimum size, 50' x 100' on average. It was a fair price, not great but not bad either.

I used the same message but modified it for realtors. Compared to the investor community, realtors are a bit touchy. So, when it comes to the realtors, I methodically send out 250 realtor emails a day instead of hitting the entire group at one time. Let's do the math.

I have about 8,000 realtor email addresses, I send out 250 a day, I don't have to create a new message for thirty-two days. Actually, it's even longer than that because I don't send out emails on the weekends or on holidays. (I'm not in the office.)

Why don't I blast all the realtors at once? I actually spread it out for several reasons.

1. I don't want to create more leads than I can respectfully handle. Nothing will hurt your business faster than asking for help and then *not* responding when help calls you.

Even if a realtor brings you a deal that is a complete loser, you need to take the time to respectfully decline. Imagine a person holding out their hand to shake hands with you and then you decline to extend your own hand. That's what it's like if you don't reply to an email that has responded to your request.

2. I don't want to beat my list of realtors up every day because they'll soon block me—or request to be *removed* from my list. Nobody likes to get hit with an endless barrage of emails day after day. *You* don't like it and *they* don't like it. *Nobody* likes it!
3. At the most, I want to stay in front of my network every three to four weeks with a different, viable message. By presenting myself every three or four weeks, I have a better chance of staying in the forefront of their minds. "Top of mind awareness" is what I want to accomplish. When people in my network run across a deal, I want them to think of me, *Mitch Stephen*.
4. Some realtors in the community tend to frown on an investor if they think they're available to every other agent out there. I don't know why that is, but it's true. When confronted with agents who want me to sign up with them exclusively, I always ask them, "My dear Mr. Agent, could you live with only *one* client?" If they don't understand where I'm coming from after that question, I move on without them.

HINT: It works against you if you put a multitude of email addresses from one real estate office in the same distribution list. That's another reason why I have thirty-two folders for 8,000 realtors, 250 email addresses to each folder. By having this many folders, I can easily spread an office with fifteen agents into separate email distribution lists. This way, all the agents in one office won't get the same email on the same day. If fifteen agents in one office get the same email on the same day, they'll stand around the coffee machine and cuss you for asking all of them for an opportunity to work with you. Go figure!

Imagine how easy it is for me to generate leads! Imagine how many people recognize my name after a few months! Imagine how many people think of me during the day as deals come across their desks! I simply go to my site, select another 250 realtors, copy and paste the same message into the email and hit send. I can send that same message to a 250 different realtors a day for well over a month before I have to change the message. It takes about thirty seconds a day to send out that message. I do it first thing in the morning before I start my daily adventures. Sometime during the day or in the evening, I check my email in box for favorable responses. If I have a lot of responses, I won't send another email message until I've contacted every responder and opted in or out of their proposal or offer.

As for my email about my desire to buy small lots in the south side of San Antonio, it wasn't until about forty-five days later that I got the reply I'd been looking for. I received an email from an investor named David whom I'd met at the local real estate investment club, San Antonio Real Estate Investment Association (SAREIA), many, many months before. (I can't tell you how many email addresses I harvest from my local RE club, but I'd guess it is well over 800.)

David wanted to know if I was still looking for lots. He went on to explain that he had received my email several weeks ago and that he'd saved it just in case he ran across what I was looking for. As luck would have it, he'd bumped into a family trying to settle an estate. They needed to sell sixteen small lots on the south side of San Antonio to close out the estate.

I responded with a phone call to David, and he explained the situation. The estate had sixteen lots they needed to sell as soon as possible. Selling the lots was the last step in closing out an arduous estate. He asked me how much I could pay per lot and still come out good on the deal. I told him that I could pay up to $12,000 a lot, but for it to be a *good* deal for me it needed to be around $8,000. David was a smart, shrewd investor. He knew that if he gave me a *good deal*, I'd be more likely to strike and strike fast. He also knew he could get the lots at a good price. David asked me if I would be upset if he negotiated a deal to purchase the lots for $4,000 and then sold them to me for the $8,000. I told him, as I had stated before, that $8,000 would be a very good deal for me. After all, he offered me the best price in the range I'd offered to pay. He settled for $8,000 when I told him I'd pay as much as $12,000. I never begrudge the amount of money anyone else makes on the deal if I am happy with my position. I agreed to buy the lots at $8,000 if he could get a contract for less, no matter how much less.

Later that week, David had consummated a deal with the estate at exactly his target price of $4,000 per lot. I contracted to buy the lots for $8,000 if everything was fine legally and if I could get a title commitment on each lot. Let's do the math.

David would contract the sixteen lots at $4,000 each, total strike price of $64,000.
I would agree to buy the sixteen lots at 8,000 each, a total price of $128,000.

David had set himself up to make a cool $64,000 in one transaction covering sixteen lots, and I would have sixteen lots at a killer price to build affordable homes on. Did it bother me that David was going to make so much so fast? Not in the least. I would make my money too, eventually.

We had already met with some success building two houses from the same set of plans on two separate lots. We intended to build that same house yet again on every lot David was offering to sell me. Obviously, my building costs would be very predictable. Our contractors had already absorbed the learning curve and, therefore, would be able to build the new homes in a cookie-cutter fashion. The previous experience told me that the homes would be sold before the paint was even dry, and that I could expect about a $20,000 minimum profit per home. Let's do that math:

Sixteen homes x $20,000 profit each = $320,000

Needless to say, Carlos and I were very happy with the deal. We figured to complete the building and the sales of the homes in about twelve months. Both of us were ecstatic about the location of the lots. They were in exactly the type of lower-income areas we were looking for and they were close to a very poplar, main thoroughfare. I signed the commitment letter for David immediately and awaited closing instructions.

Things took a turn for the worse when we discovered that the lots were smaller than the size requested in my first email to my investor list. In my email to solicit lots, I had asked that the lots be at least 50' x 100' wide and a minimum of 4,000 square feet in size. These lots measured only 25' x 100' and that was way short of what we needed. I couldn't build a decent home on a lot that was only 25' wide. Furthermore, the city code wouldn't allow anyone to build a house on lots that small.

I called David and explained to him that no one could build on a lot that was 25' x 100' and that it would take two lots to build one house. He acknowledged my previous email and that I had, in fact, requested lots that were at least 50' x 100' to build on.

As luck would have it, many of the lots were contiguous. There was a group of lots on the main street and a group of lots across the block and yet another group just down the street from there. The lots could easily be paired up to create eight lots measuring 50' x 100' and thus we made a plan "B." David would go back to the estate and re-negotiate the deal, explaining to the executrix of the estate that their sales price would have to be cut in half because the lots were too small to build on individually. My hat was off to David.

The big problem with all of this negotiating and then re-negotiating was that the estate consisted of thirteen heirs. Thirteen heirs had to agree! I have dealt with my fair share of estates and, believe me when I tell you, it's hard enough to get two heirs to agree on a sale, much less thirteen heirs. Still, David persisted and, several weeks later, I had a revised contract in my hand, and we were off to the races yet again. Now, the math looked like this.

David had contracted to buy the sixteen lots for $2,000 each (down from $4,000 each). It would take two lots to equal one building site, so the eight building sites would cost me $8,000 each. We had lost 50% of my potential sites, but we were still at a price per building site to be excited about.

David had re-contracted with the estate to buy sixteen lots for $2,000 each, which meant we'd obtain eight building sites for a grand total of $64,000

My partner and I were down to eight lots to build on instead of sixteen, but we were still happy with the prospect of building eight homes at a profit of $20,000 each.
Eight homes x $20,000 profit each = $160,000 profit

Everything seemed to move quickly after that. Soon it was time to close and I was off to the title company to sign docs. It was turning out to be a routine closing when, suddenly, the escrow agent asked me to sign a disclaimer acknowledging that the lots were situated over the Kelly Plume.

Now, exactly what is the Kelly Plume? Well, as it turns out, the Kelly Plume is a regional water table that has been affected by chemicals used by the Kelly Air Force Base to clean and rebuild jet engines. A chemical used by the Air Force beginning in the 1950s (a practice that ended years ago) had been steadily soaking into the ground and had affected a water table some eighty feet below the surface. Over the years, it had spread. It had permeated out under numerous neighborhoods throughout the south side. Apparently, it was gaining some media attention at the time. They wanted me to sign off on a disclaimer and, more specifically, they wanted me to acknowledge some newspaper articles that proclaimed this as potential problem.

Needless to say, this deal started choking then and there. All the paper signing stopped at that moment, and the deal was soon left dead on the table. I cited undo duress as my reason for not closing because there had been no mention of this in the events leading up to the closing. Nobody argued my reasoning.

I called David to tell him of the unfortunate events. As you can imagine, he was deflated as well. After all, he was a day away from receiving a nice paycheck for his entrepreneurial efforts. Now, all was lost. Nonetheless, David was a consummate pro. He took the change of events in stride and agreed that we had done the logical thing by *not* closing the deal. It was a relief that David understood, because the last thing anyone wants to do is contract for a deal and not close. It deserves repeating, David was a consummate pro.

It took me a day or two to get over the loss. Never letting deals die easily, I began to rationalize the prospect of going ahead with the deal.

1. We could build the homes at a cost of $60,000 total investment (land included) and sell them with a disclaimer acknowledging the Plume. It was a reasonable thought because I could feasibly explain away the concerns. The city, or anyone else for that matter, did *not* use that water. Every restaurant, YMCA, school, hospital, and household in the region used water piped from a completely different source (the Edwards Aquifer). In fact, the only way that specific water would be a problem was if someone actually drilled a well that tapped the contaminated water. People were not going to drill a private well in an inner city that offers clean water at the faucet. The deal was still over stressed. I would have too much money invested to take that kind of risk as *the builder.*
2. We could buy the lots and sell the lots *only*. If we didn't have to build a house on the lots, we would only be into each building site for $4,000. We could possibly sell the lots for as much as $15,000 each (maybe), but still, it didn't meet my risk-reward comfort level.

Carlos and I did our best to consider all options, but as far as we were concerned, the deal died at the closing. There was nothing left to do about it. Having to sell a new home as the builder with a disclaimer was too much. The financial liability was too great. If we were going to sell lots only, we'd have to pay less.

I can't tell you how many days passed after that, maybe a month or two or three, but one day I got yet another call from David. He told me that the estate was desperate to sell the lots and bring an end to their dilemma. They wanted me to make an offer. I told David that

I did not want to be insensitive but if I had to make an offer I would offer the estate $500 per building site ($4,000 Total). Plus, we agreed I would pay David an additional $4,000 for his efforts. My total investment for the eight building sites would be $8,000 ($1,000 per site). My thoughts were this.

1. People living in that area knew that the Plume was not affecting their lives.
2. We could definitely sell the building sites for something over $1,000 per building site, even if we had to give a disclaimer. My immediate calculations said we could possibly sell the sites for as much as $15,000 to someone who understood #1 above, even with the disclaimer.
3. If we could not sell the lots *today,* we could sell them in the future. Clean up plans for the plume were being worked on, be it in a year or ten years from now, and the $8,000 we had invested would pay us back before all was said and done.
4. If we lost $8,000 ($4,000 each) it would not be the end of the world.

With that mindset, I consummated a deal with David. David managed to strike yet another deal with the estate, and finally we all got what we had agreed too. In the proceeding months, I sold all of the eight building sites with *full disclosures* for roughly $15,000 each. Once again, let's do the math.

We had $8,000 invested in eight building sites ($4,000 to the estate and $4,000 to David). Because we were offering such a low price, we had to incur all of the closing costs, which totaled an additional $4,000. Including the closing costs we had $12,000 invested in eight building sites.

We sold the eight sites for $15,000 each.
Eight x $15,000 = $120,000
Less the $12,000 investment
Total profit = $108,000

Of course we had some advertising and some sign expenses and some gas and some time involved, as well, but let's not trip over the pennies on the way to the dollars. It was a very good deal. And the moral of the story?

1 *Never* let a deal die on your side of the table. Because David exercised that theory, too, we were able to make a huge profit from it.
2. Using the Internet to find deals works!

SIDE NOTE: I never expected that the building sites would actually sell for what they eventually sold for. I had a hunch that they could be worth as much as $15,000 per site but, given the fact that I had to sell with such an ominous disclaimer, I wasn't certain what would happen. The advertised price was at the top of our expectations knowing that the price could be reduced if the market was staunch. We had purchased the lots at a very low price because we were afraid of what the local sentiment would be. That low purchase price (low risk) made the deal fly. This time, my calculated risk worked out better than I had planned—by a long shot.

STORY 6
OFF THE COAST OF AUSTRALIA

• • •

With the Internet, the world is your marketplace.

Having your very own office open to the world 24/7 is *not* just a bunch of hype. Don't think for one minute that people all over the world aren't shopping the Internet at all hours of the day and night. In other parts of the world, the sun is up while it's down in your town. If you aren't open for business on the Internet arena, you won't get any of those customers.

This particular deal was going to prove hands down that my cyber office, my website, was worth every penny I'd ever put into it. This deal happened because I was open for business in the wee hours of the morning, and I was available for anyone in the world with an Internet connection.

This story begins with a man, Mr. Randy Randall, working off the coast of Australia on an oil rig. As a major means of communication, the oil company provided Internet services and a computer for the workers so that they could keep in contact with their family and friends in their off hours. These men are often out at sea for weeks, even months. During Mr. Randall's time off, he was using the computer to help solve a problem.

His problem was that his mother desperately needed to get on Medicaid but, before she could qualify for that assistance, she needed to rid herself of all of her assets. Randy was trapped in the ocean waters miles from civilization. To make matters worse, his aging mother, in all her dementia, had given his heroin-addicted brother power of attorney over her last remaining asset, her homestead.

Mr. Randall found me on the Internet and emailed me about his dilemma. He explained that his drug-addicted brother, Virgil, was well aware that the property needed to be sold. In fact, Virgil was trying to sell the property in his own little messed up way but couldn't seem to get the job done. The mother was in terrible shape, and the convalescent home where she resided was threatening to put her bed on the street any day now.

Mr. Randall was in complete agony over his mother's situation. He explained to me that he had done everything he knew to do to help his poor mother. He had spent everything he had in an effort to make sure that his dear mother had decent care and that she would rest comfortably until her time came. However, Virgil had found his way to the money and had used it to buy more drugs. Working on the rig was the only way Mr. Randall knew to make money. The convalescent home was costing him $3,500 per month, and no other job he was skilled at could come close to paying her expenses plus his own. Because of Virgil, he had fallen behind and couldn't catch up fast enough.

I ask Mr. Randall what his goals were and what would be the perfect solution. This is what he told me:

"I want my mother to be comfortable. I want her in a decent place. I've tried but I haven't done well by her—and I am sick over it. Everything would have been fine, but I underestimated the evil of my brother's addiction. Now, I'm broke and stuck on this rig, trying to get money that's coming too slow. Even if I get the money, I can't send it home. My mother has lost her mental abilities completely, and my brother can't be trusted to be even near the money.

"I don't want anything out of this. I don't care about the money from my mother's home. I want my mother on Medicaid. In order to get this done, my brother has to take the home from my mother and then sell it to someone. He has the power of attorney and all the legal rights to do it. Only *he* can do it. The problem is this: Virgil is a drug addict, and he can't hold a thought or a rational intention long enough to get it done. I need *you* to go find Virgil at my mother's address. I need *you* to buy that house from Virgil, using Virgil's Power of Attorney. When it's done, *you* need to let the state know that my mother's estate has been dissolved so that they can begin to assist her."

I asked Mr. Randall how much he thought I should pay for this property that I hadn't even seen yet. He said it didn't matter to him. Virgil and I had to decide. And then he said something I'll never forget. Mr. Randall said, "The less you give Virgil, the better chance he has of surviving. Anything Virgil gets from the transaction will be spent on heroin, and I don't know how much more he can take. If you can get him to sell you the property for $1.00 then buy it from him for $1.00. No matter what you give him, it will be gone in an instant. I'm actually afraid that if he gets too much money he'll overdose."

That being said, Mr. Randall gave me directions to his mother's home and assured me that I would find his brother, Virgil, there. He was right.

When I arrived at the property, I was stunned at the poverty amongst such beauty. The property was just off the main road and consisted of fourteen acres, two large stone houses, and one smaller stone guest house. I immediately saw beyond the trash and neglect. The setting was beautiful. The oak trees were huge and tall and everything was positioned perfectly below the green canopies created by those massive trunks and limbs.

As I got to the crest of the hill, a wonderful view of the lake came into sight. For a moment I could feel how this place must have felt in the good ol' days, back when Mr. and Mrs. Randall were young and vibrant and in love, with two beautiful, healthy sons (Randy and Virgil) in the yard, watching them play as they sipped lemonade on the front porch. How wonderful this home must have been in its time. I imagined it filled with love and happiness and sunny days, better days.

I was almost right there with the young Randalls when I was startled out of my daydream by the slam of a screen door. A voice from behind me demanded answers, "Who the hell are you and why are you on my property?"

I turned to see a very tall man dressed only in some ragged shorts walking towards me. He had bags under his eyes and his wildly contorted head of hair suggested he had just gotten out of bed. He was approaching me fast with not-so-friendly steps. I hurried to explain, "I'm Mitch. Mitch Stephen. I've been talking to your brother via email, and he says you could use some help. I'm here to see if I can help you."

He looked at me with suspicion. "My brother never helped me in his life so you better start tellin' me the truth real soon."

I thought to myself I'd better keep talking. "Your brother told me that your mother is in a bad situation. He asked me if I would come here and buy the property from *you* so that she could get her Medicaid assistance. Does any of this make sense to you?"

Vigil indirectly answered my question. "You got cash?"

I had been warned by Mr. Randall in his email, but the harsh reality was coming into full view. I was dealing with the "Black Sheep" of the family. To make matters worse, he was a Black Sheep with *power*.

I've seen this before. It's some type of phenomena that probably happens to more families than we think. Everyone is doing quite well in the pecking order of life except for this one family member. And this one family member thinks the other family members owe them something. Black Sheep see themselves as victims. Black Sheep never take responsibility for themselves. Black Sheep are Black Sheep because they label themselves the Black Sheep. Black Sheep are usually no problem until they get into a position of power. Virgil was aware of his position of power. I could tell by the way he was wielding his words. Virgil was giving no time or effort to be polite or courteous because for once in his life he controlled something.

On that day, Virgil controlled his mother's property, which put him in control of his mother's disposition, which in turn, put him in control of his older brother's emotions. For a while, he even began to control me.

I can almost tell you how the rift between these two brothers got started. I have no doubt that the older brother had pleaded time and time again with the younger brother, trying to help. I can almost guarantee you that the older brother had bailed the younger brother out so many times that it was admirable. Virgil's addictions had blinded him. Virgil perceived the benevolent actions and thoughtful scoldings by his older brother as hate and not as *love*. There's your wall, the wall between the healthy brother and the sick brother.

To navigate between these two siblings, I was going to have to tread lightly, especially on Virgil's side of the road. I could have been wrong but until further data proved different, this was how I pegged the two personalities:

Mr. Randall (older brother) - rational, self-sufficient

Virgil (younger brother) - irrational, needy, black-sheep syndrome

So, where were we? Oh yes, we're at the point in a conversation where Virgil was inquiring as to the color of my money. "Do you have cash?" Virgil asked. I was nodding my head as the smell of his approaching body took my words away.

Impulsively I stuck out my hand to greet him. He had gotten so close to me by now I didn't know what else to do. He smelled so bad I didn't even want to think about where his hands had been or how long it had been since he'd washed them. At best his fingernails were black at the ends because they had dirt under them. I had to fight to not grimace as our palms touched. I told myself to get over it, and so I did, immediately.

Virgil's handshake was hugely unimpressive. It was like squeezing a dead fish. Right or wrong, I've always associated a person's handshake with their character. Virgil's handshake was empty, lifeless, disappointing. His handshake could have changed my opinion of him somewhat but, instead, it confirmed what I already suspected.

After much wrangling we finally agreed on a price, and we signed a contract.

As it is with most closings of magnitude it took awhile for things to come together. The problem with closing quickly was compounded by some very different realities that I had never faced before.

1. I was dealing with a heroin addict whose very interaction with anyone (like the title company or his mother's health providers) could send the deal into the gutter.
2. The heat of Texas summer was at its peak. Temperatures were reaching into the hundreds, and humidity was almost unbearable. Virgil was living on the property without electricity or water. The toilets had long since been filled to the brim and the bathtub had become the second choice for relief. There were flies by the thousands. Living conditions were horrid. The conditions were enough to make a heroin addict worse than irrational. Many times Virgil was livid. He simply would not (or chose not to) understand why I couldn't just give him cash, *right now!* Sometimes he'd scream at me for money. It was difficult to maintain my composure.
3. The property hadn't been surveyed in years, and the real estate boom had everyone waiting weeks for services. Surveys were no exception.
4. The senile mother was on the verge of getting put out onto the street by the hospice where she was staying. The money sent by Randall had never made it to the rest home, and the bills were months behind. I was constantly aware there was an innocent old woman who couldn't take care of her own well being, and the clock was ticking. As if all of this weren't bad enough.
5. The title company wanted a "CYA" document to be signed by Mr. Randall in front of a U.S. notary public. Normally not a problem, but he was on an oil rig off the coast of Australia, and the closest U.S. Embassy wasn't close or easy to get to from an oil rig.

Yes, this deal wasn't going to happen as fast as I thought it would. I had already made the mistake of catering to Virgil's daily demands for rations. I thought the closing would only take a day or two when I made that decision, but now it looked like it was going to take a few weeks. Virgil had already threatened to pull the deal. He called me at all hours of the day and night demanding money (probably because he needed heroin). I never gave him money. As an act of charity, I did continue to take food in ice chests now and then, but I must admit, I'd tell him I was out of town from time to time to keep him off my back because he was so relentless with his position of power.

I called a friend for a favor to get the survey done almost over night. I continued to email Mr. Randall, and after some ten or fifteen emails, he finally accepted the fact that he was going to have to fly to an embassy and sign a single piece of paper in front of a U.S. notary public. I called the mother's rest home and assured them that I was *very capable* of closing the deal and that I would have Virgil sign a piece of paper giving the title company the right to take the money they were owed out at closing and send it to them. Everything was moving in the right direction, except for Virgil.

Virgil was demanding a meeting or else. I figured something had to happen so I went to meet him. He tried the same thing again. He demanded money or the deal was off. I tried to rationalize with him, but I knew before I started that wasn't going to work. Even so, I gave it a try. I told Virgil that there weren't a handful of people that could pull this deal off faster than me. No bank in the world would loan money on a property the condition his was in and even if they would, institutions were notoriously slow. Thirty to forty-five days to get a new loan would be normal. I had $80,000 *cash* and I was ready to close, but we were all at the mercy of other people right now. Virgil got very upset, and his tone escalated. I couldn't take it anymore. I had to take his power away from him or he was going to run me into the ground. I looked at him squarely in his eyes and spoke softly but very sternly and with authority.

"Virgil, you are *really* starting to upset me. I have bought and brought you food and water. I have ordered surveys that I've paid for. I have gotten your brother to fly to an embassy and sign papers. I've made arrangements with your mother's caregivers so they won't put her onto the street. I have bent over backwards for you. Furthermore, I am doing everything as fast as I can for your poor mother's sake. You don't seem to appreciate any of that, so I am going to tell you how the cow is going to eat the cabbage. I have a contract at the title company signed by *you* in your own handwriting. I will not be treated this way by you any longer. If you don't close with me when its time to close, then you will *not* close this property with *anyone* for a long, long time."

In an effort to trump his undeserved power and negate his position, I put forth a calculated bluff that actually had merit. "I will take you to court and tie up this property for *years* before you can sell. Do you understand me, Virgil?"

I am *not* a litigious person, and this option wasn't going to be exercised because of my compassion for his deteriorating mother. Still, it was the only card I had. A man wielding power only understands superior power. I played my card and it worked.

In a single moment of clarity, Virgil apologized to me. He became humane to me for the first time. For the first time, I could see this deal closing and the mother spending her last days in some level of comfort that Medicaid could provide.

Figuring that Virgil's money management skills weren't so great, I tried to get him to accept payments instead of cash at closing. My reasoning was that he would have an income for a long, long time to come. It would have been good for my business but more importantly, I felt it would be the best thing for him. My words fell on deaf ears. Unfortunately, he pressed for a lump sum of cash, and thus he got it. If I had succeeded in arranging payments he would still have an income today and for years to come.

All the while, during all of the events described above, I had been marketing my position on the property. I actually had the property contracted for sale before I closed. Shortly after my heart-to-heart conversation with Virgil I simultaneously bought and sold the property on the same day. Everyone got what they wanted, and Virgil walked out of closing with a very large some of money. I never saw Virgil again but about a month later I heard from credible sources that he was broke. I hated to hear that but it was foretold by Mr. Randall, and I had figured as much.

Today, under the new ownership, the old house is a show place. The people who purchased it did a wonderful job restoring it back to its natural potential and beyond. A lot of things happened during and after that transaction—some good and some sad. I profited $92,000 (much better than I thought I'd do). It all started with a Google search and an email sent to me from somewhere off the coast of Australia. Once again, I pose this question to investors across the nation and the world: Are *you* open to the world 24/7, 365 days a year? You might be well served to visit:

www.Homes2Go.NET/FreeVideo

STORY 7
OLD DOGS – NEW TRICKS

• • •

Finding the owner of an abandoned property.

I've found that if I don't attend at least two seminars per year I start to get stagnant. The seminars aren't cheap, but I never fail to profit from the knowledge I gain in the end. You can learn as much or more from the other attendees as you can from the speaker himself. In one particular seminar I learned a few things not on the agenda.

I once attended a Ron Le Grand seminar in Florida where about 250 people showed up. It's typical for most speakers to start out their three-day seminar with informal introductions and a sizing up of the audience. Ron likes to ask, "How many of you are looking to purchase your very first property?" At this point, the majority of the hands in the room will go up. "How many of you have purchased at least one property?" Another set of hands go up, but fewer. "How many of you buy three houses a month?" even fewer hands go up.

At this seminar, by the time he had gotten to, "Who buys eight houses or more per month?" I was the last guy in the room with his hand up. Ron asked me to stand up and introduce myself.

ME: My name is Mitch Stephen and I'm from San Antonio, Texas.

RON: Mitch, how many houses do you buy per year?

ME: Last year I bought exactly 150 homes.

A slight gasp ran through the crowd and I was beaming with pride.

RON: You're an idiot!

It took me a second to reassess what I thought he had just said. Yep, I heard him right. Ron Le Grand had just called me an idiot in front of 250 people! The air was tense and a few nervous laughs could be heard scattered throughout the room but most everyone including myself didn't quite know how to respond. Luckily I regained my composure.

ME: Gees, Ron, don't hold back. Tell me what you really think!

The crowd laughed and everyone was grateful the silence had been broken. I felt their relief *ten fold!* Ron lit up and then gave me an overdue accolade.

RON: There are a lot of you in this room who would be truly blessed if you were as dumb as this guy.

Ron went on to explain that I had mastered the art of quantity but suggested that my life would be better if I mastered quality. His advice was that I buy *only* the cream of the crop, control my expenses, sell my homes faster, and make more money off of 50 homes than I had made on 150 homes. To this day I don't think in terms of volume when it comes to buying and selling houses.

The next day, Ron was talking about how to find the owners of abandoned properties. He went on about checking the tax rolls, talking to the neighbors, weaseling information from the mailman, on to the more expensive ideas like getting a skip trace done on the last known owner all the way through hiring a private detective. At the end of the section he asked the audience if anyone had any other way to find the owners of abandoned properties. After the pummeling I had taken the day before, I couldn't believe I was raising my hand again. Ron's face lit up when he saw it was me.

RON: Well, well, well, the *150-houses-per-year man* knows a technique we've never heard of before. Mr. Stephen, are you telling me that after all of these years and thousands of seminars that you have something I haven't heard?

My thoughts: (Why, oh why, oh why did I raise my hand?)

ME: Did you tell us everything you know about finding owners of abandoned houses?

RON: Yes, that's what I get paid for…to tell you everything I've learned over the years.

ME: Well then, I guess I *do* have a way you haven't heard of.

RON: Bless us with your knowledge, Mr. Stephen. How do you find the owner?

ME: I put a "FOR SALE" sign in the front yard of the abandoned home with *my* phone number on it. The owner calls me every time."

The audience reacted with a "Wow" kind of rumble, and then Ron broke the sound barrier.

RON: You do WHAT?

ME: I put a plastic sign, a hand-written plastic sign, in the front yard that reads: FOR SALE and *my* phone number. The owner calls me every time!

RON: When the owner finally calls you, is he *upset?*

ME: Well, the first time I did it, the owner was so mad that I couldn't deal with him, so I have since modified my technique.

RON: What do you do now?

ME: I put a very small question mark after the words FOR SALE. That way, when the owner calls very mad I can explain. I'm not trying to sell your home. I'm asking you if your home is for sale. Didn't you see the question mark I put on the sign? The sign reads FOR SALE? 210-669-xxxx. I've been trying to find you for weeks. I really want to help you with this house. I saw the city inspector out here last week writing something. Have you gotten assessed a clean-up bill from the city yet? Have you ever considered selling this old house?

RON: And the owner calls you *every* time?

ME: Well, one time I kept the sign out for three months and no one ever called.

RON: So what did you do?

ME: I moved a renter in and I've been collecting $800 per month for the last six months. It's called adverse possession.

RON: You're collecting rent on a home you don't own?

ME: Yeah, I like adverse possession because it has a very high profit margin.

RON: I bet! You have no cost in the property. But I imagine you better be very well versed in the state laws governing this subject correct?

ME: Yes, I don't suggest you try this if you are just starting out.

RON: (Looking towards the back of the room) Give this man a coupon for a free dinner at Ruth's Chris Steak House. I have never heard of that technique for finding the owner of an abandoned property. I assure you, Mr. Stephen that technique will be in the next issue of this course and in the next book.

Later that evening, Ron joined my friends and me for dinner at Ruth's Chris Steak House. The steak was almost as good as my redemption that day in class.

STORY 8
DO WHAT YOUR PIE HOLE SAYS

• • •

Don't let your bulldog mouth overload your poodle dog butt.

Keeping everything on the up and up is the most important thing. I find that the best way to keep friends, clients, family relationships, business associates, and private and institutional lenders is to tell it like it is. You don't have to be disrespectful or rude. Sometimes, I don't like how it is and sometimes they don't like how it is, but the truth is always the best policy. Walking with the truth is always better than running from lies.

Another thing I really appreciate as a businessperson is when people who do what they say they're going to do. Being trustworthy means you do what you say. You don't have to be wealthy to be trustworthy. You don't have to be a businessman to be trustworthy. Being trustworthy means you have a mouth that makes commitments, and you have two arms, two legs, a heart, and a butt that gets whatever your mouth said it was going to do—done. My mouth has caused my legs to walk in directions I really didn't want to go. My mouth has caused my arms to lift a lot of pounds I really didn't want to lift. My mouth has caused my heart to do the opposite of what my selfish mind wanted to do.

Now and then in my investing career, I've had a house that just won't go away. One particular house, in a subdivision named Garden Ridge, kept coming back to me on a regular basis. I had sold the home-owner financed three times but, each time, the buyers would *not* do what they'd promised—*make the payments!* By the time the third would-be buyer moved out, I had a bad attitude about the house. Don't get me wrong. The house was fine. Everything in the house worked. It was a nice house, built well, with plenty of acreage and trees and romance. It just seemed to have a black cloud over it as far as I was concerned. There was no reason for it, but I just wasn't having any luck with this house.

Sometimes when I find myself in this situation, I'll try to change the blood. You know, switch it up a little. I was going to try a tactic that had worked for me before. In the past when I was having trouble moving a property, I'd trade problems with a friend of mine, Martin Wallace. This was the arrangement: I'd trade my hard-to-move house for one of his hard-to-move houses. We'd simply give each other an option on each other's home and then I'd go to work selling his, and he'd go to work selling mine. The rule was, we'd convey the necessary information and any disclosures that needed to be given on the properties to each other. But past that, we never discussed our highs or lows concerning the property. After all, we wanted each other to begin the task of selling without the mental road-blocks we were having about the properties ourselves.

Martin had recently moved to Dallas, and he didn't have any properties in town. So, in this case, I was not able to trade problems with him. However, Martin had been having some luck selling properties on eBay and he wanted to take a run at selling my property using that technique. I told Martin that I'd give him an option to buy the property for $237,000. Anything he could get over $237,000 he could keep for himself. With my "verbal" handshake (over the phone from 200 miles away) he went to work.

I don't know how he did it, but shortly after that conversation, Martin sold the property for $287,000. Since the commitment was given over the phone, I suppose I could have changed my mind or conveniently not remembered, like so many people I've dealt with in the past have done. Many people would have tried to renegotiate or come up with some technical reasons why the deal was going to change. But NO! You do what your mouth said you were going to do. In this case, my arms, legs, and heart made sure Mr. Wallace got what my mouth had agreed to—$50,000.

Not letting your bulldog mouth overload your poodle dog butt is an art that takes years of practice. The more times it hurts when you honor your word, the more you'll think before you open your pie hole and start committing to things.

This is especially true if you like to have a drink or two, or three or four. I'm not proud to inform you that I've made deals at parties I really wished I hadn't. What made everything good is that I've honored those festive agreements without any hint of regret to the outside world.

You'd be amazed at how many investors would have turned this deal into a mess over the money that was being made by someone else. Those same people are probably reading this and calling me a fool. I'll always differ with them. I had struggled and struggled with that house. By changing the blood and making it worthwhile for another investor to get involved, I was able to accomplish my goal of getting rid of the dang thing without a loss and moving on! I'll admit, I didn't think he would make anywhere near that much money—and I got out of the deal with a little money. Exactly what I wanted to happen happened. I made a little and in the process he hit a home run. I asked to get rid of my property for $237,000, and he did it in short order. In all honesty, I was happy.

Why should I be conflicted about it? Because he did it right away, made a lot of money, and made it look easy? When the people in your network know your word is good, the deals just start rolling in. Your word is so valuable that you'll never be able to put a price tag on it. When you honor your verbal commitments without renegotiating, you become known as a person of principle. Your reputation will bring opportunities back to you in spades.

STORY 9
CAPTAIN STEPHEN'S MAIDEN VOYAGE FAIRWELL

• • •

There are two good things about owning a boat:
The day you buy it and the day you…

It seems that everyone fantasizes about the treasures you can find in abandoned storage units. I think it's some kind of urban legend because, as storage facility owners, we have strict guidelines we have to follow in order to dispose of a unit. You don't just confiscate the belongings of delinquent or abandoned storage units and take the contents for your own. More often than not we try to strike a deal with the owner before we get down to auctioning the units because, when you consider the time and effort, it's better just to get *some* pay and get them to clear out the unit themselves. That being said, I have to tell you about the time a boat storage tenant gave us his boat in lieu of payment.

This boat storage tenant (let's call him Mr. Boatman) was about $1,700 behind in payments. As a general rule, we don't let storages get that far behind, but when we have an abundance of vacant units, we're not in a hurry to clear out delinquent accounts and rack up their debt to us. In short, it's better to have tenants rack up their bills than to have no tenants at all. As this particular facility approached 100% occupancy, we felt the need to start hounding the past-due tenants. Tommi made phone contact with Mr. Boatman, and he was very level headed in his approach to the problem. He explained that he had recently gone through a divorce and was now living in Houston, Texas. He had a new residence, a new job, and a new life. Simply put, Mr. Boatman was so far from owning a boat in Canyon Lake, Texas, that he just wanted to give us the boat and call it even. It sounded good to me. WOW! How cool is that? The Stephen family was about to own a boat for FREE!

I checked out the boat and it was an ugly old thing. But having lived on the lake for years and not owning a boat, the idea of owning a boat free and clear was a unique proposition for me. Despite the appearance of the boat, we agreed to the deal and Mr. Boatman sent us the title. Not knowing much about boats I soon discovered the boat was one of those old cable-steering-type boats, and the cables had long since rotted. I checked into getting the cable steering replaced and, within a week or so, I had the 75-horsepower engine running like a charm, and the steering rigged with new cabling. We joked about being prominent boat owners and we christened the ugly duckling dingy with the name Lullabelle. It seemed like a befitting name, and we waited for the next sunny weekend that we could take her out to sea.

A few days later, my excitement overcame me and I cut out early one workday to take our new little boat for a private test drive. It was about 3:00 p.m. when I backed down the boat ramp and set our new toy into the water. After parking the truck and trailer, I trotted over the dock and jumped into the good ship Lullabelle. I was very encouraged when she started up in an instant. Her 75-horsepower, Evinrude engine purred like a kitten and I made my way through the No Wake Zone and toward the open waters. When I got past the No Wake Zone, I took in the beautiful day. The sun was shining, white clouds dotted a perfect Texas sky, and the air was light and breezy. It was the perfect day to cruise the lake. I thought to myself, "Let's see what she can do," and with that thought I pushed the throttle full forward.

Lullabelle was gaining speed and about to get on top of the water when she started shaking like a California earthquake. I immediately looked back at the engine and was reaching blindly for the throttle when I saw something that sent my adrenaline surging. The torque from the engine was ripping the transom of the boat completely off.

Note: For those of you who don't know what the transom is, it's literally *the back end of the boat.*

My eyes were fixated on the destruction and, by the time my hand found the throttle, it was too late. Both the engine and the transom had disappeared into the lake. I might not need to explain to you what happens when the back end of your boat falls off but let's just say you start taking on water very fast.

As if that weren't enough to worry about, the engine was still running full blast under water and trying to accelerate past the front end of the boat. Since the steering cables were still attached to the engine, it shot the nose of the boat straight into the air before I could actually shut down the power. When I shut down the power, the boat was purely vertical. Without power and still attached by the cables, the engine started to sink straight down to the bottom of the lake pulling the boat with it. It might sound funny right now, but, it's taking more time for me to describe this than it took for the entire boat to sink.

My first fear was that I'd get dumped into the water and caught up in the mess of boat, cables, and a roaring engine. I was afraid the engine would shred me to pieces if I ended up in the water with it. Now I had a second fear, and it was right on top of me. The water was coming up, the boat was vertical and sinking fast, and I was about to get sucked under the steering wheel into the hollow area, the hull, at the front (now the top) of the boat. If I got sucked into the hull under the steering wheel I was going to drown. I lunged over the steering wheel far enough to get my feet onto it. Then I pushed off the steering wheel and zoomed skyward, reaching for the nose of the boat. I grabbed the nose with both hands. By now the water was coming up over my waist. The last time I touched that boat it was with my feet, pushing off the nose to keep my head above the lake. Within seconds, Lullabelle was at the bottom of the lake, but luckily, I wasn't.

I was starting to feel a sense of relief. "Wow, that was a close one," I thought. Then suddenly, BAM! The next surge of adrenaline hit me so hard it about blew the top of my head off. Mother Nature kicked in the "Go Juice" the second my eyes found the shore. "Holy Smoke!" I was a long way from the shore, with no life jacket. The life jackets were still in the hull, at the bottom of the lake.

Luckily, I had dressed light. I was wearing shorts, T-shirt and tennis shoes. I shed the shoes and the shirt and told myself not to panic as I headed toward the shore. In my younger days, this wouldn't have been a problem at all, but years of work and not much physical exercise had me a bit worried. By now, a small group of hooky-playin' picnickers had gathered at the shore and were cheering me on. It was small comfort because they were too far away to help me.

I paced myself and eventually made it to dry land. When I got there, between breaths, I asked the small crowd if any of them needed a boat trailer. A few of them said yes, and I told them that the first person to get it unhitched from my truck could have it, for FREE! I pointed at my rig and they all took off running for the prize, leaving me to fight for my breath alone. I was plum worn out and, by the time I got to my truck, there wasn't a trailer in sight. I was happy to find my wallet and keys still in my pockets.

Once inside the truck, I pulled my cellular phone out of my glove compartment to call Tommi and tell her what had happened. Half-way through the labor of dialing her number I started laughing so hard I couldn't finish dialing. What was I going to tell her exactly? I had always heard about what a pain in the butt a boat could be, but this story topped all. I figured the story of Lullabelle could wait until I got home.

"There are two good things about owning a boat:

The day you buy it and the day you sink it."

Rest in peace Lullabelle. Rest in peace.

STORY 10
WHERE'S YOUR HAMMER?

• • •

Contracts don't get honored
if there isn't a hammer behind the words.

There are subtle differences in the types of properties you can buy. There are also different strategies you can apply to each of the different types of properties. Each strategy creates a different paradigm shift in the way the unwritten laws of real estate work on or with those properties. For instance, I don't like renting houses. Why? Because the person inside the house places all the responsibility for that house on *me* and therefore tends to take less care of the house than an owner would. Another reason I don't like renting houses is because I've never seen anyone leave a house and not walk right into another one. Seems like no matter how crummy the tenant is there is always some crummier landlord ignorant or desperate enough to take a chance on them. Personally, if I'm going to generate cash flow by putting someone into a house, I'm going to put that person in as an owner (who owes me mortgage payments) or I'm not putting them in at all. I do NOT rent homes, as a general rule.

On the other hand, I love renting boat storages and mini storages. One time, Tommi was foreclosing on a mini storage and the owner called incessantly trying to make a deal with us. I took note that I had never seen a rental house tenant be so concerned about being evicted, so I waited for the next time the mini storage tenant called to ask him the question that was burning me up, "Why on earth is this pile of junk you have in storage so deathly important to you?"

Although I didn't ask the question that directly I still got a viable answer. I will never forget that answer. It's the reason why I don't like being a house landlord and why I love being a storage landlord. This is what my storage tenant said to me. "Mr. Stephen, I have come on hard times, and I know that's *neither your fault nor* your problem perse, but I simply must make some type of deal with you so that I can get my stuff out of your storage. You see, there are things in that storage that aren't worth anything to you, or to anyone else in the world for that matter, but those things are irreplaceable to me."

Finally, I understood the difference between renting houses and renting storage units, why I hated renting houses, and why I loved renting storage units! I thought what my tenants had in those storage units was junk, but to the tenant, it was a lifetime of collectibles. I couldn't sell that Marine uniform or that wedding dress for even a few dollars, but to my tenants these items were priceless family heirlooms.

People keep a lot of different kinds of stuff in storage. I once found an urn in storage, sitting on the seat of a Harley Davidson motorcycle. The tenant rented the space from us and then eventually, virtually vanished, never to be seen again. WOW, I know exactly what to do with a Harley. You ride it! But what to you do with the ashes of Uncle Ernie? I know one thing for sure: He's not putting on a helmet and riding with me!

Another time I was digging through a unit this guy had stiffed me on. It was yet another person's stack of junk that I was going to have to get rid of at my own expense. You won't believe how much trash costs these days. I was flipping through the pages of a bunch of books when my luck changed. I found some homegrown, Polaroid pictures of a reasonably attractive, female in a compromising position! I figured it was the guy's wife and, about the time I figured that, I also figured out how I was going to get the $800 this guy owed me.

After I took a deep breath, I placed the call. When my tenant answered the phone, I basically offered to trade him some Polaroids of his wife for the $800 he owed me. He laughed at me and, apparently without thinking, said, "That ain't my wife."

I laughed back at him mocking his exact tone and cadence and replied, "I wonder how much *your wife* will pay for them?"

There was a long period of silence and then my not-so-glib tenant asked me for my address so he could send me a money order. Sometimes, the littlest thing can turn your day completely around!

I think Visa/MasterCard should use this scenario to make their next commercial.

SETTING: Picture the image of a sign stuck in the lawn that reads "Storage Sale." The camera zooms into the inside of the storage. The narrator speaks as the camera passes over the contents of the storage.

"Silverware set – Two Hundred and Fifty Dollars

Antique dresser with mirror – Six Hundred and Seventy Five dollars

Time dated pictures of the delinquent tenants mistress—NAKED! Priceless"

Hey, it worked for me!

STORY 11
WHAT A BLESSING!

• • •

More often than not, their perception is your reality.

I have noticed that deals come to investors as the result of change—change in marital status, economic status, health and legal situations. You name it and it *will* change eventually. Wherever there is change, there is opportunity. I once read, "Wealth comes from chaos." Right off the bat everyone thinks that this change has to be negative for an opportunity to present itself, but that's not true. Change does not have to be negative. In fact, some of the most positive kinds of change can result in good deals for sharp investors. I've made great deals with professionals who were taking job transfers for a raise in salary. I've made deals with glowing newlyweds who were selling their individual houses in an effort to buy one home together. I've made deals with people who had inherited large sums of money and were now free to dump property they were really tired of dealing with. Don't think for a minute that a great deal can't be made with a wealthy or savvy businessman. The *best* deals are made with wealthy and savvy business- minded people. It happens every day! Let's not confuse the art of *win-win deal making* with the character flaw of *outsmarting or swindling others.*

I felt compelled to address the issue of change because some people out there have the idea that real estate investors make a living by hovering like buzzards over the misfortunate, waiting for a meal. I suppose there are some investors with that mindset, but by and large real estate investors deal with all types of change, *good* and *bad*, and they do it with integrity. The challenge of life is to treat everyone the way you'd like to be treated in that situation. It's not rocket science. The author of the book, *The Richest Man in Babylon* by George S. Clason, suggests a novel idea: If you treat everyone in your business ventures with dignity and integrity, you'll never have to look for customers. They'll be lined up at your door every day of the week.

You don't have to be pressing, deceitful, or cunning to make a fabulous deal. Think about it. Have you ever sold something for a price when you knew you should be getting more for it? There's a time in people's lives when a quick sale is the answer to whatever ails them. There are a million reasons why but, whatever the reason, the price is lower because the need for cash is *now*. I think everyone has been at that point in his or her life some time or other.

A professional investor has the resources (the money or the means) to capitalize on just that type of situation, when it's worth it to the buyer, and the seller wants or needs it now. Investors don't hold a gun to anyone's head or beat people up to get the price they want. They simply state what they are willing to do and let the sellers decide if they want to do it. The art is in finding as many of those situations as possible and making an offer every time. You can't catch a fish if your hook isn't in the water, and professional investors find ways to keep their hooks in the water! Like everything else, it's a numbers game.

In my career, I've made my fair share of deals that were a direct result of someone dying. That's not morbid, that's life. It makes perfect sense that real estate investors would make plenty of deals in this situation because dying is, and will always be, a major source of change. Like it or not, people die every day. Like it or not, you and I are going to die one day. The properties I own when I die can't simply stand empty like multiple headstones in my honor. Someone is going to take over, by fee or by decree. I'll certainly not be worried about it. I'll be too busy being dead.

I'm not superstitious about death and/or evil spirits lurking or haunting. Don't get me wrong, I believe in the spirit. I just don't believe in my actually connecting with one, and it being evil. Over the years, I've bought plenty of homes in which someone had passed away. I'm sure I've purchased way more of them than I'm even aware of because in these parts, you don't have to disclose a death in or on the property unless it was due to a violent crime. And by the way, suicides are not considered to be violent crimes. That being said, I have knowingly purchased properties that have sheltered the suicidal up to and after that final moment.

Like a lot of things in life, I don't give this negative energy much time at all. I blow right past it. Clean it up and move on as fast as possible. I find the less energy you feed a problem, the less of a problem it becomes. The neighbors, on the other hand, are a different story. They're going to tell everyone they see. Depending on the neighbors, you can have a hard sale on your hands.

One time I was trying to sell a home. I'd found a very good buyer. Mr. and Mrs. Martinez had given me $5,000 down, and we had agreed on the monthly terms of payment. Everyone was very happy with the deal. After I had everyone signed up, I got a phone call from Mrs. Martinez. Apparently she and her husband were about to move in when the neighbor informed them that the previous owner had died in the house. This was of great concern to the Martinez family, and they were certain they could not and would not live in a house in which someone had died. They were requesting a full refund. I, on the other hand, never knew that anyone had died in the home and set out to see if this were really true and if it were, what were the circumstances.

I contacted the neighbor and learned that the previous lady of the house had indeed passed away in her bed while sleeping one night. She was up in years and had died of old age. I was thinking that perhaps Mr. and Mrs. Martinez would be comforted when I informed them that the death was not violent or brutal and, in fact, was a natural event. It didn't seem to make much difference to them. They didn't want to live in a house that might be inhabited by a spirit of non-Christian virtue. In short, they were afraid of a mean ghost. El Diablo. The Devil.

I thought about this for awhile and then came up with an idea. This objection was new to me. I'd never been in this position before. Being afraid of ghosts seemed very superstitious and somewhat childish to me. I'm just not very superstitious. However, I wasn't the one who was going to live in the home. If the Martinez family were going to live in that home, I had to make it comfortable for them—not me. I had to help the Martinez family live with their own reality, not mine. I made a phone call to the Martinez family.

MR. MARTINEZ: Hello.

ME: Hi, Mr. Martinez. This is Mitch. I would like to speak to you and your wife if I may. Is there anyway you can get her to pick up on another phone so we can all talk together?

After a few seconds we're all the line together.

ME: Mr. and Mrs. Martinez, I would like to talk to you about your new home and the problem we have with it. Before we start I would like for you to know this: I will give you your money back if you are not completely satisfied. Knowing that

I will refund 100% of your money, will you please listen to me with an open mind?

MR. & MRS. MARTINEZ: Yes, we'll listen but how can you change the fact that the lady died in the house?

ME: I can't change that, but I can change the house.

MR. & MRS. MARTINEZ: We don't understand but we'll listen to you.

ME: Good! That is all I'm asking of you. Just hear me out. I need to ask you some questions. Is that all right?

MR. & MRS. MARTINEZ: Yes, we'll answer your questions if you think it'll help.

ME: Well, I'm not really sure but I think I can. I need to know, do you, Mr. & Mrs. Martinez, believe in the God and the Lord Jesus as our savior?

MR. & MRS. MARTINEZ: With all our hearts, yes, we do! Of that we are sure.

ME: Do you believe in the power of God almighty and the Lord Jesus?

MR. & MRS. MARTINEZ: Yes, Yes. YES. Certainly we do!

ME: Do you believe in the supreme power of our Father and that no evil spirit can stand up against the power of God and our Lord Jesus?

MR. & MRS. MARTINEZ: Yes, we believe. We believe there is no greater power than God and our Lord Jesus. Evil never wins.

ME: Before the news about the old lady, was that home the right home for you? Was it the right size? Did it have the right amount of bedrooms? Did it have the right school? Was this the right house for you and your family before the bad news?

MR. & MRS. MARTINEZ: We loved that house, and we really wanted to live there.

ME: So it was the right house?

MR. & MRS. MARTINEZ: Yes, it was going to be our home.

ME: Do you go to church near here?

MR. & MRS. MARTINEZ: Yes, we love our church. We've been there for over twenty years.

ME: Do you know and respect your priest?

MR. & MRS. MARTINEZ: Yes, he's the most holy man we know and we love him dearly.

ME: Mr. and Mrs. Martinez, I have an idea that will get you your home. This is what I propose. I think you should invite your priest over to that house. I believe that your priest can bless the house, every bedroom, every bathroom, the kitchen, the closets, and even the attic. I believe that with his holy water and prayers, along with your prayers, that no evil could possibly remain in that house, not against the power of the cross. With those blessings and the protection of God Almighty and our savior Jesus Christ, that house can be your home forever in peace. There is no way you can lose. What do you believe?

MR. & MRS. MARTINEZ: We'll call our father tonight and ask for his presence here.

ME: Will you let me know how it goes?

MR. & MRS. MARTINEZ: We'll call you when we're finished.

ME: I know this is the right thing to do. I'll wait for your call.

About a week later I got a call from the Martinez family. They had waited for the most holy day to bless their house, and on Sunday that house became their home. It was a very good day for the Martinez family and me. I think we all felt good inside. Since they weren't moving in until a week after we'd signed the original papers, I offered to redo the paperwork and change the pay dates. The Martinez family declined and stated they would make the payment on the original date we'd agreed upon, and that I had done enough for them.

My problems with the phone started at a very young age

STORY 12
CELLULAR PHONE CRISIS

• • •

Sometimes you can measure your success with the simplest data.

It was 1998 and things were really moving. Sam and I were buying houses like most people buy rolls of toilet paper. We were learning to adjust to the new pace and volume of life. We were frugal but, as a business grows, you spend more. I'm not talking about spending more on luxuries. I'm talking about just spending more for necessities. For example, my gas bill tripled. I was driving an average of 55,000 miles per year. In conjunction with that, my phone bill skyrocketed.

In the mid-to-late 90's, cellular phone programs were still expensive. The very best plan I could find at the time was $200 for 2,000 minutes per month. It sounds reasonable, except I was racking up 4,500 and 6,700 minutes per month. Every minute over the 2,000-minute mark would cost something outrageous, like 25 to 50 cents per minute *extra!*

I was driving around the city one day when I got a frantic call from my wife, Tommi. She was audibly shaken and in a panic. Her hysteria started after she'd opened our cell phone bill. Apparently the bill for the last month was over $1,800! Tommi was livid.

TOMMI: These phone bills are outrageous! We cannot continue to use cell phones. I want you to come home right this very minute and hand over your phone. I'll have them disconnected by the end of the day.

ME: Tommi, how am I going to work without a cell phone?

TOMMI: We'll just have to figure some other way to do business. I'm not paying $1,800 a month for a stupid phone! We pay three times more for your phone than for our house. It's ridiculous!

Now don't get me wrong. I was not happy to hear that our phone bill was over $1,800. It *was* ridiculous. But there was more to it than that, and I'd subdued my own panic just long enough to figure it out. At least I thought I had it figured out and a little confirmation would do us both good.

ME: Hey, Thomas, is this the most expensive phone bill we've ever had?

TOMMI: Yes, by a long shot!

ME: What was the next highest bill?

TOMMI: That would be last month's ridiculous phone bill…$1,200.

ME: What was the bill before that?

TOMMI: $800. And I thought *that* was bad!

ME: I'm going to start heading toward you and the house but can you please do me favor while I'm on my way? Could you please pull up our financial statements for the past three months? I want to see something.

TOMMI: We are *not* keeping these phones!

ME: $1,800 is a lot of money. I agree. Can you pull the financials?

I had a pretty good handle on what I was looking for from the financials. I didn't really need to see them but for the sake of everyone involved I wanted to go through the exercise in real time. She called me back a few minutes later.

TOMMI: It's me. I have the three months of financials. What do you want to know?

ME: The first month, when my phone bill was $800, what did we profit that month?

TOMMI: We profited about $12,000.

ME: OK, good. What did we profit the month I had the $1,200 phone bill?

TOMMI: We made just over $18,600.

ME: Okay. Now last month the phone bill was $1,800. How much did we make last month?

TOMMI: You had your best month ever, $28,000 in profit.

ME: Tommi, the way I see it, if I can get this phone bill up to $3,000 per month, we're gonna be doin' just fine!

I turned my truck around and headed back into town.

My poor Tommi never adds up both sides of the equation. To this day, she only adds up the bills. To this very day! It took a little doing but she finally looked at the phone bill as a cost of doing business. For a while there, it was almost uncanny. The higher my phone bills got, the more we made. Her lopsided way of looking at things was not all bad, though. It did point out to me that having a phone bill three times that of our house payment did seem out of whack. Subconsciously, I started working on a way to resolve the issue. Coming up with a plan to solve the cellular phone crisis led to something neither of us could ever have imagined in a million years.

STORY 13
BEATING THE PHONE BILL

• • •

A think tank to beat the phone bill turns into the San Antonio Real Estate Investor's Association (SAREIA).

After having a $1,800 phone bill, I started contemplating what on earth we could do to mitigate this expense. Don't get me wrong. The higher my phone bill, the more we made in net profit, but it seemed ridiculous to pay so much for a phone. I finally decided we needed help to solve the problem. We just weren't able to come up with any alternative that made any sense whatsoever.

One day, the idea of sponsoring a lunch popped into my head. I called some of the smartest guys in the business and asked them if they were experiencing the same kind of phone bills we were. Everyone was paying way more than they cared to pay, so we all agreed to get together and see what solution we could come up with.

Here's what I proposed: I would pay for lunch if everyone agreed to stick to the subject. Knowing the personalities involved and how most of my entrepreneurial friends seem to have Attention-Deficit Disorder, I knew that sticking to the subject wasn't going to be an easy task. I decided to throw in a little caveat. I'd pay for lunch *until* someone changed the subject, and then that person would inherit the lunch bill. Everyone really liked the new twist and agreed to show up. These investors are very competitive and making this meeting into a game got their attention.

When the day came, we all met at the Golden Wok Chinese restaurant. Right off the bat someone asked about somebody's family. I immediately announced that I was no longer responsible for the lunch bill. Everyone started laughing and one other guy asked, "Dude, we can't even ask about each other's families?" Then I informed him that he now had the bill! That set the tone for the afternoon. Everyone was having a good time with it, and the bill bounced rapidly from one person to the next, to the next, to the next, until we sat down at the table and started to get serious. I gave everyone immunity to speak to the waitress and order but after that the rule was back in play again.

I reiterated that the intent of this meeting was to see if we could collectively come up with a way to outsmart the phone companies. I started off the official think tank session by informing everyone of how many minutes I was using per month and how much my last cellular phone bill had been ($1,800). I also explained that the best cellular phone plan I was able to find was $200 for 2,000 minutes. Nobody had a plan with more minutes for less money. There were several things in play at the time we were discussing this problem.

1. You couldn't change phone companies without losing your phone number.
2. Right when you'd make a deal and sign up for a plan, the next company would come up with a slightly better plan but you were locked into a plan and phone number. And it was almost impossible to change your number without losing all your contacts.
3. Last but not least, not every cell phone company had good reception in parts of the county. Some of us (namely me) lived in areas where certain companies had serious reception problems.

It was amazing to watch the think tank process work. We were getting a lot of good information from each other, and the ideas were starting to flow. Within the hour over lunch we had the problem hammered. This is what we came up with:

You get a new land line installed at your home with call forwarding capability. Even though this was a land line at your home, this number was going to be designated as your new cellular number—forever! You could forward this land line (your designated cell phone number) to any cellular phone number and/or company you happened to have at the time. Now, when you changed phone companies, your number wouldn't have to change. You were free to change companies without losing your phone number. That meant you could start putting your cellular number on business cards, letterhead, car signs, yellow pages—everywhere you were afraid to put it before because you were afraid of having to change your number

The next step was to get three different colored cellular phones with three separate plans: Each phone getting 2,000 minutes for $200.

On the first of the month, you forward your land line to the white phone and get 2,000 minutes for $200. On the 10th of each month, you forward the land line to the blue phone and get 2,000 minutes for $200. Then on the 20th of each month, you would forward the land line to the black cell phone and get yet another 2,000 minutes for $200.

That's how we beat the phone companies one day over lunch. The end result: We were getting 6,000 minutes for $600 plus $35 for the extra phone line at our homes. At the time, that was a real coup. It was very little work to save anywhere from $1,000 to $1,200 a month. I was very satisfied with what we'd come up with, but, more importantly, I thought if getting together could solve that problem, what else could we solve?

We all agreed to meet once a month to talk about real estate and our problems and how to solve them. We agreed to meet the first Tuesday of every month. Within a few meetings there were 20 to 30 people showing up and then 50 to 60 and on and on. We constantly had to switch meeting places to accommodate our ever-growing numbers. Eventually, it led to the formation of the San Antonio Real Estate Investor's Association (SAREIA). Today, there are more than 800 members, and an average of 150 to 300 people show up on any given first Tuesday of the month for the SAREIA meetings.

I recall the day SARIEA was formed. Elmer Diaz was helping get everything organized, and we needed to elect a president. During the actual forming of the nonprofit organization, there were about twelve people in the room. When Elmer asked who wanted to be president of the organization, no one raised their hand. After all, we were all independent entrepreneurs and not about to get tied up in the red tape of running an organization. One of the guys in the room was named Harley Davis (that really is his name). I didn't know a lot about him, but he had been attending the meetings regularly and seemed genuinely interested in real estate. He had been quietly sitting on the sidelines during this meeting when I looked over at Harley.

ME: Hey, Harley, would you like to be the first president of the San Antonio Real Estate Investor's Association?

Harley looked at me with puzzled features.

HARLEY: Mitch, I've never bought a house in my life. I've never even bought my own house.

ME: Harley, the question is; "Would you like to be the first president of SAREIA?"

HARLEY: Well I'd love to but... but...

ME: Everyone voting for Harley Davis as President of SAREIA say, "Aye."

Everyone in the room responded with a resounding "Aye" and Harley Davis became the first President of the San Antonio Real Estate Investor's Association. I thought the poor guy was going to cry he was so proud. It wasn't long before Harley was buying houses. He did a fine job as the first president of SAREIA. As far as I was concerned, he got the group down the road to where it needed to be at the time.

In January of 2007, Orlando Rodriguez, acting President of SAREIA, asked me to come discuss real estate and answer investment questions at their regular monthly meeting. Approximately 300 people were in attendance and I showed up ready to do just that. Much to my surprise that is not at all why I was invited. When it was time for my appearance, I took the stage only to find out that I was there to receive a very special honor. Orlando Rodriguez and the San Antonio Investor's Association presented me with a plaque that read:

MITCH STEPHEN INVESTMENT CENTER

In February of 2001, Mitch Stephen gathered a group of investors for lunch. The purpose of this lunch was simply to mastermind a way to reduce their cell phone bills. The meeting was productive so Mitch was inspired to do it again. Mitch invited more real estate investors to discuss and share their investing experiences. By the fourth meeting, the San Antonio Real Estate Investors Association was born. This facility is a reality because of the initiative, vision,

and commitment of Mitch Stephen to have a group of like-minded individuals working together.

This facility is dedicated to the man that started it all – Mitch Stephen

9 January 2007

Today, you may visit the Mitch Stephen Investment Center at 2379 NE Loop 410, Suite 14, San Antonio, Texas 78217. You can join SAREIA or attend their meetings and investor-education events. Their membership approaches 800, and many people have garnered the beginnings of their financial freedom from this starting point. I am very proud to be associated with SAREIA and to have been given such an honor. You'd think with all my connections and my network someone would have clued me in. But, when the award was presented, I was speechless for perhaps the first time in my life.

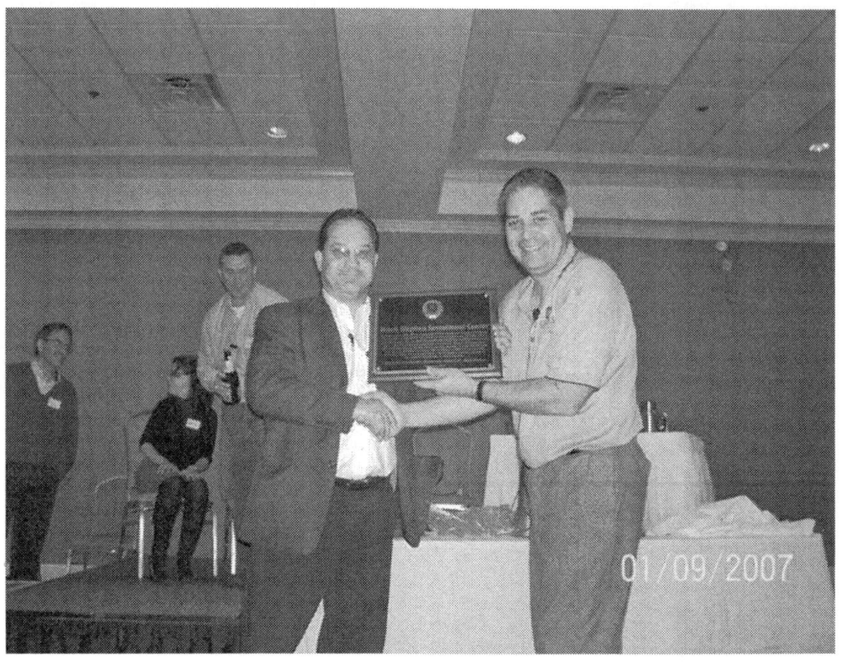

SAREIA President, Orlando Rodriquez, presenting me with a plaque to mark the commemorative day.

STORY 14
CONTRACTORS

• • •

Can't live with them. Can't live without them.

I suppose one of my personality traits is that I absolutely do not like conflict or friction in my relationships. It has been said that I'm a gentle person, and it's true that I'll do almost anything to avoid uncomfortable confrontations. In a way, it goes right along with not dwelling in the negative and always moving on to the positive. There is a delicate balance between that concept and not standing up for yourself and getting run over all the time.

If being accommodating has been a great asset (which I know in my heart it has), it has also been one of my biggest faults in business. There are some people in my life that absolutely should have had a baseball bat taken to them but, for whatever reason, I didn't do it. I think I react passively because my personal disappointment in them would not be satisfied with their blood. I'm still friendly with some of the people who have hurt me the most financially. I don't do business with them anymore, but they still send me business, and that part makes me feel better about the passive ways in which I've handled some things. It's not always easy to forgive or move on. For me, the art of it is to come to terms with your loss (both financially and in terms of the relationship) quickly. Then, move gracefully and quietly away, to a safe distance. Just because I've wasted time trusting a person in business doesn't mean I have to waste even more time hating them or trying to get even with them. I just don't know where to find the energy for that. I consciously choose to funnel that same energy into the next rewarding relationship or venture. In short, the sooner we forget about our losses, the sooner we get on with the business of being successful, emotionally as well as financially.

One time I tried to get even with a contractor by stringing him out on the next job. Then, when the job was complete, I didn't pay him. It worked well by the numbers, and I gained back what I'd lost, but it turned into a duel of mental gymnastics, and it simply wasn't worth the brain power I spent on a negative situation. Furthermore, even though I conceivably had the right to get back at the contractor, I now had a person walking around town saying I didn't pay him. Having to explain to people why I didn't pay him caused more wasted energy. I'll never do that again—not because it didn't work financially, but because I'd have felt better about myself and my reputation would have been better off, if I'd taken my lumps and moved on. Using all that time and energy to find another contractor or great investment would have been a better use of both time and energy.

One of my favorite contractors asked me for a $10,000 loan to pay his property taxes before he lost his home. Of course I was assured I'd get it back in a relatively short period of time, yadda, yadda, yadda. But I knew the loan was *not* a business move. It was something I was doing as a friend. He had worked for me for ten years as a subcontractor, and I had become close to him and his family. Shortly after I loaned him the $10,000, it became apparent that I was going to have to have a conversation with him about his ever-increasing prices. In my preparation for that conversation I also discovered that some rather large advances I'd paid out to him for certain jobs were not getting spent on those jobs. Suddenly it hit me like a ton of bricks. He made his money working for me. If he was going to pay me back, he was going to have to get the money from *me*! I wasn't feeling very smart when that revelation struck me.

In short, I'd let my contractor's problems become my problems and that can't happen in a business relationship. After he finished the job he was on, I simply never contracted with him again. When he asked why I wasn't giving him any more work, I told him that apparently we *were too* good of friends for us to do business anymore. I told him I'd have lunch with him, have a beer with him, even sit and dine with him and his family at his home, but we were done doing business together. I knew he was smart enough to know that my business could be his again if he'd honor his word, but I'm under no illusions. The truth is, I don't expect to see him working on one of my jobsites anytime soon. If I sound hurt, it's because I am. But you'll notice there's no anger or revenge in my tone. We're still friends, just not the business friends we could have been.

It has always been difficult for me to keep distance between any of my relationships. Emotionally, I'm either in or I'm out. It has served me well at times and hurt me at times. I know this: I can live with myself just fine. I sleep very well.

Today, I pay attention when I hear or see that my contractors are in personal financial trouble. When you see this happening, it's a sure signal that you're about to start having troubles on your jobs, as well. If you don't keep a tight rein on the contractors and everything about the job they're working on, *you* are going to be the one who pays their deficits, especially if the only jobs they do are for you! It's smarter to let them solve their financial problems while working on someone else's job, and then let them start back with you when they get back on their feet. It sounds ruthless right? Well, just try helping them through their financial difficulties and send me an email as to how it works out. I'm all ears. This is the part of business I hate, having to choose between business and friendship. Then I think, if they really were friends, they wouldn't have put me in a position where I had to choose.

There is a popular saying in the industry:

You make your money when you BUY.

I modified this one. It reads like this in my book:

You make your money when you BUY. You lose it in the REMODEL

(If you're not careful)

STORY 15
CONNING THE CONS

• • •

When you're dealing with a con man you have to take the gloves off...
Anything goes when you're conning a con.

I've had my fair share of Jr. Partners who weren't on the up and up, either. Most of the people who haven't reciprocated in our relationship simply ran out of whatever it was they needed to reciprocate with. They simply couldn't pay their part or get the job at hand done. Those failed partnerships are much easier to get past than partners who premeditated or schemed to scam you from the start. Those guys are cons.

The ones that tend to get me out of my better judgment are the ones who are obviously and blatantly deceiving people, like they have some kind of immunity to the law. It is the pathological, repeat offender who really gets me fired up. These guys know exactly what they're doing and have plans to take you before they ever meet you. They are constantly looking for their next victim. I've run into several of them but I've only been drawn in by two in my career.

In the mid 90's, during the very first days of my investing career, I ran into a guy we'll call T.H. (short for "Turd Head"). T.H. was buying up the town and offering to split with investors who came up with the money. T.H. would find the deals, you would bring the money, and you'd both do the work and split 50/50. For me it was a great opportunity. I had longed for the chance to work alongside a successful investor and garner all the knowledge my curious and observant mind could absorb. The first deal we did together was made possible because I was able to borrow $20,000 from my father. I made huge mistakes during the acquisition of that property, and I lost control of the money. It's not that I was that dumb. It was because I was young and gullible and trusting, and my new mentor was an Olympic-caliber con. He didn't do what he said he was going to do, and the property ended up in his name instead of mine. From that minute on, my gut didn't feel so good. We completed the flip in a very short period of time. Soon there was a closing, and it was time to get my father's money back (with interest) and for me to get my 50% of the profit. I bet you can already guess what was happening to me, but humor me for a bit.

T.H. kept coming up with reasons why he couldn't get a check out to me. It rolled into a week, and I was beginning to get a really bad feeling. I was determined to get in front of T.H. and get the situation resolved. The next day, I drove over to his fancy home in an elite part of town. At the back of his property, there was a structure that was meant to be maid's quarters, but T.H. had turned it into an office. Once inside, I found myself sitting in a waiting room with a handful of other people ahead of me. While I was sitting there an old friend walked in. He recognized me before he found a chair and stood there staring at me with a look of disappointment on his face.

ME: Hey Lou, what's wrong?

LOU (in a whisper): What are *you* doing here?

ME: I'm here to see T.H.

LOU: Does T.H. owe you money, too?

I nodded my head "yes." Lou shook his head as if to say, "No, No, No."

LOU (in a whisper): Everyone in this room is here for the same reason. He owes everyone money and I hate to tell you this, but he's not going to pay you either.

ME: Does he owe *you* money, Lou?

LOU (looking at the ground scratching his head): Yep, $50,000, and I don't have time to wait to see him today either. He'll hold us out here in this waiting room trying to get us to give up and leave. If you sit here for a few hours he'll finally see you.

Lou said he was really sorry to see me there and then he left.

The reality of everything was sinking in so hard that my ears were ringing. What can I do to get my money back? What on earth can I possibly do? I sat with my head in my hands. I simply could *not* fail with my father's money—that was not an option. I was starting to beat myself up for letting this happen when T.H. called one of the guys in the waiting room into his office. I thought, "Maybe I won't have to wait too long today." I kept repeating in my head, "Think, Mitch, think!…Think! Think!"

Then I started to focus.

QUESTION: Okay, I've got a con man on my hands. How do you get to a con? What is his Achilles heel? Where is the chink in his armor? What's his weak spot?

ANSWER: GREED! Greed and easy money!

QUESTION: So how can you use this con man's greed to get your money back, Mitch?

ANSWER: Promise him a bigger deal. Make him believe he can get to you for even more money, a lot more money. And easily!

The two men ahead of me in line looked at their watches and left. I was on deck. The next person in that office was going to be me. My ears were still ringing, "Think Mitch Think! You don't have much time. You're only going to get one shot at this."

About that time the office door opened and a very disgruntled man walked feverishly toward the exit and left. I heard my name called from inside the office. I took a deep breath and paused for a moment. Just before I stood up to go in, I spoke to myself. It was like talking to my father/football coach when I was a kid in the Pop Warner Football League, just before the game started, just before I walked toward the end zone to receive the opening kickoff.

"Alright baby. Here we go now. Here we go. It's time to strap it on. Time to hit somebody baby. Time to shove it down their throats." I had made up my mind and I was ready to do it. "We're gonna con this con man, right now!"

By the time I reached the office door I was overflowing with excitement. My walk was brisk, my smile was huge and confident, and I greeted T.H. with all the enthusiasm a person could possibly exude. "Hey, Mr. T.H. Man-o-man, do I have some great news for you!"

T.H. looked a little surprised to hear that sentiment coming from a guy I'm sure he thought was there to confront him. T.H. stood up to shake my extended hand, "Well tell me about it!"

My dog and pony show kicked into high gear, "I have this deal that will make us an easy $100,000 - $50,000 each! I even have it sold already! Here's the problem: Today is Monday. Tomorrow is

Tuesday—foreclosure day—and I have to solve the problems right now before foreclosure tomorrow!" T.H. was all smiles. I could see the gears turning in that little con man brain of his. He had already sized up the deal. He was going to get the entire $100,000.

T.H. jumped at the chance to con me for more, "So what do we need to do?"

I'm thinking, "*Bait's in the mouth, time to set the hook.*"

I said, "I have to go pick up the contract from the seller right now and pay the $25,000 in back payments to the mortgage company's attorney before the end of the day. I need you to give me the $20,000 principle and my $10,000 profit from the house we just sold so I can tie this thing up. Dude, this is an easy 100 GRAND!"

T.H. started to show signs of concern but I knew exactly what he was waiting to hear. I fed it to him like a fish eats a purple rubber worm, "I've done the contract just like we did the last one. You know, with your company being the buyer and everything, just like the last one." I could see a twinkle in his eye as he reached for his checkbook. Then I asked the question that made him pull his pen out of his shirt pocket, "Is your company a Corp or an LLP? I want to make sure we don't have problems at the title company." When T.H. heard that he bit—hook, line, and sinker. The bait was so far down into his gullet he cut me the check for $30,000, plus interest! I could hardly believe my eyes as I glanced over the check for accuracy. It was perfect. It was written out to *me*, Mitch Stephen. Unbelievable! Is this for real?

As you can imagine, I ran to his bank as fast as possible to see if this check was actually good. It was, and I cashed his check within minutes. It was made in the shade. Not only had I picked up the principle with interest, I picked up my profit as well! I had conned the con! When I got back to my car in the bank parking lot the customers around there must have thought I'd gone crazy. I was dancing around my car like Mohammad Ali, jabbing and ducking and weaving, throwing flurries of combination punches into an invisible, imaginary boxing opponent.

As I arrived at my driver's side door, I threw up my arms above my head and shouted, "I'm Champion of the World!" I ended my extended dance with the famous Ali shuffle, and some people at the front door stopped to vaguely applaud. I know they were thinking I was some kind of nut but I was so high I didn't care. My adrenaline was rushing. I felt like I'd just knocked out Joe Frazier in The World Heavyweight Boxing Championship! I could hear Howard Cosell shouting, "He's done it! He's done it! Ladies and Gentlemen, he's conned the con!"

Later that day, T.H. called me to see why I hadn't brought the contract over yet. I told him the deal had fallen apart. You could hear his jaw hit the floor from over the phone. I never saw him again. Later, I learned he had gone to prison for fraud. I hope he learned his lesson. I learned mine!

STORY 16
CONNING THE CONS (PART II)

• • •

Sometime, you have to strike a deal with the devil.

A friend of mine, Martin Wallace, called me one day and asked for my opinion. He had been dealing with a crooked contractor (herein after referred to as "Mr. Wacko") who had filed a mechanic's lien on his property making it impossible for him to sell it without taking a huge loss. Martin explained that he had paid the contractor for some work, but the work had never gotten even close to being finished. My friend let me listen in on a phone call to mitigate the problem but, as he said, the contractor just went ballistic!

Martin said that every time he tried to hold a conversation with the contractor about the issue, the contractor would fly off into some tirade and become impossible to communicate with. I believed Martin. I've known him long enough to know he doesn't refuse to pay contractors for the heck of it. I also know the propensity of some contractors to use this legal maneuver in a very unfair and criminal way. I did some research on Mr. Wacko and it didn't take long to figure out that he was doing this to people all over town.

To make matters worse, Martin had this property sold but the mechanic's lien popped up in the title search and now it was a huge problem. Martin was about to lose his buyer.

I thought about Martin's situation for a day or so and came up with a plan. I'd send out letters in the neighborhood to see if I could con the con into selling me the lien on Martin's property for a little bit of nothing. If I could pull it off it would be much, much faster and much, much cheaper than Martin's having to go to court. I told Martin my plan.

Martin liked the idea, so we sat down together and designed a very professional flyer. In unmistakable, bold letters we put the words **"I BUY MECHANIC'S LIENS"** at the very top of the flyer. At the bottom I used a 1-800 phone number and invited people to call "Mark Hamill" for more information. Whenever someone called me and asked for "Mark" or "Mr. Hamill" I'd know what the call was in reference to. In addition, the flyer portrayed Mr. Hamill as an out-of-state buyer so I would *not* have to confront the contractor in person. Why you might ask? Because I heard the phone call Martin had made to the contractor earlier, and this contractor truly was a wacko! That same day, we made about twenty-five copies of the flyer and mailed them to every house on Mr. Wacko's street, including Mr. Wacko's house.

In addition, I had to prepare for my role as a mechanic's lien buyer. I programmed Mr. Wacko's phone number into my phone so that hopefully my caller ID would warn me if it were Mr. Wacko calling. I also changed the greeting on my cellular to reflect my new role. Then, last but not least, instead of answering with my signature drawl, "Thiiis iiis Mitch" I began to practice answering my phone generically. After all that was done, we waited.

Well, we didn't have to wait long. The very next day my phone rang. My caller ID did its job, and I knew it was Mr. Wacko calling. When I answered the call a familiar voice on the other end of the line asked for *Mr. Hamill.* I could hardly believe it! Mr. Wacko had taken the bait! I gathered my composure and started to do my best to strike a deal with the devil.

ME: Hello, this is Mark Hamill

MR. WACKO: Hi, I'm calling about a mechanic's lien I'd like to sell.

ME: Great! Did you get my flyer in the mail?

MR. WACKO: Yes, I got your flyer yesterday and I'm very interested. I may have several of these for you.

ME: I send these out all over the country. What city are you in?

MR. WACKO: I'm in San Antonio, Texas.

ME: So you have several? Wow, that'd be great! Do you have one for me today?

MR. WACKO: Yes, I have one.

ME: What property address do you have a lien on?

MR. WACKO: I have a lien on a home at 1245 Gorman Street in San Antonio.

I almost lost my breath! That was Martin's property!

ME: How much is the lien for?

MR. WACKO: $10,700.

ME: I'll need a copy of your contract signed by you and the owner and a copy of your lien.

I gave Mr. Wacko a 1-800 fax number.

ME: I'll also need a copy of the demand letter you sent to the owner.

I already knew Mr. Wacko had never sent any demand letters. I didn't even know if you have to give notice or not. I was just making all this up.

ME: Meanwhile, I'll have my office pull an original copy of the lien from the courthouse using the computer. I need to do some research.

With that I got Mr. Wacko's personal information and I told him I'd call him back the next day. When I called the conversation went something like this.

ME: Hello, Mr. Wacko?

MR. WACKO: Yes, this is Mr. Wacko.

ME: Mr. Wacko, this is Mark Hamill. I'm sorry to inform you of this, but I won't be able to buy your mechanic's lien on 1245 Gorman Street. It appears that your contract with the owner, Mr. Martin, is missing some very significant pieces. There's no way your contract is going to hold up in court.

MR. WACKO: What's wrong with my contract?

ME: Well, first of all the owner's real name is "Martine" with an "E" at the end and you have it spelled "Martin." That's just *one* problem. Another problem is you must send demand letters, and you didn't send any demand letters. The biggest problem is that the signatures on the contract aren't notarized. There are some other small problems as well but not sending a demand letter and having no notary makes your contract worth nothing right off the bat.

MR. WACKO: My lien is worth nothing?

ME: Well, I might be able to give you a little something but not much. I'd be gambling on bluffing Mr. Wallace but that's going to be a huge gamble. I searched his name at the courthouse and judging by his holdings and the fact that he's a trustee for others on several properties, he appears to be a very successful, smart, and respected man. I don't feel the chance that Mr. Wallace will fall for my bluff is very good. And no court in the world is going to go against him because of your weak paperwork. On the other hand, whoever shows up in court against him, *you* or *me*, may have to pay his legal fees when he wins. I don't have to tell you how expensive that could be, do I?

MR. WACKO: So you said you could pay me a little. How much is that?

ME: I really don't want to do this deal because it's too small dollar wise, and the chances aren't good.

MR. WACKO: So you're not even going to offer anything?

ME: Look, Mr. WACKO, I don't want to disappoint you so I'll offer $1,000, but please don't be insulted and *please* don't try to get my offer up. I really don't want this deal.

MR. WACKO: If I say yes how and when can I get my money?

ME: I'll have the money and the assignment of the lien sent to a bail bonds company with a notary public that's open for business 24/7 in San Antonio. You go there and present your Texas driver's license, sign the docs in front of the notary public, and collect your $1,000. You just need to tell me exactly how to make out the money order.

Mr. Wacko agreed to sell me the lien that day and within a matter of hours we had control of that mechanic's lien. To short-cut the paper work, I actually had Mr. Wacko assign the lien to another company Martin Wallace owned. While it did cost Mr. Wallace an extra $1,000 to get things turned around, he was able to remove the mechanic's lien and sell his property for a profit later that week. I got the satisfaction of helping a friend and conning a con, and a fantastic dinner for two at the famous (and very expensive) Ruth's Chris Steak House. I would tell this story to my wife over dinner that night. I'm not sure she enjoyed the story all that much but she sure did like her steak!

STORY 17
THE ART OF WAR

• • •

Knowledge is power.

You'd think that investors would have been happy with the arrangement Sam Hombre and I had made for them. Jr. Investors could partner on as many properties as they could find, and they enjoyed a 50/50 profit split. They had no real monetary risk that could be enforced against them and no overhead to speak of. Still, that wasn't good enough for some of them. I caught several Jr. Investors padding the contractors' bids.

One day, my main contractor came to me and said that one of our Jr. Investors had asked him to mark up the price on the bid sheet. As I recall, the investor wanted to increase the bid by $2,000. The Jr. Investor was offering to pay the contractors a little something extra if the deal went through. Apparently the same thing was being offered to the electrician and the plumber, but they weren't so honest and had taken the deal offered by the Jr. Investor. When the contractor came to my office and reported this to me, I told him not to say anything about our meeting to anyone.

Everyone completed their job, and I wrote checks to all the contractors as if nothing had ever happened. For easy math let's say the deal appeared to make a net profit of $18,000, so the Jr. Investor made $9,000, and Sam and I made $9,000. What really happened is the Jr. Investor padded both the electric and the plumbing bill an extra $2,000 total, and the property should have made a net profit of $20,000 ($10,000 each). In the end, the Jr. Investor made $11,000 and we made only $9,000.

The next time that Jr. Investor showed up with a deal, we informed him that we weren't doing as much partnering as we used to and that we could only buy the property from him at a wholesale price. Basically, we offered to buy his contracts for $2,000, and we would convert the properties ourselves. Since no one else in town was partnering like we were, and because he was most likely known as a liar and a cheat around the investment community, this Jr. Investor had no place to turn. Over the months, we eventually purchased all of his contracts for $2,000 each, never partnering with him again. This worked out perfectly for Sam and me. We made back way more than the Jr. Investor had scammed from us. Now, instead of partnering with this slime-ball and getting $9,000 from a house that profited $20,000, we were paying him $2,000 and making $18,000 of the $20,000 profit. Of course we had to do those houses with different electricians and plumbers, too.

I once read a book called *The Art of War* by Sun Tzu, a Chinese military strategist who wrote this work in the 6th Century B.C. The book suggests that knowledge is power and that we shouldn't be quick to give up everything we know about a person or a situation until we've had time to think about it. In the above scenario, my immediate instinct was to rush toward the cheating Jr. Investor, call him some choice names and cut him out of the deal all together, burning the bridge completely to the ground! But when I stepped back and stopped to think about it, I came up with a much better plan. These Jr. Investors were very prolific house finders. While no one could appreciate their business ethic whatsoever, I really didn't want to lose the properties they could bring to the table. I decided to subdue my temper and bite my tongue. It's all right to deal with a snake if you can find a way to stay behind the fangs. If I had boldly confronted the thief he would have surely run and never shown his face again. Since I kept my knowledge of his cheating to myself and changed the way I did business with him, I could recoup my losses and create an even better business arrangement for our company in the future. That is exactly what happened, many times over. To this day, when I see these guys, I still say, "Hi" to them with a legitimate smile on my face. I'm very happy to explore the potential deals they have in store for me.

STORY 18
HOUSE ON HAUSMAN ROAD

• • •

When you can't go back, there is only one way left to go... forward

When I first moved to Texas I was in the 6th grade. I came from a modern split level school in Diamond Bar, CA to Lockehill Elementary in San Antonio, Texas. My new school was way out in the sticks and it was built from natural stone and no Central Heat or A/C. I say it was at least one million years old when I arrived. It was very different from what I'd been used to in California and I guess you could say I was in a bit of a culture shock for the first several days. I remember a very scary portrait of Mr. Lockehill hung over a very large fire place in the cafeteria. I always wondered who chopped the wood that burned there in the winter and I never did find out what Mr. Lockehill did to get a school named after him.

I made some steadfast friends and eventually we'd end up staying the night at each others home from time to time. My friend George lived on a ranch in a stone home not so different from the school we went to. It was old and way out in the sticks too. It was smothered under huge old oak trees. In the summer I'd stay for a few days and we'd be gone for hours exploring or hunting rabbits, shooting sling shots or BB guns or our bows. It must have been 100 degrees out there during the summer but for the life of me I never remember anyone complaining about it. George's dad was a tough man and didn't put up with much tomfoolery. Whenever the music would get too loud or it would start to get late he'd be sure to let us know. My own father was no *softy* either so that didn't bother me much. I actually thought that was just how the world spun 'round.

I spent my fair share of time with George on that land. Later, as we got older, we'd use the back part of the place and had high school parties with bonfires and such. I got to know Mr. Salazar better and he taught me a lot about hunting. He was an avid bow hunter and he showed me how he made arrows and strings and all sorts of things. A boy could spend hours in that old barn and never get tired of everything that was in it… everything from old car parts to shotgun shells, to reloading equipment.

After high school everyone kind of went their own way. I bounced around in and out of San Antonio and George became an airplane mechanic and moved to Dallas. I don't know exactly how it happened but Mr. Salazar and I became hunting partners. We did a little deer hunting with bows and a whole bunch of dove hunting together. Mr. Salazar was the best shot I'd ever seen. Later he introduced me to sheet shooting and that was where I learned just how he'd become so handy with a shotgun. We did a lot of clay shooting!

As I started to achieve some success in real estate I introduced Mr. Salazar to the wonderful world of house flipping. He was a good deal finder and we did our fair share of deals over the years. I guess we'd progressed into business partners at some level. We did everything on a handshake and everything always worked out fine. Who'd have ever guessed so many years ago that we'd be buying real estate together? Not Mr. Salazar I'm sure.

As the years rolled along the population kept expanding westward from the city and by the early 90's Mr. Salazar's land was completely surrounded by modern day neighborhoods and housing developments. His land had become so valuable that the major developers were starting to make offers and then one day it happened. On offer came over that was just too good to refuse. Money like that is enough to give a man peace of mind and a well deserved freedom after 60 some odd years of work and toil. Even so, it was a difficult decision. He was born in that house on that land and he had never called any other place home his entire life. There might have been a few different places he'd lived for a spell but there was only one home… and it was always on Hausman Rd.

I spoke to Mr. Salazar often and we'd talk about the offer and the paperwork and the taxes and the *what if this* and the *what if that* and by the time we were finished talking the papers were all signed and the closing was done. Mr. Salazar had been given ample time to remove all of his belongings but I guess he just didn't want to face the inevitable turning of that page. As the deadline loomed I got a call:

ME: Hello

Mr. SALAZAR: Hey Mitch

ME: What's up my Mr. Salazar? You wanna go shootin'?

Mr. SALAZAR: Yea, I wish… but I've got myself in a small jam and I need some help.

ME: I'll help, what do you need?

Mr. SALAZAR: I was wondering if you might come over and help me pack a few things? I really want to take a few more things from my property before they mow this place down but I can't do it by myself. I need an extra hand.

ME: When do you want me to come?

Mr. SALAZAR: Well, I'm sorry for waiting 'til so late but the truth is they are sitting in their bull dozers revving the engines. They really aren't to happy with me right now and as soon as I leave they're gonna push the place over I'm sure.

ME: I'll be right over… maybe take me 10 minutes.

Mr. SALAZAR: Thanks my friend.

Mr. Salazar wasn't joking. When I pulled up the black smoke was pouring out of the 2 bulldozer's smoke stacks and they were poised for the demolition. I got out of my truck and see some stress on my friends face. He motioned me inside the home and once inside he started telling me everything he wanted removed; the front door, the mantle over the fire place and some other things here and there. As we worked together moving everything from the house to the truck he started talking. It just kind of came out of the blue. He started from the very beginning and began telling about the history of the old place as it related to him. I immediately recognized that I should not speak… that I was there to listen.

This had happened to me once before when I'd gone to see my ailing Grandfather for the last time. We both knew we'd never see each other again and there, in his bed, with his long white hair, he spoke to me for hours. He too started at the beginning and slowly, methodically, never missing a beat, told me the story of his life. Then, as now, I was proud that I had been chosen to hear such things spoken with such emotion and quiet dignity.

As Mr. Salazar spoke time just sorta stopped. It was surreal. Outside the dozers raged but inside we were taking some type of immunity from the world. Yep, the whole universe just had to stop until this story got told… and there wasn't going to be a time limit either. It was just understood. "You know my daddy bought this place in 1931?" Mr. Salazar was not looking for an answer and in fact he was not even looking at me. He was gazing around the old home as if he'd never seen it before. "Old man Gerfers landed on hard times and needed to sell so my daddy bought it from him." He ran his hand over the kitchen counter as he meandered out of the kitchen, "My daddy paid $3,800 and that was hard earned money back then." I followed at a distance. "I was born in this house you know." He took a few steps into the hall and stopped at a doorway. "I was born right here, in this room, February 4, 1937." I stood quiet and notice how the floor creaked when he moved. "This is the only home our children ever knew. They never had another home besides this one, 'til they moved out." "A lot of livin's been done in this place… and some dyin' too." Moving to the end of the hall to the doorway of the master bedroom, "Both my mother and my father died here."

I don't know how long he talked but I guess it was eventually long enough. When we finally stepped outside it was like a bubble had popped or something. Suddenly we were back in the real world and the smell of diesel exhaust and the grumble of idling machinery took front and center. "It's now or never Mr. Salazar. Anything else you want we better get it now." He stood and look around a short bit, "Na, I guess that's it." I jumped in the passenger side of his truck and just about the time we got to the main road Mr. Salazar stopped and put the truck into park. He opened his door and got out just enough to stand up. He was looking back at the old home. One dozer was already knocking over some grand old oak tress and the other was approaching the side of the house rather quickly. I watch as the 2nd dozer struck the house but noticed that Mr. Salazar turned away and got back in the truck just before impact. He clearly did not want to see that. He put the truck in gear and then, his hands on the wheel in perfect 10 and 2 driving position, we went nowhere. He stared out the front windshield and we didn't move. "You alright Mr. Salazar?"

A few seconds later we started moving towards my truck, "Yea, let's get outta hear. I can take it from here. Thanks for your help. I really appreciate you being here today." I got out of Mr. Salazar's truck and he left out of sight. I turned to see the house all but leveled and watched the big machines stir up the dust and finish of the job. I felt sad for Mr. Salazar. A slow, haunting melody began to reach my lips and I thought…that man will never ever be able to go home again.

"House on Hausman Road"

Written by Mitch Stephen

My Daddy bought this place, in 1931
When Old Man "Gus" had to sell off
I used to hunt this land, back when I was young
And long before the urban sprawl
My grandchildren like to play, right there on that swing
Where Daddy drank his beer...
And Momma loved her shade...
Now they'll cut down those old oak trees today

CHORUS:
Another road is being paved, another high-rise bein' raised
Some monumental feat, in some developer's grand scheme
Another page tore from my past, Erased off of the map
I don't think they could ever know...
They'll tear down much more than stick and stones
When they lay low that house on Hausman Road

The bulldozer operator's scraping off the ground
Beyond what I can recognize
The demolition man is taking out the doors
An all the windows and the lights
Every piece could tell a story, but most will go untold
Except the trinkets in my pick-up truck
And their stories will grow old

(REPEAT CHORUS)

BRIDGE:
Burger Kings and Texacos
A famous hotel chain built right across the road
It makes me think, when I'm alone
There is no place I can go home
I can't go home

(MODIVIED CHORUS: Modify last 3 lines)
Another road is being paved, another high-rise bein' raised
Some monumental feat, in some developer's grand scheme
Another page tore from my past, Erased off of the map
I know, that they will never know...
They tore down much more than sticks and stones
When they laid low that house on Hausman Road.

Listen: http://www.mitchstephen.com/houseonhausmanrd.asp?music=on Piano/Cello version, Sung by Kevin Hughes
Listen: http://www.mitchstephen.com/houseonhausmanrda.asp?music=on Alternative Version, Sung by Kevin Hughes

www.MitchStephen.com

AFTERWORD

So there you have it. A glimpse into what happened to a guy after he watched the "you too can be rich" real estate info-mercial and charged the CD set on his credit card. Did I fail to mention that I've invested at least $50,000 in my real estate education? It's true. A man once told me, "If you think education is expensive, try being stupid." I never forgot that. I can't tell you how many people have asked me if those seminars and courses really work. To which I'd have to say, "Most of them work if *you* work…and none of them work if *you* don't work." If I've had any success at all I think I've made it abundantly clear, it didn't happen over night, I got out of my comfort zone, it wasn't always easy, and I've worked at it. What makes it all worth it? It's not the money as much as it is the freedom, the passion, the people, the journey.

Mitch Stephen

FREE LIST

125+ WAYS TO FIND BARGAIN PROPERTIES

To receive the list; ***125 ways to find bargain properties*** go to;

WWW.HOMES2GO.NET/125WAYS

and submit your email address. Your email address will not be sold and you will not receive an endless stream of emails everyday as a result of email request.

FREE LIST

On my journey I read many books that changed my life for the better. Many of those books were about *real estate,* some were about *self help,* some were from *other entrepreneurs* whose accomplishments were nothing short of phenomenal. I was not able to include all of the writings that helped mold me in my book BUT if you would like a free list of my favorite books go to;

WWW.HOMES2GO.NET/ FAVORITEBOOKS

Your email address will not be sold and you will not receive an endless stream of emails everyday as a result of your request.

FREE

PRIVATE LENDER'S REPORT

This report describes exactly how Mitch Stephen deals with private investors that lend their money to his companies. Private money is the key to success. This report is a valuable tool for anyone looking to raise capital for their investment endeavors. For your free report Click on:

WWW.HOMES2GO.NET/ PRIVATELENDERS

Your email address will not be sold and you will not receive an endless stream of emails everyday as a result of your request.

If you have a copy of this book and it
did NOT include a copy of the CD

Songs from the Book
"My Life & 1,000 Houses"

You may complete the following form and mail $12.50 (U.S. dollars), which includes shipping and handling, to:

Make Payable to:

Mitch Stephen

P.O. Box 171174

San Antonio, TX 78217

Please send me my CD to:

Name:______________________________

Street Address:______________________________

City:____________________ State__________ ZIP____

Email Address:______________________________

Phone Number:______________________________

Listen to much of Mitch Stephen's music at;

WWW.MITCHSTEPHEN.COM

ACKNOWLEDGEMENTS:

Tommi and I consider our lives to be a direct reflection of the time, effort, work and love that we have given and that we have received. We would like to thank the following people for their contributions to our lives.

Jason & Shannon Stephen	Terry & Dorothy Hall	Glenn Reed
Alexis Stephen	Tom Salazar	Eli Call
Tina Stephen	Candice Peyton & Tony Rodriguez	Dennis Shelly
Shelby Stephen	Jack & Sue Rogers	Tracy Calvert
Rod & Rita Stephen	Jack Word	Kathryn Modisette
Stan & Jean Stephen	Ruthann Coveney & Dario Navaira	Paul & Diane Schaffenberger
Brian & Leslie Stephen	Abie & Angela Epstein	Jack Biegler
Charles & Diana Hall	Gerald Winakur & Lee Robinson	Mark Colaw
Steve & Terri Edlund	Daniel Kruger	Marc & Sara Faulkner
Raymond & Janie Braun	Marty & Betty Brant	Kriss Brown
Carlos & Leslie Balido	Albert McKnight	Jim Clayton
Billy & Jackie O'Rourke	Yulanee McKnight	Jackie Browning
David Lee Garza	Johnny Gabriel	Rita Dressell
Bill & Debbie Green	Eddie & Martha Speed	John & Tommi Leonard
Orlando Rodriguez	Mary Peterson	John Collins
Bill Crawford	Bill & Nieves Oakley	Mike & Lori Rhodes
Dick & Judy Gilby	Davie & Kris Held	Mike Walloch
Rick & Dawn Olsen	James & Annette Allison	Mick Ochsner
Sam & Elisa Madrid	Mike & Gay Ryan	Jarrett Hale
Tom & Peggy Hennigan	Albert McNeel	Adriana Vann

Made in the USA
Lexington, KY
08 December 2016